Kirtley Library
Columbia College
8th and Rogers
Columbia, MO. 65201

Congress
in the
American
System

WITHDRAWN

Congress

in the
American
System

Carl P. Chelf

Nelson-Hall nh Chicago

LIBRARY OF CONGRESS CATALOGING IN PUBLICATION DATA

Chelf, Carl P
   Congress in the American system.

   Bibliography: p. 249
   Includes index.
   1. United States. Congress. I. Title.
JK1061.C47   328.73   77-1084
ISBN 0-88229-210-2 *(cloth)*
ISBN 0-88229-517-9 *(paper)*

Copyright © 1977 by Carl P. Chelf

All rights reserved. No part of this book may be reproduced in any
form without permission in writing from the publisher, except by a
reviewer who wishes to quote brief passages in connection with a
review written for broadcast or for inclusion in a magazine or newspaper.
For information address Nelson-Hall Inc., Publishers, 325 West
Jackson Boulevard, Chicago, Illinois 60606.

Manufactured in the United States of America.

328.73
CHE

02859

Contents

Preface
vii

Acknowledgments
ix

Introduction
xi

I
Congress and Representation
1

II
The Personnel of Congress
29

III
Structure, Organization, Rules, and Procedures
57

IV
The Committees of Congress
87

V
Debate and Floor Action
121

VI
Political Parties in Congress
147

VII
Organized Interests and Congress
165

VIII
Congress and the Judiciary
189

IX
Congress and the Executive
199

X
Rx: Reform
223

Bibliography
249

Index
251

Preface

THIS WORK IS largely an outgrowth of the author's own experience
as a Congressional Fellow of the American Political Science Association and a teacher of courses in the legislative process at the
undergraduate level for a number of years. Designed both for the
serious student of Congress and for the interested lay observer, this
book is an attempt to bring together in one volume a wide variety
of interesting and meaningful material on the Congress and its role
in our total political system.

The United States Congress is a highly interesting institution,
steeped in custom and tradition, intricate in rules, procedures and
rituals, and completely submerged in the arts and crafts of practical politics. Often in the center of controversy, Congress is a volatile and exciting place, full of drama, conflict and history. No account of Congress and its members would be complete which failed
to capture at least some of the atmosphere of the legislative arena.
This collection attempts to provide the reader with some "feel"
for the legislative process by exposing him to a Congress composed
of living, breathing human beings. This book is not designed as
a history or an analysis of the formal structure, organization, and
procedures—though these are not ignored altogether—but emphasizes the human and practical aspects of the Congress and its
functions. It attempts to add flesh, muscles and vital organs to the
structural framework of the United States Congress, a body once
described by Mark Twain as our only "distinctly native American
criminal class."

So intricate and complex in its operations that it can remain largely incomprehensible even to some who have spent a greater part of a lifetime in and around it, Congress simply cannot be studied thoroughly from any one perspective. Traditional literature on the subject emphasizes the descriptive approach: viewing Congress primarily as a law-making body and describing it largely in terms of its constitutional powers, responsibilities, organization and procedures. Too often, as John Morley, distinguished English statesman and man of letters, once observed, "The great fault of political writers is their too close adherence to the forms of the system of state which they happen to be expounding or examining. They stop short at the anatomy of institutions, and do not penetrate to the secret of their functions." By drawing from a wide variety of sources and examples, this work attempts to answer some of the questions not generally answered in other works on the Congress and its functions. The examples used have been chosen to provide the reader with tangible and striking examples of the Congress at work in our system. It is hoped that they will provide some insight and understanding of the true dynamics of Congress and its functions.

Reflecting that Congress is but a part of a larger political system, outside groups are given almost as much attention as the Congress itself. Much of the book is devoted to analyzing and depicting the relationships between Congress and the executive branch, special interest groups, political parties and the courts. Congress is presented in the light of its total environment and its role in an all-inclusive political system.

The author of this volume is fully aware of its limitations. It is by no means thorough and complete in its analysis of the Congress, nor is it comprehensive or exhaustive of the materials available. Appreciating that legislative politics is too voluminous and ubiquitous to be confined within the covers of one book, no effort was made to make this work encyclopedic. However, the format of the book provides for more flexibility and selectivity than the demands for symmetry and comprehensiveness in a text would allow. It is hoped that this highly selective exposure to the legislative process not only will provide the reader with a better understanding, but will above all stimulate a desire to read further and more widely on the topic.

Acknowledgments

THE AUTHOR ACKNOWLEDGES his indebtedness to the authors and publishers of the following previously published works from which materials are used: *Public and Republic* by Alfred de Grazia, © 1951, Alfred Knopf; *Both Your Houses: The Truth About Congress* by Warren Weaver, © 1972, Praeger Publishers; *Representation* by Hanna Pitkin, © 1969, Atherton Press; *The Congressman: His Work as He Sees It* by Charles Clapp, © 1963, Doubleday; Articles from Congressional Quarterly Service; "Pressure Groups in Congress" by Emanuel Cellar in *Annals of the American Academy of Political and Social Sciences* V 319 (1958); *Congressman From Mississippi* by Frank Smith, © 1964, Pantheon Books, a division of Random House, Inc.; *The Public Philosophy* by Walter Lippmann, published by the Atlantic Monthly Press in association with Little, Brown and Company; *The Representative: Trustee? Partisan? Politico?* by Neal Riemer, © 1967, D. C. Heath; *Considerations on Representative Government* by John Stuart Mill (Everyman's Library edition) published in the United States by E. P. Dutton & Company, Inc., used with their permission; *The Federalist* © 1937, Modern Library, a division of Random House, Inc.; "The Shame of the States" by John Kennedy in the *New York Times Magazine* (May 18, 1958); "Putting the Houses in Order" by George Merry in the *Christian Science Monitor* (October 29, 1968); *The Role of the Congressman* by Roger Davidson, © 1969, Pegasus; *Congress Makes a Law* by Stephen Bailey, © 1950, Columbia University Press; *To Be a Congressman: The Promise and the Power* edited by Sven Groennings and Jonathan Hawley, © 1973, Acropolis Books, Ltd., Washington, D.C.; "When

Congress Throttles the Executive" by Walter Lippmann, © 1963, The Washington Post Company; "An Exodus From Congress: 'No Longer Any Fun,' " © 1974, the Washington Post Company; *My First Fifty Years in Politics* by Joe Martin, © 1960, used with permission of the McGraw-Hill Book Company; *Professional Staffs of Congress,* © 1962 by Purdue Research Foundation, West Lafayette, Indiana; "The House" by Richard Bolling, in *Playboy* magazine (November, 1969); "The Shadow Congress" by Robert Sherrill in the *Courier-Journal and Times* Magazine (January 24, 1971); *The Center Magazine,* Center for the Study of Democratic Institutions, © 1974, The Fund for The Republic, Inc.: *O Congress* by Don Riegle, © 1972, Doubleday; "Modern Saga: The Old Man and Capitol Hill" by Russell Baker, © 1968, New York Times Company. Reprinted by permission; "Inside Capitol Hill: How the House Really Works" by Larry King in *Harper's* magazine (October, 1968); *Congress the Sapless Branch* by Joseph Clark, © 1965, Harper & Row; "Office Cheers Perkins' Aide for 'Protecting Committee' "; by Charles Babcock in the *Courier-Journal* (October, 1974); *Profiles in Courage* by John Kennedy (Pocket Books edition), © 1955, Harper & Row; "Why I'm Quitting Congress" by Everett Burkhalter in *Family Weekly* magazine (December 27, 1964); *The Washington Lobbyists* by Lester Milbrath, © 1963, Rand-McNally & Co.; "Wastington's Money Birds" by Larry King in *Harper's* (August, 1965); *Congressional Government* by Woodrow Wilson, © 1956, Meridian Books; "The Shape of American Politics" by Richard Goodwin, © 1967, *Commentary* magazine; "The Congress . . . What Is Its Role in the 20th Century?" by Tom Wicker, © 1965, New York Times Company. Reprinted by permission; "The American Presidency a Defective Institution" by Marcus Cunliffe, © 1968, *Commentary* magazine; "A Heartland GOP District Sways Toward Impeachment" by David Hacker in *The National Observer* (August 3, 1974); "The Congress and America's Future," published by the Twenty-sixth American Assembly in cooperation with Prentice-Hall; "Reforming Congress" in the *Courier-Journal* (April 21, 1974); "Representative Perkins to Oppose House Committee Division Proposal" by Bill Peterson in *The Courier-Journal* (March 20, 1974); "It's the Presidency That Wields Power Now" by James Reston, © 1966, New York Times Company. Reprinted by permission.

Introduction

TODAY OUR GOVERNMENT is at a most crucial point in the history of our constitutional system of separated powers and checks and balances. In 1887, as a young graduate student in political science, Woodrow Wilson had published a classic study of the legislative-executive relationship entitled *Congressional Government* in which he saw our system hamstrung with the President overshadowed by a domineering Congress. The passing years and far-reaching changes in our society and in the international situation brought about dramatic changes in the balance of power among the branches of our government. In 1974 Arthur Schlesinger, Jr., wrote a work called *The Imperial Presidency* in which he painted a bleak picture of the almost total dominance in our system by the executive branch.

The years following World War II have seen a rather steady withering of the legislative branch as more and more governmental initiative and power have shifted to the executive. This overshadowing of the Congress by the executive has meant that those elected representatives, who in theory should be most aware of and sensitive to the impact of governmental policies on citizen interests, are, in reality, least able to determine how programs are being carried out and what their real impact is. That branch of government supposedly closest to the voters often appears the least able to act decisively and effectively. A disturbing consequence has been a sharp decline in public respect for the "people's branch" of government. Polls over the last decade have repeatedly shown that Congress is held in low esteem.

The time is now ripe for the Congress to assert itself and to regain much of its lost power and prestige. Recent revelations of the misuse of power by the CIA, the FBI, and other agencies of the federal bureaucracy dramatically illustrate the urgent need for the Congress to provide more effective oversight of these agencies and to demand more executive responsibility. Congress can no longer afford to ignore its responsibility in this and other important areas, but must move quickly and vigorously to reassure the public against further abuses and to restore an element of credibility and confidence in our governmental institutions. Can and will the Congress move and become, once again, an effective partner in the system of checks and balances? This is a question to which the following chapters are addressed.

Chapter I

Congress
and Representation

TODAY MOST AMERICANS who give the matter much thought think of the republican form of government as being an essential element in a democratic system. A look at the history of representative bodies reveals that, at least in their earliest forms, they probably did not spring up out of desires for self-government. Though unknown to the ancients, various forms of representative assemblies have appeared throughout history. It is probable that such assemblies go back beyond the Greek city-states, and that they existed in both Greek and Roman governments at an early date. There is also some evidence of representative assemblies among the early American Indians.

These early assemblies, however, did not possess true "representative authority." The modern concept of representative government most likely evolved from the assemblies called into being by medieval monarchs. Realizing that they must strengthen their bases of support and operate with some degree of cooperation from those they ruled, the medieval monarchs brought together "representative" councils to ratify their taxes and to provide advice. These early bodies were not truly "representative" nor were they democratic, but by gradual steps they evolved into law-making bodies and a representative function began to emerge. Their petitions eventually became bills and their control over taxes and revenues provided them with considerable leverage.

Thus in the late Middle Ages political philosophies of representation began to develop, and by the sixteenth century "represent" had acquired a political meaning similar to the modern concept. The seventeenth century saw the emergence of the doctrine of legislative supremacy, and the nineteenth century produced elective representative councils as strong governmental institutions.

The spread of the concepts of popular government brought a new significance to the role of representative. The American and French revolutions proclaimed the equality of men and their right to an equal share in government. How were men to exercise this universal right to share in their government? Some, like the Frenchman Rousseau, believed only in direct participation. He concluded that representation was a great fraud, fatal to individual liberty. According to Rousseau, no representative could enact laws on behalf of the people because their sovereign power to make laws could not be delegated. Writing in *The Social Contract,* Rousseau observed that when the people named deputies to serve in their behalf and then stayed home, they soon lost interest in governmental affairs. He concluded that the moment a people allowed themselves to be represented, they were no longer free. Every law that had not been ratified by the people themselves, he felt, was null and void. Reflecting Rousseau's earlier sentiments, a noted Oxford professor and author, the late G. D. H. Cole, stated that no man could represent another man, nor could one man's will be substituted for the wills of others.

Representation in the U.S.

In spite of some distinguished dissenters, concepts of representative government had gained widespread acceptance by the nineteenth century. When the Founding Fathers assembled in Philadelphia to frame the U.S. Constitution, the concept of representative government was not only accepted, it was dictated by vivid memories of a revolution against the nonrepresentative structure of the British government and "taxation without representation." The framers were, therefore, quite explicit in their intent to establish a republican form of government deriving its powers from the citizens but administered by elected representatives. While they believed, on the whole, in the representative principle, another prime motivating factor for adopting the republican form was the framers' fear of the masses. The republican form would break the force of mass majority rule by filtering it through a more elite representative body. The framers felt this system would provide far more thorough deliberation while reducing the tendency to act brashly out of current passions. Also, the system adapted well for the governing of a large area and population.

While making the republican form explicit in the Constitution, the framers did not answer the much more difficult question which goes to the very heart of representative government: What is the proper role of the elected representative?

Concepts of Representation

The idea of representation involves a variety of concepts and is more easily discussed than defined. Despite centuries of discussion, even the most astute philosophers have experienced difficulty in defining precisely and completely the meaning of representation. James Wilson, probably the leading spokesman for democracy among the Constitution framers at Philadelphia, defined representation as the chain of communication between the people and those to whom the important charge of exercising the delegated powers for the administration of public affairs had been committed.[1] According to social scientist Seymour Lipset, representation is a process of interaction between social groupings and political decision-makers. Alfred de Grazia writes that representation is "a condition which exists when the characteristics and acts of one vested with public functions are in accord with the desires of one or more persons to whom the functions have . . . importance."[2] Distinguished social scientist Max Weber introduces the element of legitimacy into the discussion when he says that by representation, we mean that the action of certain members of a group, the "representatives," is ascribed to the others, or is regarded as legitimate so its results must be accepted as binding on all.

All the definitions of representation center around the fact that in most societies pure, direct democracy is impractical and governmental authority must be delegated to a group of leaders and their leadership legitimized in some way. Thus, in liberal democracies the formulation and administration of public policy is normally a task restricted directly to officials freely chosen and authorized to act for the society. A major problem in such systems of popular government is how to maintain the responsiveness and responsibility of the elected representatives once they are chosen and granted authority. In such a system, what is the proper relationship between the elected representative and his constituency? In a federal system with representatives selected from geographical districts, what is his constituency? His district? His state? The nation?

The Representative's Role

The question which has intrigued political philosophers and practicing politicians alike since the rise of representative institutions has been, does the elected legislator act on the basis of constituency desires, or does he make decisions on the basis of his own knowledge, insight and judgment? Expressed another way, does he function as an agent, reflecting only his constituents' wishes, or as a trustee, exercising his own judgment? Was he elected to office because of his ability and good judgment, or because he is seen as a man who will mirror the district's sentiments?

When one looks at the United States Congress, it quickly becomes apparent that the styles of representation reflected there are many and varied. Many congressmen like to view themselves as trustees in the Burkean concept, but when the chips are down, few have the intestinal fortitude to tell their constituents, as Burke did in his November 3, 1774, speech to his Bristol constituents, that he would not be their rubber stamp, but if elected would exercise his own best judgment in their behalf. Speaking of the representative's role, Burke argued:

> ... his unbiased opinion, his mature judgment, his enlightened conscience, he ought not to sacrifice to you, to any man, or to any set of men living. . . . Your representative owes you, not his industry only, but his judgment; and he betrays, instead of serving you, if he sacrifices it to your opinion.[3]

In Burke's view the elected lawmaker represented the nation as a whole first and his particular constituency second. In his opinion, Parliament was to represent, not local interests and local prejudices, but the general good of the nation.

Many United States congressmen share this philosophical concept of the representative role, but encounter difficulties in putting it into effect. Their local constituencies may insist that they be effective local representatives rather than national statesmen. The individual representative's role will depend to a great extent upon his district and the specific issue involved. One California Democrat, not at all pleased with his newly reapportioned district, complained, "Now I'll have to continue going this way and that way, back and forth. I'm a cracker-assed congressman, and I could have been a statesman."[4] But to be a statesman one must get elected, and to insure this one may have to court his particular constituency. Anyway, in the final analysis, statesmanship may, in the words of Speaker Reed, "not consist in doing the best thing, but in doing the best possible thing."

It is a lofty goal to share with Woodrow Wilson the feeling that nothing is "more honorable than to be driven from power because one was right." However, more elected representatives are probably inclined to agree with Lloyd George that they do not relish being "crucified" at home. As Senator Ashurst of Arizona once told a colleague, "You must learn that there are times when a man in public life is compelled to rise above his principles." This is not to say that the man in public life must abandon his principles altogether. It is simply saying that in the American system, before you can be a good representative you must be elected. Frequently this requires a rather pragmatic approach to the concept of one's role as a representative. Faced with the expectations of their constituents and the brevity of their two-year term, many members of the House of Representatives may not quite manage Burke's lofty view and independence.

The Representative as Agent

At the other end of the spectrum we have the concept of the representative as the agent of his constituents. He is expected to act in their behalf, to be their instrument for getting things done. In describing this representative role Hilaire Belloc and G. K. Chesterton wrote:

> Either the representative must vote as his constituents would vote if consulted, or he must vote in the opposite sense. In the latter case, he is not a representative at all, but merely an oligarch; for it is surely ridiculous to say that a man represents Bethnal Green if he is in the habit of saying "Aye" when the people of Bethnal Green would say "no."[5]

In his maiden speech in the House, John Tyler asked how one could be regarded as representing the people when he spoke not their views, but his own. Then he represents himself alone and not the people, said Tyler. Addressing this same question, John Kennedy asked in his work *Profiles in Courage,* are we rightfully entitled to ignore the demands of our constituents even if we are able and willing to do so? The idea of the congressman as agent actually is built into the representative system. Members of the House are elected from districts rather than at-large, and senators are recognized by the vice-president as the senator from Kentucky, the senator from Texas. If the representative or senator does not look out for his own district and state, who will? Former Speaker Joe Martin observed that he was not about to sit back and let representatives from some other part of the country decide what was good for his New England district which he knew more intimately than anyone else in the Congress. On many occasions most members will find themselves saying as John Sherman Cooper said of himself, "Today it is my duty and my desire to support the people of Kentucky, the people whom I represent."

The difficulty for some arises in that under the federal system, the elected representative must serve double duty, performing as both a local and a national representative. Which should take priority? For some this poses no problem. A Southern Democrat says his job is to serve the best interests of his district as well as those of the nation, but he sees no conflict because what is good for a segment of the country is good for the whole. A colleague from the West, however, feels members of Congress are too parochial and tend to represent only specific districts when they should represent the state and nation as well.[6] Can a member serve both local interests and national interests at the same time? If not, which should take a backseat? Lyndon Johnson, speaking of his economic program, observed, "Many congressmen and senators understood my concerns for the economy as a whole, but each legislator had one overriding concern—to make a record with the people who sent him to office."[7] Can the elected representative serve his local constituency and the national interest at the same time?

Viewed in another light, if we embrace the concept of the representative solely as agent, in our day of modern technology we probably do not need representatives at all, but simply some electronic means or computerized sampling technique for determining the will of the majority on specific issues. This concept when focused too narrowly misses the point of the much broader scope of the representative function in a highly complex and pluralistic society. The complete representative in our system is not exclusively either trustee or agent. On one issue he will reflect constituent interests, on another he will go along with his party, and on still another he will exercise his independent judgment. The Congress is a problem-solving place where there must be a lot of give-and-take. "The 'good' representative," writes Emanuel Celler, "is he who effectively accommodates opposing interests within his constituency; who successfully relates the needs of his constituents to those of the people as a whole; and who harmonizes his responses to the demands made upon him with the dictates of his conscience."[8]

On occasion the representative may experience some real cross-pressures between the demands of his constituents and his job as he sees it. Under usual circumstances, however, he will have considerable flexibility as to just how he performs his representative function. While many legislators do reflect the interests of their districts on many matters, they are free to maneuver on a wide range of other issues coming before the Congress. Even though the legislator may be quite willing to be a rubber stamp, constituents speak with a really clear voice on relatively few issues. On a vast majority of the issues they are neither well enough informed nor interested enough to insist that their congressman vote a certain way. By far the largest portion of the matters a congressman votes on affect his constituency only indirectly. Thus, many representatives will find that as far as specific issues are concerned, they can pretty well follow their own judgments as to how they should vote.

Just how the individual legislator performs his role will depend largely upon his interpretation of the job and the nature of his district. Congressmen from safe districts can usually afford to be somewhat less constituent-oriented than those from closely competitive districts. A grave mistake of the elected representative, however, is neglect of his state or district, and even the most secure do so at their own risk, as such national stalwarts as Albert Gore and William Fulbright discovered. The representative is expected to maintain a first-hand familiarity with the home district or state and its problems. He does not necessarily have to confine his functions to local interests, but he must convince his constituents he is functioning in their best interest.

In addition to this, the representative's constituency may establish certain constraints within which he must work, like them or not. Most members are keenly aware that their particular constituencies impose certain boundaries beyond which they proceed at their own risk. For example, with only a few exceptions, members of Congress from the South for the past fifteen years have opposed civil rights legislation. In the final showdown the moderates and conservatives from the South have voted the same way. Former Congressman from Mississippi, Frank Smith, says, "In the American South, . . . race is the controlling element in a political structure dedicated to the preservation of inequality among men."[9] As a member of Congress, Smith sent literature to Negro constituents but could not address them as Mr. or Mrs. To do so in Mississippi was considered a cardinal sin which could arouse the wrath of the White Citizen's Councils. Therefore, Smith used the salutation, "Dear Friend." While some might view this as an unnecessary surrender to constituent prejudices, Smith, at least for a time, did save his state from having another totally racist representative.

What many critics fail to appreciate fully is the political nature of the job of the elected representative. Many people are inclined to forget that members of Congress are chosen in a highly volatile electoral process, and no matter what their goals and personal philosophies, their decisions must be considered in the light of electoral implications. This leads some critics to be overly harsh in their evaluations of democratic politicians. Take for instance, Walter Lippmann in *The Public Philosophy* where he describes them in these terms:

> They advance politically only as they placate, appease, bribe, seduce, bamboozle, or otherwise manage to manipulate the demanding and threatening elements in their constituencies. The decisive consideration is not whether the proposition is good but whether it is popular—not whether it will work well and prove itself but whether the active talking constituents like it immediately. Politicians rationalize this servitude by saying that in a democracy public men are the servants of the people.[10]

What Lippmann, and other critics like him, miss is that our system provides for government, not by philosopher kings, but by elected representatives. And what the critics see as unnecessary catering to constituent wishes for the sake of votes may really be a reflection of the legislator's true representative character and closeness to the needs and desires of his district. Most congressmen are not simply rubber stamps for the sake of re-election; they are rather more in tune with their respective states and districts than anyone else. They tend to reflect the prejudices, values and interests of the districts from which they are elected. This can hardly be a condemnation of them as representatives of the people.

The political process is too important to be left to the politicians, say some critics. So somehow they would like to depoliticize the representative. To whom do we leave the process? The lawyers, a profession whose members played a key role in Watergate? The businessmen, who have contributed such recent successes as the energy crisis and the Penn Central Railroad? In the final analysis, it is the political element that makes the system function. It is the politics of the situation that ensures that the representative represents. Without this, an essential ingredient would be lacking.

Thus the average American legislator is not wholly agent or trustee, but politician, or in the words of one writer, a politico. According to Frank Sorauf, he makes no firm commitments to constituency, party, or self. His response to their demands on him and sanctions over him shifts from issue to issue. The shifting political demands made of him and the finely balanced choices available compel him to choose cautiously and tentatively, one issue at a time.[11]

Types of Representation

While theories of representation have been a topic of considerable discussion for centuries, an equally difficult problem has been the more practical matter of engineering really efficient machinery for representation. What formula for apportioning members and what methods of selection best insure proper representation of a constituency? Must all segments of society have members in the legislature to be represented? That is, must each ethnic, racial, religious, professional, economic, social and political group composing our society have a member in the legislature in order to be represented? Again, opinions as to what system provides the best representation vary considerably.

John Adams said, "A representative legislature should be an exact portrait, in miniature, of the people at large, as it should think, feel, reason and act like them."[12] In a similar vein, John Stuart Mill said the legislature should serve as "an arena in which not only the general opinion of the nation, but that of every section of it, and, as far as possible, of every eminent individual whom it contains, can produce itself in full light and challenge discussion, where every person in the country may count upon finding somebody who speaks his mind as well or better than he could speak it himself. . . ."[13] He went on to note that the legislature should be a place where every interest and every shade of opinion could have its cause pleaded.

One group of theorists feel that this type of representation can be achieved only when the legislature contains within it the same elements, in the same proportion, as are found in the body politic at large. The advocates of functional representation feel the way to achieve this is to establish a system of representation which provides representatives for all segments or interests in the society as a whole. Another, somewhat similar approach, is the concept of proportional representation under which seats in the legislature are allocated among parties on the basis of the portion of the votes each polls. Thus if party A polls 45 percent; party B, 40 percent; party C, 10 percent, then seats in the legislature would be assigned in essentially the same proportion.

The functional and proportional methods of selecting representatives no doubt result in legislatures which are more accurate cross-sections of the societies they represent, but they may have other defects. In some European countries where these methods are used, representative systems appear to contribute to multi-party systems and tend to encourage the fragmentation rather than aggregation of interests, thereby contributing to governmental instability.

With their misgivings about mass majority rule, the framers of the American Constitution probably had no desire to create a system that would make the legislature an accurate cross-section of the general populace. A delegate to the Philadelphia Convention, Alexander Hamilton, wrote in *Federalist* Number 35:

> It is said to be necessary, that all classes of citizens should have some of their own number in the representative body, in order that their feelings and interests may be the better un-

derstood and attended to. But we have seen that this will never happen under any arrangement that leaves the votes of the people free. Where this is the case, the representative body, with too few exceptions to have any influence on the spirit of the government will be composed of landholders, merchants, and men of the learned professions. But where is the danger that the interests and feelings of the different classes of citizens will not be understood or attended to by these three descriptions of men?[14]

Though the system for choosing members of Congress has been changed somewhat, with senators now being popularly elected and representatives being elected from districts rather than at large, several of Hamilton's predictions appear to be borne out. Congress, whose members have varied backgrounds and talents, is not a microcosm of the nation but a rather elite group. Dominated by white, middle-aged males, Congress does not very accurately reflect the populace of the nation. In a country whose population has as average age of something under twenty-five years, the average age for House members is fifty-one and for the Senate fifty-eight. Congress is dominated by professionals, with lawyers being most numerous, followed by businessmen and bankers, teachers, farmers and journalists. Few persons from the lower and lower-middle classes are elected to Congress. A member of the national legislature becomes a sort of symbol for his constituents and in many instances the voters appear inclined to select as representatives those from superior class positions. This is essentially what Hamilton predicted.

One thing the framers of the Constitution may not have anticipated is the highly parochial nature of the Congress. This parochialism of the national legislature is a direct and unmistakable result of the localism of the political system itself. The political base of the member of Congress is local; his political success depends on a uniquely local constituency. This goes a long way toward explaining the strong constituent orientation of the American legislator.

Apportionment and Representation

The selection of members from geographical districts has resulted in some difficulties concerning the representativeness of the Congress. For the first fifty years after adoption of the Constitution, members of the House were allocated to the states on the basis of population and all were elected at-large. Since 1842, members have been elected from single-member geographical districts.

Following each ten-year census, the director of the census notifies each state of the number of members it is entitled to in the House of Representatives. It then becomes the responsibility of the state legislatures to divide the state into the appropriate number of districts, which are supposed to be fairly equal in population. When the first federal census was taken in 1790, 5.1 percent of the population was urban; when the last census was conducted in 1970, it revealed 73.5 percent was urban. Over the years many state legislatures either simply neglected to redistrict after each census or failed to redraw district lines in a manner accurately reflecting the shifts in population. The census of 1910 marked the last time when rural America registered a majority in the nation's population, but rurally-controlled state legislatures continued to draw district lines which made disfranchisement of urbanites widespread. In 1928 H. L. Mencken wrote in the Baltimore *Evening Sun*:

> The yokels hang on because old apportionments give them unfair advantages. The vote of a malarious peasant on the lower Eastern Shore counts as much as the votes of twelve Baltimoreans. But that can't last. It is not only unjust and undemocratic; it is absurd.[15]

Mencken was an excellent journalist but a rather poor prophet because the malapportionment of legislatures at all levels continued to worsen. A major reason for this was that by the time the imbalances were noted, the power of correction had slipped away from those most disadvantaged. Members of the legislatures who benefited most from the malapportionment were highly reluctant to approve any changes jeopardizing their positions. When the disfranchised elements turned to the courts for remedy, both the state and federal courts showed a general reluctance to intervene. In the 1946 case of *Colegrove* v. *Green*, Justices Frankfurter and Harlan were joined by a majority on the Supreme Court in expressing the feeling that the court should stay clear of the apportionment hassle. As a consequence the situation in the state legislatures and the Congress continued to worsen.

In 1958 John Kennedy wrote in the *New York Times Magazine*:

> The apportionment of representation in our legislatures and in Congress has been either deliberately rigged or shamefully ignored so as to deny the cities and the voters that full and proportionate voice in government to which they are entitled.[16]

Finally an urban voter in Tennessee, where district lines had remained unchanged for sixty years, decided to seek redress in the courts once again. At this time six other states had not reapportioned for a quarter century, and in many states a minority of the voters chose a majority of the elected representatives. The Supreme Court's decision in the Tennessee case in 1962 was the first in a series of landmark decisions relating to apportionment and representation. In *Baker* v. *Carr* the high court ruled that federal courts could and must decide constitutional challenges to state legislative apportionment when qualified voters claimed impairment of their right of franchise. While deciding only that there was power in the federal courts to decide these claims, the *Baker* decision opened the doors to a series of cases of momentous import to representative government.

In 1964, in two significant cases, the Supreme Court elaborated further on the apportioning of representatives in legislative bodies. In *Reynolds* v. *Sims* and *Wesberry* v. *Sanders* the court established the principle that substantial population equality was a constitutional prerequisite in state legislative and U.S. House of Representatives districting. In *Reynolds* v. *Sims,* the majority of the court proclaimed what came to be known as the "one man, one vote" concept:

> Legislators represent people, not trees or acres. Legislators are elected by voters, not farms or cities or economic interests.
> Logically, in a society ostensibly grounded on representative government, it would seem reasonable that a majority of the people of a state could elect a majority of that state's legislators. . . . Since legislatures enact laws governing all citizens they should be bodies responsive to the popular will.
> A nation once primarily rural in character becomes predominantly urban. Representation schemes once fair and equitable become archaic and outdated. But the basic principle of representative government remains, and must remain, unchanged—the weight of a citizen's vote cannot be made to depend on where he lives.[17]

In *Wesberry* v. *Sanders* the same concept was applied to the U.S. House of Representatives. The court stated:

> The right to vote is too important in our free society to be stripped of judicial protection.
>
> . . . one man's vote in a congressional election is to be worth as much as another's.
>
> To say that a vote is worth more in one district than in another would not only run counter to our fundamental ideas of democratic government, it would cast aside the principle of a house of representatives elected by the People.
>
> While it may not be possible to draw congressional districts with mathematical precision, that is no excuse for ignoring our Constitution's plain objective of making equal representation for equal numbers of people the fundamental goal for the house of representatives.[18]

In a series of subsequent decisions, the court elaborated on these basic principles, finally concluding in *Kirkpatrick* v. *Preisler* in 1969 that the states must justify each variance in population, no matter how small, unless such variances resulted in spite of careful efforts by the state to draw congressional districts of equal population.[19]

Following the court's decision in *Baker* v. *Carr,* the Chattanooga *Times* proclaimed, "Urban America had its day yesterday. The fact that we are now a predominantly urban society has received inevitably, fundamentally, significant recognition." The *Times* overlooked the fact that this recognition only came five decades after the census reports had indicated such a change. While the court's decisions in the reapportionment cases did have considerable impact on legislatures across the nation, they have not transformed these bodies into highly representative assemblies overnight. Following the court's decisions, virtually every state in the union was redistricted, some several times. The 1970 census required nine states to relinquish eleven House seats, meaning they had to redistrict. Even those states not gaining or losing seats usually had to redraw lines to more accurately reflect shifts in population. As a result of redistricting, in a number of instances long-time incumbents decided not to seek re-election. Other changes resulting have been a growing voice for the suburbs and a reduced one for the inner cities and rural areas. As the changes occur, the legislatures begin to show more concern for such issues as tax reform, crime, narcotics, consumer protection, environmental protection and mass transit.

While the court's decisions have resulted in substantial improvement of legislative representativeness in some respects, the job is still only partially done. The federal courts, including the Supreme Court, have, unfortunately, shown little inclination to expand the "one man, one vote" concept to the legislative practice of gerrymandering. The result of allowing the state legislatures to manipulate the drawing of district lines for partisan or individual advantage has been to undermine the overall impact of the reapportionment drive. For example, in a number of southern states where the Democratic party-controlled legislatures have redrawn district lines, the Republicans have gained substantial numbers of voters but only a few seats in Congress. The Democratic majorities in the legislatures have been quite adept at drawing district boundaries to bunch the voters in a very few districts or disperse them widely in a number of districts so they are heavily outnumbered.

Since it can change the makeup of his constituency sufficiently overnight to possibly bring defeat in the next election, redistricting is the nightmare of the incumbent representative. The governors and state legislatures may use redistricting as a means of rewarding their incumbent friends or making things difficult for those they dislike. Bella Abzug, outspoken liberal Democrat from New York, was virtually "dedistricted" by the state legislature. Governor Rockefeller and conservative Democrats set out to get her, splitting her existing district four different ways. She won re-election anyway. In Wisconsin, Bill Steiger, a loyal team player who votes with his party consistently, was well protected by the state legislature when the members drew district lincs. On the other hand, Al O'Konski, who frequently votes his own mind, was redistricted in such a manner that his re-election was put in real jeopardy. As long as the state legislatures are free to approach the drawing of representative districts in this manner, it appears doubtful that the spirit of "one man, one vote" can be fully achieved. In an article in the *Christian Science Monitor* in 1968, George B. Merry reported that gerrymandering was evident to some extent in over half the recently redistricted states.[20]

Tennessee state legislator James Cummings lamented that *Baker* v. *Carr* marked "the end of good, clean rural government."

To the contrary, reapportionment has not been the death knell for rural interests in American legislatures. In the year that the census reports revealed that urban Americans outnumbered rural Americans, the United States Congress launched the tradition that would insure rural domination for decades. In a time when the nation's populace is heavily metropolitan and the norm of American family life is suburban living, because of seniority, Congress is dominated by a few powerful individuals, most of whom represent rural districts. A nation whose population is young, urban and geographically mobile is governed by a Congress dominated by committee chairmen who are old, rural and strongly regional in their orientations. While thirty of the fifty states are 60 percent or more urban, many of the committees of Congress are headed by members representing districts less than 30 percent urban. George Mahon, chairman of the powerful House Appropriations Committee, serves a district approximately 36 percent urban, and Carl Perkins, head of the Education and Labor Committee, comes from a district less than 35 percent urban. While recent reapportionments have expanded urban representation, the upper echelons of most standing committees have been only gradually altered, and the committee chairmanships remain for the most part the solid bastion of rural America and a minority way of life. This is in no way a condemnation of rural Americans or their representatives, but is simply to point up the fact that legislatures dominated by these interests are less inclined to give tax dollars to urban America and grapple with such tough urban problems as transportation, public facilities, housing, recreation, crime and drugs.

Thus, reapportionment is really only a partial answer for achieving fairer representation. The fact that powerful chairmen come from districts that are often atypical, that state legislatures are inclined to show favoritism in drawing district lines, and that seniority is a powerful element in the distribution of power and influence in Congress won't be changed very dramatically or very quickly by reapportionment. In the final analysis, reform of the institutional structure of the Congress will not alone bring complete reform to the legislative process. Since representation includes a substantive as well as an institutional element, no particular device or institutional arrangement can guarantee equal representation. The effectiveness depends to a great extent on how individuals perceive and perform their roles as representatives.

The Job of the Congressman

To fully appreciate the representative role, the legislature must be viewed as a part of the larger political system. Most people immediately perceive the representative as a lawmaker, and, while law-making is certainly a prime function of the legislator, it is only one of several roles he fills. Today's legislator, faced with the increasing size and complexity of the governmental operation—federal expenditures have tripled in just the last decade—has less and less time to devote to legislating. There is no absence, however, of ideas for legislation. The faith of Americans in legal solutions leads them to seek to guarantee everything from good health to good morals by enacting yet another law. The problem is that other functions come to compete more and more with the legislative functions for time and attention.

As the complexity of the federal government grows, more and more people turn to their congressmen for help in dealing with it. Where the average member used to get perhaps ten to fifteen letters per day, from constituents, he now gets several hundred. He finds himself inevitably becoming more and more a prisoner of the mailbag and a spokesman for district interests. This role, however, involves a number of legitimate functions for the elected representative.

Since it becomes impossible for the average citizen to effectively keep up with government, the legislator becomes a vital connecting link between the government and the governed. In this respect he plays a number of roles important to the successful functioning of our democratic system. He is a broker, an overseer, and an agent for his constituency. Sometimes the distinction between these various roles may be blurred. For example, while acting on behalf of a constituent on some problem, the representative is also involved in oversight of the bureaucracy and the administration of the laws. The performance of casework for constituents provides the legislators with some of their best insights as to how well their policies are being carried out by federal administrators. This function also encourages more bureaucratic responsiveness to the Congress.

According to John Stuart Mill, the oversight function was really the primary role of the legislature. In *Representative Government* he wrote:

Instead of the function of governing, for which it is radically unfit, the proper office of a representative assembly is to watch and control the government; to throw the light of publicity on its acts; to compel a full exposition and justification of all of them which any one considers questionable; to censure them if found condemnable, and, if the men who compose the government abuse their trust, or fulfill it in a manner which conflicts with the deliberate sense of the nation, to expel them from office. . . .[21]

In the Congress this is a role performed only sporadically and on the whole rather ineffectively, usually as an adjunct to some other function.

In functioning as a broker or ombudsman for his constituents, the representative performs a vital function for both his constituents and the governmental system. The average citizen doesn't know where to start, or is highly apprehensive about coping with the faceless bureaucracy of a remote governmental giant in Washington. He feels much more at ease sitting down to write a letter to Representative Smith whose hand he shook last November, and Representative Smith or someone on his staff is more likely to get a speedy and satisfactory response from a governmental agency.

The processing of constituent requests, casework, has become a substantial task for congressional offices. Individual members react to this demand on their time differently, and some delegate this task almost completely to their staffs. A Southern Democrat says, "I feel the errand boy function is contrary to the Founding Father's intent, but it's necessary for election."[22] A Western Republican, describing his job, said it consisted of "taking care of home problems. Casework, not necessarily having anything to do with legislation at all. Taking care of constituents."[23] A Missouri congressman stated:

I learned soon after coming to Washington that it was just as important to get a certain document for somebody back home as for some European diplomat—hell, *more* important, because that little guy back home votes.[24]

In this same vein, Representative Edward Koch of New York remarked, "I'm not a congressman, I'm a printer," and Representative James Burke said, "I'm not a congressman, I'm a mail-order house." Most members feel that engaging in casework, which ranges all the way from legitimate claims to absolutely ridiculous requests, is a tremendous drain on valuable time. However, many see themselves as being the only really responsive element in the vast federal structure, and they find such work personally gratifying. In the words of one member:

> The government has gotten too big and any degree of compassion and humility that we can bring to it all the better. Some of these bureaucrats think government jobs were created just for them, and they forget that they are to serve the people. I guess we are the last true servants that the people can turn to.[25]

Not all the representative's casework involves individuals. He is also an agent and spokesman for his state and district. Former Speaker Joe Martin observes in his autobiography that as a young congressman from Massachusetts he scurried all over Washington doing chores for his district. Many others are equally vigorous as they seek to help local officials, agencies and civic groups seeking grants, loans, projects, contracts and information that will be helpful in their operations. In many of these endeavors it helps considerably if the member has seniority and the accompanying prestige and power. For example, North American Aviation and General Dynamics have both opened plants in lonely rural southeastern Oklahoma. Both are large federal contractors and their plants just happen to be located in the home district of former House Speaker Carl Albert. Some years back a $32 million federal building was constructed in Kansas City and a multi-million dollar dam in the district of Richard Bolling. It just happened that Bolling was a confidant and close friend of Speaker Sam Rayburn. Had this not been the case, these choice projects might have gone elsewhere. So being an "insider" helps in these endeavors, but all members are in there pitching on behalf of their constituents.

For some, this aspect of the representative's role is totally distasteful. They see the legislator as simply buying votes by delivering personal or corporate favors. There is no question but that the system is subject to abuse and some members use poor judgment in the manner in which they perform the functions. On the other hand, there are too few places in the vast federal bureaucracy where grievances can be registered, heard, and resolved. It is a perfectly legitimate representative function to seek redress from the federal bureaucracy for some governmental injustice. In the words of Hubert H. Humphrey:

> . . . the main job of Congress is to redress grievances, to right wrongs, to make freedom and justice living realities for all. This is the essence of politics: to translate the concerns and the creative responses of a vast citizenry into effective and humane laws.[26]

Thus the broker and errand boy functions enable members to perform a number of valuable and worthwhile services for their constituents. Members are enabled to use their power and influence in constructive and satisfying ways by righting wrongs that otherwise might well go unchallenged. Engaging in these efforts also enables congressmen to keep closer tabs on the bureaucracy and to see the impact of laws enacted by them. Besides this, members of Congress are electorally oriented, and errand running is good politics. As long as they are elected by local constituencies, the representatives are going to try to bring home the bacon. While it may have some undesirable aspects, this system lends an element of accountability to the representative role that might otherwise be lacking.

While such activities may be personally rewarding, a major disadvantage is the valuable time they consume. The increasing volume of constituent demands takes a heavy toll on the time frequently needed for other important duties. Errand running may consume anywhere from 40 to 75 percent of a member's and his staff's time. Because of their greater electoral vulnerability, freshmen are more likely to be errand boys than veterans, but many members spend a substantial portion of their time in these activities. While a majority in the Congress emphasize their law-making function, a significant minority emphasize constituent services.

Because he is an elective official, the life of a member of Congress, especially the representative who serves a two-year term, is one of a constant campaigner. The politician's basic instinct is self-preservation; consequently the elected representative's every move must be weighed in terms of its electoral implications. As former U.S. Representative Walter Judd used to say, you must be re-elected to be a good congressman. The job security of the member of Congress is closely tied to how well he satisfies his constituents. He may come to Washington with aspirations of becoming a great national statesman, but he must first of all develop a good relationship with the voters at home who will determine whether he continues in office or not. In this respect, Speaker William Bankhead's advice to a freshman member is still sound. He advised:

> It is a simple secret. Give close and prompt attention to your mail. Your votes and speeches may make you well known and give you a reputation, but it's the way you handle your mail that determines your re-election.[27]

Every member has his own special constituency to keep happy and he must keep his "fences mended" or even the most popular and well-known find themselves with re-election problems.

One aspect of the representative's job that sometimes brings him under criticism is that legislators must constantly engage in compromise. Politics is the art of the possible, and no one is more aware of this than he who must enact our public policies. Seldom do individual members get everything they would like in a measure, but to achieve a goal, they must give a little here, bend a little there. This is the key to getting policies through the Congress. To many idealists this is unacceptable because they feel decisions should be a matter of principle, not compromise. However, in our highly pluralistic society, compromise and the aggregation of competing interests are major functions of our legislators. They must find the common grounds on which a majority of our citizens can agree, or at least, accept. Madison's concept of the legislature was that its principal role would be the regulation of conflicting economic interests and that these interests would be the major influences in proposing and opposing legislation. While this is not the total function of the legislature, it is an important facet of the legislator's contribution to the functioning of our democratic system.

This leads us to another vital role of the representative in a democratic system. While the legislator has a duty to learn what his constituents desire in the way of public policy, he has an equally important responsibility to educate them and keep them informed of governmental policies and activities. He is, or should be, a vital source of information and influence in a democratic government. Effective two-way communication between the representative and his constituents is an essential ingredient of the representative function. The banks of telephone booths in the congressional cloakrooms serve as constant reminders that the representative's role is communication. Also, the rules of each house reflect this responsibility by providing each senator twelve round trips to his home state each year, and one trip for each month Congress is in session for each representative. Most members far exceed this number of visits back home each year.

Speaker Reed once noted, "It is a very lonely life that a man leads who becomes aware of truths before their time." Because of their position and the nature of their jobs, most congressmen are usually ahead of their constituents in anticipating national problems and are better informed on most issues. In fact, the representative frequently deals with issues on which his constituents have expressed no will and have little or no interest. Thus, on occasion, the representative must lead, inform, educate and correct his constituents and their thinking. He is obliged to help his constituents grasp the real issues and make the political world of Washington as understandable for them as possible. In light of the complexity of the issues and procedures involved, the fragmentation and obscuring of decision-making by such devices as seniority and committee structure, the apathetic lack of interest on the part of constituents, and the press of time on the representative himself, keeping the folks back home informed is no simple task.

For these and other reasons, one of the chief areas of congressional irresponsibility is the failure of individual members to assume responsibility for fully and honestly informing their constituents. As the late Representative Clem Miller observed, members are sometimes hesitant to give their constituents the blunt facts. In fact, members may on occasion try to obscure the real issues and divert constituent attention from questions they don't want raised. Frank Smith reports that not long after coming to the House he asked a colleague how he was going to explain his vote on a public power issue to REA members in his district who would be displeased with the vote. His colleague's response, "I'll tell them that the Secretary of the Interior integrated the swimming pools in Washington." Unfortunately this kind of tactic still works on many issues and is resorted to much too often by some members. As a consequence, the gap between the real issues being faced by the policy-makers and the public's understanding appears to grow rather than shrink. In this day of credibility gaps and erosion of faith in governmental institutions, our representatives must do a better and more responsible job of communicating and educating.

In addition to all these roles, the member of Congress must also find time to be a member of one or more committees. Some members feel that effectiveness in one's committees is the most important part of the job. On occasion the member must function as a judge in cases involving the punishment or expulsion of members, impeachment, contempt and contested elections. On occasion he functions as an elector, choosing President or Vice President under provisions of the twelfth and twenty-fifth amendments. Thus the role of the elected representative is much, much broader than simply enacting laws on behalf of his constituents. The particular role depends to a great extent on the individual member, but he certainly won't lack things to occupy his time.

Conclusion

As a representative body, the United States Congress is a highly complex organization which can remain almost incomprehensible even to those who have spent most of their lives in and around it. Intricate, colorful, steeped in tradition, rich in controversy, highly significant in the political process, it is a superbly interesting institution of representatve government. It is probably the most honored legislative body in the world today; at the same time, the most harshly criticized. It can make the transition from the heights of lofty statesmanship to the level of complete mediocrity in a matter of hours. It can be highly representative or almost totally unrepresentative.

In theory at least, the ideal system of government would be a pure democracy in which the citizens make all decisions directly. Because the republican form is only "second best," there is a persistent tension between the ideal and the actual practice of representation. Since in the republican form the citizens cannot act directly for themselves, their interests must be maximized by their duly elected representatives. While presidents and bureaucrats have representative functions, the focus of those analyzing representative government has been the legislature. Since the origins of representative government, society has experienced such dramatic changes as the industrial and technological revolutions. Economic institutions have become highly centralized and governmental activities have multiplied in number and complexity. Have these far-

reaching changes rendered representative government incapable
of coping with the problems of modern society? As Walter
Lippmann noted in a December 12, 1963, article:

> Democratic government based on the popular election of rep-
> resentative assemblies is a difficult form of government . . .
> there are serious reasons for asking ourselves whether the
> system as it exists today will be able to cope with the world
> as it is in the middle of the twentieth century.[28]

America's tremendous growth since 1789 has unquestionably
made the Congress a rather cumbersome and, in several respects,
unrepresentative policy-maker for so pluralistic a society. The
urbanization of the American populace in the twentieth century
brought about considerable change in the nation's political structure. The Congress fails to reflect the full impact of these changes.
In spite of reapportionment in the 1960's, Congress is still inclined
to favor rural and military America over urban and poor America.
Representatives from safe rural districts continue to be re-elected
and build seniority which brings them to positions of considerable
power and influence. Their effect is reflected in the policies enacted by the Congress. While only about 4.5 percent of our population remains on the farm, the U.S. Department of Agriculture
employs 86,000 persons; the Department of Housing and Urban
Development, 16,000. While every cow on every farm in America
must be tested for TB, this is not required for every child. In one
year Congress approved expenditures of $27 million for weed con-
trol, $3.2 million to eradicate witchweed, and $6.7 million to keep
the water hyacinth from Southern waterways. This is about $37
million to control weeds, considerably more than was appropriated
for rat control or fighting juvenile delinquency.

While the reapportionment ordered by the courts has made
the population of districts more nearly equal, it has not substantially altered the distribution of power within the Congress. This
malapportionment of power within may well pose more of a problem for really effective representative government than the malapportionment of districts. The impact of such traditional practices
as seniority tends to give disproportionate power to representatives
from those states and districts which in many instances are least
typical of the whole Congress or the nation generally.

Have modern technology and methods of communication rendered our imperfect system of representation obsolete? Should we, as commentator David Brinkley has suggested, now have a national referendum or poll on many issues rather than rely on elected representatives to make the decisions? Is the average citizen familiar enough with the issues and well enough informed to make a wise decision on the complex issues faced by government today? Would we be better served by developing a new system, untried and still imperfect, than by reforming and improving the present one?

Modern technology and the electronic media have already made an enormous impact on the representative role of Congress. Because of his position and his access to the press and broadcast media, the President has developed a much more direct relationship with the people than was possible in the time before radio and television. To a great degree this has altered the traditional relationship between Congress and the executive, in that the President no longer answers to the legislature but to the people directly. Because of this, such intermediary agencies as political parties, special interest groups, and other political organizations on which members of Congress depend for input and direction, have lost some of their power. Consequently, the elected members of Congress, who should be the most sensitive of all officials to the impact of governmental policies and programs on the citizen, are really least able to determine how programs are being administered and are affecting their constituents. That arm of government which is supposed to be closest to the people thus appears the least able to act effectively and decisively. This is why the polls repeatedly show the Congress to be held in low esteem.

The keys to the rehabilitation of the legislature as an effective branch of government are the attitudes of the citizens and of the Congress. As we have noted, in our system questions of public policy are resolved not through public referenda but by elected representatives. It is the role of the constituents to chart the course of government for the elected representatives. In our rapidly changing and complex society this is a critical task requiring considerable skill on the part of the electorate. To perform this task effectively the voters must take it seriously. The idea of representative government carries with it the idea of an interested and informed electorate. Rousseau said in a well-ordered city every man flies to the assemblies. The citizens must understand and appreciate the significance of governmental actions on their lives because, as Rousseau noted, when men begin to say of the affairs of state *what does it matter to me?* the state is on its way to being lost. Unfortunately, public concern and knowledge of congressional action in the United States are woefully low. One of the greatest tragedies of the Watergate episode is that it has "turned-off" so many citizens' interest and desire to participate in the political process. They are convinced the whole process is "dirty business" and they want no part of it. A democratic system can ill afford such neglect on the part of its citizens. The masses of the citizens must decide to take an active part in the process, to demand responsiveness and responsibility from their elected representatives, to rid the system of its "bad apples," and to insist on high moral standards and levels of performance from their public officials. When an informed and concerned electorate does this, the elected office holders will take note.

Members of the legislative branch can make a significant contribution to the restoration of faith in governmental institutions. Currently the lack of strong leadership at the top, both in terms of national goals and general operating principles, has undermined public faith in government. Though Congress has allowed its power to erode, it still plays a vital role in government. As long as major decisions with broad social consequences, such as tax rates, welfare spending, and federal construction projects, are made through the political process, the Congress will have a role to perform. The time is ripe for the legislative branch to assert itself with a new vigor and to provide at least some of the leadership currently so badly needed in our system. The legislature is still a vital link on our system between the governed and those who govern, and some leadership on its part would do more than anything else to restore some of its lost esteem.

Notes

1. James Wilson, *Works,* ed. James Andrews (Chicago: Collaghan & Co., 1896), V. I, p. 389.
2. Alfred de Grazia, *Public and Republic* (New York, Alfred Knopf, 1951), p. 4.
3. Edmund Burke, Speech to Electors of Bristol (1774).

4. Warren Weaver, Jr., *Both Your Houses: The Truth About Congress* (New York: Praeger Publishers, 1972), p. 143.
5. As quoted in Hanna Pitkin, *Representation* (New York: Atherton Press, 1969), p. 177.
6. Charles Clapp, *The Congressman: His Work As He Sees It* (Garden City, N.Y.: Doubleday, 1963), pp. 123–124.
7. *Congressional Quarterly* (January 27, 1973), p. 129.
8. Emanuel Celler, "Pressure Groups in Congress," *Annals of the American Academy of Political and Social Sciences* 319 (1958): 1 ff.
9. Frank Smith, *Congressman From Mississippi* (New York: Pantheon Books, 1964), p. 108.
10. Walter Lippmann, *The Public Philosophy* (New York: The New American Library, 1956), p. 28.
11. Frank Sorauf as quoted by Neal Riemer in *The Representative: Trustee? Partisan? Politics?* (Boston: D. C. Heath and Company, 1967), p. viii.
12. As quoted in Pitkin, *Representation*, p. 73.
13. John Stuart Mill, *Considerations on Representative Government* (New York: Everyman's Library).
14. *The Federalist* (New York: The Modern Library, 1937), p. 214.
15. H. L. Mencken, "A Carnival of Buncombe," Baltimore *Evening Sun* (July 23, 1928), p. 15.
16. John Kennedy, "The Shame of the States," *New York Times Magazine* (May 18, 1958), p. 12.
17. *Reynolds* v. *Sims,* 377 U.S. 533 (1964).
18. *Wesberry* v. *Sanders,* 376 U.S. 1 (1964).
19. *Kirkpatrick* v. *Preisler,* 394 U.S. 526, 546 (1969).
20. George B. Merry, "Putting the Houses in Order," *Christian Science Monitor* (October 29, 1968).
21. See John Stuart Mill, *Representative Government*, pp. 308–321.
22. As quoted by Roger Davidson in *The Role of the Congressman* (New York: Pegasus, 1969), p. 101.
23. *Ibid.,* p. 80.
24. As quoted in Stephen Bailey, *Congress Makes a Law* (New York: Columbia University Press, 1950), p. 215.
25. T. Edward Westen, "The Constituent Needs Help: Casework in the House of Representatives" in Sven Groennings and Jonathan Hawley, *To Be a Congressman: The Promise and the Power* (Washington: Acropolis Books, Ltd., 1973), p. 64.
26. Hubert H. Humphrey, "What It Means to Be in Congress," Introduction in Sven Groennings and Jonathan Hawley, *To Be a Congressman: The Promise and the Power* (Washington: Acropolis Books, Ltd., 1973), p. xvii.
27. As quoted by the Joint Committee on Congress, *Hearings* (1946), p. 1524.
28. Walter Lippmann, "When a Congress Throttles the Executive," *Courier-Journal,* Louisville, Kentucky (December 12, 1963).

Chapter II

The Personnel
of Congress

WHILE THE INSTITUTIONAL framework provided by the Constitution-makers has a significant bearing on the representativeness of the government, an equally important element is the recruitment and selection of those to sit in Congress. This is an aspect, however, that is frequently overlooked, as is evidenced by the fact that the framers of the U.S. Constitution had little to say about staffing beyond the provision for periodic elections. They apparently operated on the assumption that the desire for public office would be sufficiently widespread and strong to bring forward qualified candidates in sufficient numbers.

On the matter of qualifications, the framers were equally brief. They confined the constitutional requirements for a seat in Congress to age, citizenship, and residence. Members of the House must be at least twenty-five years of age, a citizen of the U.S. for seven years and a resident of the state from which elected. Senators must be at least thirty years old, a citizen for nine years, and a resident of the state from which elected. Thus the framers shied away from enumerating an elaborate list of requirements for holding a seat in Congress. They probably agreed with Jefferson that the best government would result from the selection of the "natural aristoi" to rule, but they apparently felt the matter would take care of itself. Thus they left membership in the Congress open, as the author of *Federalist* Number 57 states, to

> . . . every citizen whose merit may recommend him to esteem and confidence of his country. No qualification of wealth,

of birth, of religious faith, or of civil profession is permitted
to fetter the judgment or disappoint the inclination of the
people.[1]

The major devices for recruiting and staffing the legislature
are the formally competitive elections provided by the Constitution
and the informal mass political parties which grew up outside the
Constitution. While the mass parties, universal suffrage, the secret
ballot, the seventeenth amendment (direct election of U.S. Senators) and the direct primary have broadened participation and opportunities for competition, informal recruitment standards have
proven considerably more restrictive in selecting members of Congress than have the formal constitutional requirements. Despite
various efforts by reformers to make them more democratic in
terms of broader participation, elections, especially elections to the
U.S. Congress, have remained essentially, as Aristotle first noted,
oligarchic affairs. Both in terms of the candidate participants selected and the electorate voting, the process is limited to a relatively small portion of the theoretically eligible participants.

While in theory a wide range of citizens is eligible to run for
the Congress, its actual membership does not reflect such a broadly
based access to the system. Though each congressman is a unique
individual and many different types constitute the membership,
Congress is not an accurate cross-section of American society.
Congress is the stronghold of upper-middle-class America, with the
typical member being a church-going white male, fifty-two years
old, a military veteran and a college graduate. In terms of members, the Congress overrepresents lawyers, businessmen, bankers,
farmers, educators and other professionals while women, blacks,
clergymen, laborers and scientists are underrepresented. Though
different districts with varying cultures will impose different requirements for candidates, members are recruited almost wholly
in all districts from the relatively high-status occupations. Thus,
while the society is highly pluralistic, the Congress representing it,
because of informal recruitment patterns, is not a representative
cross-section. In chapter one we discussed the implications of this
relative to the representativeness of the Congress. As long as the
elected representative is responsive and responsible to those electing him, it is probably not absolutely essential that all segments of
the populace have one of their own in the Congress itself. How-

ever, it is important to the democratic process that the recruitment and selection process remain open to all qualified candidates and that the system provide sufficient qualified candidates to adequately staff the legislature.

Who Runs?

This raises the important question of who runs for Congress and why. We have already noted the higher social status of most candidates for the national legislature. What other characteristics do they possess generally? Emerson once said that people who sought public office were trying to make up for an inner insufficiency, and while a look at some members might seem to bear this out, there are numerous other factors apparent as well. Most members of Congress are veteran political activists who became interested in politics at an early age and who display a generally positive disposition toward politics. Very few members come to Congress without serving a political apprenticeship elsewhere; many as members of the state legislature, governor, or in some other state or local office. Recruitment patterns seem to favor "local boys" over "carpetbaggers"; thus most members have lengthy and rather close ties to the districts and states from which they are elected.

Motivations for seeking congressional seats are varied. Some run to advance professional careers, especially the lawyers; some "inherit" seats, and some "grew up in politics." The *Congressional Directory* is usually sprinkled with the names of families well-known in American politics—Taft, Stevenson, Pell, Symington, Kennedy, Goldwater, an indication that family background may be a most potent factor in one's seeking public office. While some members were drafted as candidates, many were self-starters. Congress has a lot of self-starters, since the parties are inclined to focus more attention on the Presidential and gubernatorial elections. The role of the party in recruiting candidates for seats in Congress will vary considerably from state to state and district to district. In some areas the parties will dominate the selection process and only candidates of the party's choice can be nominated; in other areas the party may play little or no role in recruiting and nominating candidates. A tightly-knit urban party organization may control congressional districts within the city's boundaries, but rural parties are much less likely to identify with or dominate the politics of a sprawling congressional district. Since congressional districts often tend to be one-party districts, the opposing parties may have to scramble to even come up with a candidate willing to run. Don Riegle (R. Mich.) tells how Larry Ford, a Republican party organizer in Michigan, trying to line up candidates for the party, called him. According to Riegle, Ford couldn't even find a "nice guy" willing to run and lose, so he called him as a last resort. A moderate, Riegle has since left Republican ranks to run and win as the Democratic candidate for the U.S. Senate in his home state. On the whole the parties do a rather poor job of recruiting top quality candidates for congressional offices, and more are self-starters than are genuine party recruits. In interviews with a number of congressmen, Charles Clapp reported that only a few testified to strong party influence, usually in metropolitan districts, and many felt that even opposition by the party organization was not necessarily a serious obstacle to electoral success.[2]

Tenure and Turnover

Political writer Frank R. Kent once observed that every man who held a public office either wanted to keep it or get a better one. This is certainly true of Congress where careerism is the rule rather than the exception. Even though service in Congress is highly demanding and sometimes frustrating, few members who stay for more than one or two terms leave willingly. For the first forty years of its history, turnover in the Congress was relatively high, about 41.5 percent. Until about 1900 first-termers regularly constituted 30 to 40 percent of the Congress, often as much as 50 or 60 percent. Since 1935 first-termers have constituted only about 10 to 25 percent of the Congress, and even after the Johnson landslide in 1964, only 21 percent of the 89th Congress were newcomers. More and more, congressmen have come to view membership in Congress as a career in its own right and as a consequence of this careerist trend, turnover in recent Congresses has been lower than in earlier years, causing the average age of members to rise gradually through the 70th Congress. While prior to 1901 the average tenure for members was 2.9 terms, the average member today has served about 5.5 terms. In earlier Congresses the dean of the House was often about forty years of age. In 1972 Emanuel

Cellar, dean of the House, was eighty-four and had been in Congress almost five decades. The natural attrition rate appears to have increased somewhat in recent Congresses and the median age has been reduced slightly. Reapportionment, the granting of the vote to eighteen-year-olds, and Watergate have encouraged a number of older members not to seek re-election and have contributed to the defeat of others. The 1972 elections brought in seventy-two new House members and thirteen new senators. Few changes in leadership resulted, however. Watergate and its aftermath brought the most substantial changes in more than a generation. Following Watergate and its impact on public attitudes, several members complained that they were no longer treated with the respect their office deserved and that being in Congress was no longer any fun. Former Representative Howard Robison (R. N.Y.) said, "We members of Congress are under a constant cloud of suspicion, a fairly high degree of mistrust and a lack of confidence. . . ."[3] Representative Chet Holifield (D. Calif.) noted:

> You no longer feel that it is an honor to be a member of Congress because there is so much stigma attached to all elective offices as a result of Watergate and the misdeeds of a few members of Congress. The people lack confidence in us. Everyone is suspected of being a crook. People of our capability just don't enjoy things like that.[4]

Calling the last year the most miserable he'd spent in Congress, Wendell Wyatt (R. Ore.) complained, "Watergate has made the mood of the public and their loss of confidence in government more acute. . . . I don't think people have a right to be as pissed off as they are."[5]

With more than forty members deciding not to seek re-election and Watergate haunting other incumbents, the 1974 elections produced the largest freshman class in Congress in decades—ninety-two new members in the House and thirteen in the Senate. This meant that one of every five members in the 94th Congress was a first-termer, an unusually high rate. A major significance of the trend bringing in more new and younger members has been a more activist spirit and a gradual growth in the base of support for congressional reform.

Considering all the pressures, frustrations and demands on those filling congressional offices, what are the attractions making

the motivation to stay so strong? Why is there usually an abun-
dance of candidates ready and waiting to step into the shoes of
those who retire or are defeated? The job of being a congressman
is full-time and demanding. His is a life of almost constant movement and exhausting physical activity with heavy demands upon
his time and his family life. What makes it all worthwhile?

To start with, the financial rewards and personal privileges
accorded members aren't bad. The $57,500 salary is not excessive;
many could make more in other professions. However, when all
the fringe benefits and subsidies are thrown in, the offices become
much more lucrative. The member is provided free office space
and all sorts of allowances for conducting his business. A senator
gets approximately $400,000 and a representative about $160,000
for staff; each gets allowances for telephone, stationery, postage,
travel to the home state or district and free copies of the *Congressional Record* and other government publications. They eat their
meals in subsidized dining rooms, get their hair cut in their own
barbershops at unheard of low prices, and ride almost anywhere
in the District of Columbia at taxi rates unmatched in any other
city in the nation. The federal housekeeping unit will build picture
frames, bookcases, tables, etc. upon request; the National Botan-
ical Gardens will provide plants monthly; and the National Park
Service will make available scenic photographs to brighten the walls
of members' offices. Regardless of their age and health, members
can purchase up to $45,000 worth of life insurance for only $26.82
per month; hospital care is available at reduced rates and all types
of goods and services are provided at rock-bottom prices. To cap
this all off, after thirty-two years' service a member can retire with
80 percent salary, currently $46,000.

In spite of all this, it is entirely possible that the intangibles
attract more people to run for congressional seats than do the tan-
gibles. In a nation steeped in politics, Washington, D.C., is where
the action is. It is the center of power, and its exciting, high-pressure
atmosphere attracts those who aspire to public service and national
leadership. As a member of Congress, one shares, though his role
may be minuscule, in the secrets and satisfactions derived from the
governing of the most powerful nation in the world. For those really
interested in politics and public service, few careers provide more
ample opportunities for translating dreams into reality than service

in Congress. The senator or representative is in a position to perform a great many services of importance to people who are his personal concern. For many, helping ordinary constituents solve their personal problems is the most politically rewarding work possible. Whatever the motivation—egotism, personal vanity, civic mindedness, financial gain—once contracted, "Potomac Fever" is difficult to cure. Once it gets into the bloodstream of the individual, he usually seeks re-election term after term.

Election to Congress

The formal machinery for filling the seats in Congress is the election. Again, the Constitution establishes only the bare essentials, providing that all representatives and one-third of the senators shall be elected every two years. Originally senators were elected by the state legislatures, but adoption of the seventeenth amendment made them elective by direct popular vote as were representatives. Beyond the provision for periodic elections, the Constitution leaves the procedures for selecting members largely up to the individual states. Most states have provided for the nomination of candidates for Congress through the direct primary, though a few states still select these nominees through party conventions.

Regardless of the specific procedures involved, much of the life of the individual member of Congress is devoted to elections and campaigns. To the member of Congress, especially the representative serving a two-year term, nothing is quite so ephemeral as an election victory. No sooner has he won than he is off and running again. To be a congressman is to be a campaigner; campaigns and elections are not just isolated events in his career, but an integral part of his job. For the elected representative, the campaigning never stops.

Convincing an electorate of from 100,000 to 7,000,000 that one should continue to represent them in Washington, D.C., is a complex, demanding and continuing process. No two members go about the process in exactly the same manner. Each campaign for Congress takes place in its own unique setting and is shaped by its own particular circumstances. Many different elements enter into the planning, execution and outcome of a campaign for Congress. Each candidate must decide what particular campaign style and strategy will most likely put him in Congress.

Basically there are two ways to get voters to the polls—persuasion and organization. Most campaigns rely on a combination of the two rather than one or the other. The type of campaign will depend upon the candidate, the district, the electorate and the candidate's party. While the parties may play a substantial role in campaigns for congressional offices in some districts, as a general rule congressional campaigns are more personal than party affairs. In some metropolitan areas, congressional campaigns may be an integral part of the party's total campaign effort. In fact, the seat itself may be used as a reward for long and faithful work on behalf of the party. However, such party campaigns for Congress are the exception rather than the rule. In the vast majority of cases, the individual candidate for Congress, while using his party's label, must organize, finance and conduct his own campaign. It is largely up to him to attract and organize his supporters, define his policy positions and decide whether or not to use increasingly sophisticated modern campaign techniques. Both the techniques and styles of organization in congressional campaigns are changing. The 1974 primary contest between incumbent Frank Stubblefield and challenger Carroll Hubbard for the Democratic nomination in Kentucky's first district illustrates the changing style of organization. Stubblefield's organization followed the traditional pattern for campaigns in Kentucky. He had the usual party organization with campaign chairmen and co-chairmen designated in each county in the district. Though he had the support of most local public officials, Stubblefield's local organizations were often times largely paper organizations that failed to deliver many votes. Hubbard, on the other hand, had little formal organization of the traditional type, not even appointing chairmen in all counties in the district, but had an excellent personal organization developed through long and careful cultivation of personal contacts. For years Hubbard had attended weddings, funerals and any other events where he could make contacts and gain exposure. As a state senator he sent a tremendous volume of letters and other communications to voters. In this way, Hubbard was able to build an organization and successfully challenge an entrenched incumbent, but the work was largely his own.

In some districts where party organization is strong the candidate for Congress may conduct a rather low-key personal campaign depending on a strong party effort to get him elected. He may depend on the popularity of the party's slate and the tendency of the districts' voters to vote the "straight" ticket to get him the votes he needs.

In other districts candidates will employ more sophisticated and more elaborate campaign techniques. With the parties playing less and less of a role in congressional elections, more and more candidates are turning to highly sophisticated techniques in efforts to mobilize more voters. Increasing numbers of candidates are enlisting the aid of consultants, pollsters, public relations firms, media specialists, computer experts, direct mail specialists, make-up artists and all manner of experts in their campaigns. In California particularly, more and more candidates have been hiring public relations firms to handle their campaigns. By the mid-1960's about 85 percent of the winning Senate candidates and almost half the successful House candidates made use of polls in their campaigns. Polls have a number of uses. They may simply be used to determine name familiarity, or they can be used in defining campaign themes and strategy. However, unless carefully conducted, they can be misleading, and they are quite expensive, costing $1,000 to $14,000 for a single poll.

Along these same lines, the communications media have come to play a more and more vital role in campaigns for public office. Publicity is the lifeblood of the congressman, and he must work through the media to gain the exposure he needs to survive. Since the media serve constantly as a mechanism for linking the representative with his constituency, they can be a valuable tool at campaign time. When we speak of the media today, of course, we immediately think of television. In Senate races, television may be an effective campaign medium, and some House districts with a moderate-sized, centrally located city may lend themselves to effective TV usage. On the whole, however, the House district where TV can be used effectively is rather rare, and in some states effective use becomes a problem. New Jersey, for example, is served largely by stations located in New York and Pennsylvania. Money spent with the New York stations is wasted on a lot of viewers who can't vote for the candidate. These are all factors the candidate must weigh in devising his campaign strategy and design.

The big question facing the candidate, of course, is how he

can most effectively mobilize the voters and get them to the polls on election day. It would be nice if we could say the best way to accomplish this is to have the candidate engage in a frank and candid discussion of the issues and to fully inform the voters who would then go to the polls and vote their choice. In reality, nothing could be much wider of the mark from what really takes place in a congressional campaign. Though there are some indications that voters may be gradually becoming more issue conscious, current data indicate that a majority do not view individual candidates for Congress in terms of issues and policies. The popular image of the congressman is marked by an almost total absence of policy content. As a consequence, campaigns for Congress often are largely issueless affairs and decisions as to who shall fill the representative seats are based on other factors which may have little or no relevance to representative government. Such things as appearance, ethnic background, name identification, religion and other similar factors may become the primary basis for voters' decisions. Commenting on his fifty years as a representative from Boston, Joe Martin noted that his was a good political name for his district. He recalled that on one occasion he was even introduced to an audience sprinkled with a substantial number of French-Canadians as Joseph St. Martin. He went on to note that his brogue had been a distinct political asset in Massachusetts as the Scotch had thought it was Scotch, and Irish thought it an Irish brogue. Martin opined as to how he was content to have each group of voters think as it did and take him for its own. Having such factors play a prime role in electoral decisions can, however, at times become rather confusing. In an effort to confuse his supporters, opponents of George Norris recruited a grocer of the same name to oppose the incumbent in one of his bids for re-election. Norris won, but this ploy no doubt confused a number of voters. In the 1974 Republican primary in the second district in Idaho the contestants were Orval Hansen, the incumbent, and George V. Hansen, a former representative. The Democratic candidate who opposed George V., the victor in the primary, was Max Hanson. The lack of really significant issues tends to force the candidates to resort to gimmicks, such as the "walking campaigns" of Lawton Chiles in Florida and Dick Clark in Iowa, or to focus on other matters and resort to issues and slogans that are less than clear-cut. Discussion of complex national policy issues tends to be oversimplified or subverted by catchy sloganeering such as "a younger man with younger ideas" in the Tunney-Murphy senatorial race in California.

Considering the attitude of most voters, the nature of our electoral system and the role of the media, there is little to encourage candidates to make their campaigns more issue-oriented. Since congressional elections are set by the Constitution for periodic intervals rather than being held only when significant issues are at stake, candidates may find it rather difficult to focus their campaigns on burning issues that will significantly affect the outcome of the election. Also, since we are a nation of headline readers who prefer our information in capsulated form, the communications media tend to look for the ready clichés and slogans which tend to distort and oversimplify complex issues.

Since the candidates are not compelled, in fact, not even expected, to stick to the real issues in their campaigns, congressional campaigns have had their share of mudslinging and demagoguery. Most legislative candidates are not nearly so candid as was Edmund Burke with his Bristol constituency or even Otis Pike (D. N. Y.), who wrote in his 1968 newsletter of the 90th Congress:

> It would be nice to be able to report that it [the 90th Congress] went out on a high note, doing lofty things for all the people of America. Candor compels the admission that it went out on a low note, doing tiny little acts for minor political advantage.

Unfortunately for the prospects of a well-informed electorate, too many congressional campaigns are marked by efforts to play upon the fears and prejudices of the voters and to cloud the issues rather than to enlighten and inform the electorate. Speaking of the all-too-frequent style of many of his Southern colleagues, Frank Smith noted:

> . . . intelligence, unfortunately, was no weapon to carry into the rough and tumble of a contest against the pseudo-evangelistic vulgarities and federal spending promises by which Bilbo won the support of the mass of voters who so blindly supported him. . . .[6]

While the situation has improved somewhat since Bilbo, too many campaign tactics still are designed to play upon the baser instincts of the voters. After being defeated in his 1970 bid for re-election to the Senate, Albert Gore of Tennessee remarked, "Can you imagine it, coming down here to find out not what the people wanted, what they needed, but what their fears were."[7]

Too many candidates probably feel as Joe Martin did in speaking of his 1938 bid for re-election: ". . . I couldn't allow the opposition to do all the demagoguing," he explained. At another point in his memoirs, speaking of the traditional Republican outcry against governmental spending, Martin admits this probably had little impact electorally, but "it was a handy weapon to point at the Democrats when we had no other." [8] If elections to Congress were not such serious business, some of the shenanigans would be downright amusing. When George Smathers and Claude Pepper were engaged in a heated contest for a Senate seat from Florida, Smathers' supporters circulated stories that Pepper had practiced nepotism, had a sister who was a thespian, a brother who was, of all things, a homo sapien, and when he went to college he had matriculated. Serious charges, which no doubt, caused many a voter second thoughts about voting for such a candidate. In Texas when liberal Senator Ralph Yarborough was seeking re-election, chiropractors in the state were told he favored M.D.'s; M.D.'s were told he favored chiropractors; truckers were told he favored the railroads, rail men were told he wanted to increase the weight limits for trucks; wets were told he was dry and dries were told he was a wet. If that doesn't confuse the voters, the candidates themselves may add to the confusion. After a great career as a baseball pitcher for the Washington Senators, Walter Johnson decided he would seek a seat in Congress. Joe Martin, a leader in the Republican party and a rabid baseball fan, had his speech writers compose two speeches for Johnson to use in his campaign—one for the farmers in his Maryland district and one for the industrialists. Unfortunately Johnson got the two confused, delivering the farm speech to the industrialists and the industry speech to the farmers.

While the campaigns for congressional offices do leave much to be desired, they are an essential and vital part of our representative process. The voters' periodic expressions of their choices for members of Congress constitute their principal means of shaping national policy. The campaign is the crucible of American politics. Physically and emotionally straining, the campaign exposes the candidate to close public scrutiny and tests the mettle of those who make our laws. The campaign is really an intensified version of the sort of contact the congressman has with his constituents day by day, and it puts to the ultimate test his effectiveness in relating to individuals and groups through both face-to-face encounters and the media. Through his campaigning, the candidate develops a system of contacts and sources of information, makes numerous acquaintances and establishes a network of advisers and builds support among various interests in his district. Probably most important of all, the campaign helps the candidate to better understand the needs, fears and aspirations of his constituents and thus define his function as an elected representative. Therefore the campaign becomes an important cog in the policy-making machinery of our republican system.

A number of factors have come to exert substantial influence in making elections something less than a totally open process for selecting the Congress. More and more, national leaders have shown an inclination for getting into congressional elections, which in the past were considered as largely state and local affairs in which national leaders were wary about interfering for fear of getting their fingers burned. Not all national leaders have been as confident of their positive influence as President Johnson was when compaigning for Representative Henry Gonzalez in Texas. According to Gonzalez, Johnson arrived, stalked into the airport terminal swarming with oil-rich millionaires (overwhelmingly Republican, of course) and took a poll. Not surprisingly, eight out of ten were supporters of Gonzalez' opponent. Johnson and Gonzalez then drove to a Latino neighborhood in the district where Johnson took another poll. All the people said they would vote for Gonzalez. Whereupon, LBJ turned to Gonzalez and said, "Look, I've only been here forty-five minutes and already I've reversed the trend." Gonzalez was furious. There is no doubt that under the right circumstances White House endorsements and photo sessions, Presidential visits to the home state or district, and money from the national party can help in a hard-fought congressional campaign. The ultimate impact, however, is to remove the choice of elected representatives more from the local constituents to forces outside the state and district.

Another factor of considerable impact on the outcome of elections to Congress is that of incumbency. A successful campaign for Congress usually marks the beginning of a lengthy congressional career unless one leaves voluntarily. It is usually much harder to get in than to stay in once elected. The power of congressional incumbency is frequently sufficient to bring victory even when Presidential and other party candidates are experiencing defeat. Incumbent congressmen enjoy a success rate of about 85 to 95 percent, usually winning re-election with 55 percent or more of the vote. In an average year about 400 to 435 representatives will seek re-election, and of this number approximately 370 will be successful. As a general rule, three or four senators will be unsuccessful in their bid for re-election. Some observers predicted that because of Watergate and the attitude of the voters, incumbency would be a handicap rather than an advantage in 1974. This didn't prove to be the case. In the 1974 primaries only two of ten incumbent senators failed in their bids for renomination. Thus it becomes abundantly clear that incumbency has its advantages and those challenging an incumbent face a formidable task. Dr. Robert Erikson, who heads a Ralph Nader team looking into the impact of incumbency, says its value is substantial. He says every congressman goes to the polls with a built-in 9 percent advantage over any challenger.

The candidate challenging an incumbent congressman may discover rather quickly that the vast majority of party and community leaders are more inclined to support the incumbent than to cooperate with a challenger. He will also find that they are much more willing to make an investment in the form of a campaign contribution in the incumbent's campaign than in his own. Trying to raise enough money to effectively challenge a long-time incumbent can become a really frustrating experience. Add to this the fact that the incumbent is probably already better known, has the psychological advantages of knowing the job and having conducted a winning campaign before, has prestige and respect among large numbers of voters, has performed many favors through his office and has a staff paid for by the taxpayers at his disposal to help with the campaign. Not many challengers can afford to hire the kind of professional help the incumbent has at his disposal free, and most members do not hesitate to exploit this advantage to the fullest. He is also in a position to call upon distinguished colleagues and government officials to lend a helping hand in his campaign, and many of his former staff members may be available in the district for volunteer work at campaign time. He also has available to him at little or no cost services that aid him substantially in his campaigning. Free mailing privileges under the frank* is a rather awesome privilege enabling the incumbent to inform his constituents and impress them with his hard work in their behalf. Some members have had twinges of guilt over incumbents' use of the frank for campaign purposes and have proposed that, on a limited scale, it be extended to challengers as well. In 1971 Senator Hugh Scott suggested two free mailings for both candidates. Such proposals usually have been couched so as not to give away the full advantage. The incumbent can also insert his campaign speeches in the *Congressional Record* and then get them reproduced at a fraction of what it costs his challenger to get his campaign literature printed. Or the member can go the House or Senate studios and have two one-minute color video tapes produced for something over twenty dollars, yet another advantage of incumbency. A study by the Americans for Democratic Action (ADA) concluded that in terms of salary, staff allowances, office space, franking, travel expenses and other breaks, incumbency could be worth up to $376,346 in an election year. This makes challenging an incumbent a rather up-hill battle.

Yet another factor which has tended to narrow the election as a process for filling the seats of Congress has been the ever upward spiral of campaign costs. The increasing size of the electorate, the growing use of polls, professional managers and consultants, extensive use of communications media, and steadily increasing costs of goods and services have combined to make running for Congress in many states and districts a terribly expensive business. The cost of running for all elective offices in the United States in 1952 was $140,000,000; by 1972 the figure had grown to $400,-000,000. Running for the Senate may cost anywhere from a few hundred dollars to several million. A candidate for representative may spend from virtually nothing to several hundred thousand dollars in getting elected. In 1968 Richard Ottinger spent $200,000 getting elected to the House from New York. The key is that the in-

---

*This refers to the privilege members of Congress have to send their official correspondence through the mails free. A facsimile of their signature (the "frank") in the upper right corner suffices for the normal postage.

dividual candidate for Congress is largely responsible for financing his own campaign. Though in 1972 the Michigan Republican party had a $1,575,000 budget, candidates for the House did not share in this, but had to raise their own funds. The impact of this fact, coupled with rising campaign costs, has been to substantially narrow the access to congressional elections. The myth of the poor boy growing up to become President may no longer apply. In fact, the poor boy in the future may not even hope to become a United States Representative! At least not in those competitive districts where extensive and expensive campaigning is necessary for election.

One of the most striking characteristics of congressional elections is the number in which there is no real competition. In this respect, congressional elections may be unique, as other races in the same state may be competitive while certain congressional districts remain totally safe. Though the number of one-party states has declined, congressional districts, which are more likely to be one-party areas than are entire states, have shown no dramatic change. The position of United States Representative is probably the least competitive of all political offices in the country. Election data indicate that approximately three of every four congressional districts are completely dominated by one major party. In addition, over three-fourths of the districts are relatively "safe" districts for the incumbents. This deals with two different aspects—1. Districts "safe" for the party candidate regardless of who he is. 2. Districts safe for the incumbent regardless of party. This leaves fewer than one-fourth of the 435 House seats that are genuinely competitive. Interestingly, however, though most congressional seats are rather invulnerable, few races go uncontested. The open primary nominating system and the weak party organizations facilitate the appearance of a multitude of candidates. The futility of the cause does not deter many who run out of a sense of civic or party duty, or those who seek exposure rather than victory. From 1914 to 1958, personnel changes resulted from only 23.4 percent of the congressional elections. Only 11.5 percent of these involved changes in party control of the seats in Congress. The upshot of all this is that the competitive electoral system provided by the Founding Fathers is not in the final analysis an open and highly democratic process for filling the legislature. But while it has its shortcomings and could no doubt be improved in a number of respects, it is, as Aristotle noted of democracy, the most desirable alternative available.

Professional Staffs in Congress

In any governmental structure it is not really the office-holders who provide the continuity and perform most of the routine work, but the professional staff. As Czar Nicholas said, "Not I, but 10,000 clerks rule Russia." With all their many functions, members of Congress are terribly pressed for time, and they certainly cannot begin to attend to all the demands of their offices. For the committees of Congress, staffs are absolutely essential to their effective functioning. For the individual member, a dedicated and competent staff is vital for winning and retaining a seat in Congress. Thus, it is the staff directors, the chief counsels, the legislative and administrative assistants, and the varied ranks of aides, clerks and secretaries who make the machinery of Congress go.

Congressional staffs have not always played the vital role they play today, of course. In early Congresses clerks were provided for committees by special resolution on a temporary basis. It wasn't until the start of the twentieth century that staffing really began to get attention in Congress. By 1900, staff for members and clerks for committees were established practice. In 1914 the Legislative Reference Service was created and in 1919 the Legislative Drafting Service was added. The latter was renamed the Office of the Legislative Counsel in 1924. These offices, designed to aid members in information gathering and bill drafting, were an outgrowth of the Progressive Movement of the period. On the whole, committee staff remained largely patronage positions, and prior to 1946 few committees had qualified staff with tenure. Many committees followed the practice of "borrowing" staff from executive agencies, thus undermining the concept of separation of powers. Effective oversight of the executive branch was made extremely difficult with limited committee staffs. Adoption of the Legislative Reorganization Act of 1946 marks the beginning of really "professional" staffs for congressional committees.

Over the years, as the volume and complexity of legislation has increased, congressional staffs also have grown. Today the personal and committee staffs, the Legislative Reference Service, the Office of Legislative Counsel and housekeeping personnel have reached substantial proportions. In just the last two decades, congressional staffs have tripled. In the period since the enactment of the Legislative Reorganization Act of 1970, staff and research functions have grown rapidly. The Congressional Research Service has been substantially expanded, its budget tripling to nearly $14 million for 1975. The General Accounting Office has an expanded role in program analysis and evaluation and a budget of $127 million, twice the 1970 level. GAO now has a staff of over 5,000. The newly created congressional Office of Technology Assessment already has a 1975 budget of nearly $5 million. The 1974 Budget Reform Act also created a much-needed Congressional Budget Office. So Congress' research and staff facilities have grown rapidly in the last decade. Senators are given staff allowances ranging from approximately $400,000 to $750,000, depending on the size of their constituency. Out of this allowance senators hire from eight to thirty or forty staff members; the average senate office staff numbers thirteen to sixteen. House members are allowed up to sixteen full-time employees with the average staff numbering six or seven members. The size and organization of congressional offices varies considerably. The late William T. Dawson, representative from Chicago, had at one time one staff member in Washington and a full staff in his Chicago office. In addition to those hired from their allowances, some politically prominent members are able to attract numbers of volunteer speech writers, researchers, academics, and students eager to help a U.S. Senator or Representative. This additional help can be particularly valuable, providing the member with outside expertise and advice from professionals who are free of bureaucratic restraints or executive ties.

Recruitment of professional staff in congressional offices is a largely personal task of the individual member. Many of the staff may come from the home state or district, having worked for the member before or served on his campaign staff. Newcomers are usually advised to hire at least one or more Capitol Hill "professionals" who have been around a while and know the ropes. The typical staff has one or two individuals who have prior experience on the Hill. Most members arriving for the first time are not so well-organized in their approach, nor can they afford it, as was Senator Lloyd Bentsen (D. Texas). When elected, he hired a consulting firm to make a study of the most effective senate office operations and set up his own office along these lines.

Until just recently Congress had no personnel or employment office, and employees were recruited largely by word of mouth and personal contacts. For the last three years an Office of Placement and Office Management operating under the Joint Committee on Congressional Operations has functioned as a sort of clearing house for those seeking employment on Capitol Hill. However, employment in many staff positions is still a highly selective process and many jobs remain patronage positions. According to staff in the Office of Placement and Office Management, Congress is not bound by the Equal Employment Opportunity Act. One staff member said this was so Southerners wouldn't have to hire blacks in their offices, which might embarrass them when constituents visited. Apparently a number of members include in their instructions for filling staff positions requirements which are discriminatory in nature. Some indicate on their employee request cards "no blacks" or "no minorities."

Beyond the specific requirements set by the individual member or the committee, there are no special qualifications established for congressional staff members. Consequently, congressional staff members represent a variety of professions, backgrounds and experience. In fact, from the standpoint of their socioeconomic backgrounds, the staff probably constitute a more accurate cross-section of the populace than do members of Congress. As with the members, many staff members have a legal background, but Kenneth Kofmehl, a political scientist who has made probably the most exhaustive study of congressional staffs, says the number is "not excessive." Kofmehl concludes that on the whole committee staffs are well-fitted for their posts by educaton, previous employment and aptitude. He says they compare well with groups elsewhere in the government.[9]

For the member of Congress who is hard-pressed to come up with both time and the information necessary for carrying out his role as legislator, the staff become indispensable. The role of the staff will vary, depending on the individual member, but of necessity the staff will perform many of the functions of the office. Many members assign the "errand boy" tasks largely to their staff assistants. Because of the press of time and the technical nature of many matters they consider, the elected representatives rely heavily on others for the information and judgments necessary in carrying out their functions. Staff members are able to specialize much more than the members, and consequently members must frequently rely heavily on them in dealing with complex technical matters. Thus it is often the administrative assistants, the legislative assistants, the staff counsels or the staff economists, rather than the members themselves, who think up the legislation, make the deals, listen to the lobbyists, determine what mail the member sees, who gets into his office, and handle the day-to-day operations of the offices.

It is the professional staff who provide the continuity in the legislative bureaucracy and keep the machinery functioning through changes in membership, political parties, and leadership. Many staff members have served Congress for a considerable period. Lew Deschler was parliamentarian in the House for more than forty years, serving a number of speakers, both Democrat and Republican. Joseph H. McGann went to work for the Rivers and Harbors Committee of the House in February of 1902. In 1920 he became clerk of the committee and continued as clerk of its successor, the House Committee on Public Works. His tenure on the committee has exceeded that of nine chairmen and more than 250 members. Elton Layton started his career as clerk of the House Interstate and Foreign Commerce Committee in April 1921 and served through 1954. Frequently these "middle level" staff members come to play a major role in the congressional establishment and to wield considerable influence.

The individual member or the committee chairman, preoccupied with many competing demands on his time, often delegates to his staff a major part of the responsibility for running the office or committee. Also some members and chairmen are inclined to accept a vigorous role for certain staff personnel. In many situations, a key staff member may be the "expert" and may be in a better position to be informed than anyone else. When the Democratic Policy Committee meets to decide the calendar of business in the Senate, there is usually only one person who has read all the reports and bills. That person is not the majority leader, but Charles Ferris, chief counsel for the Democratic Policy Committee. Around Congress, to be in this sort of position is to have power and influence. Ferris is indispensable to the Senate Democrats as a floor tactician.

In the committees particularly, staff members play a paramount role. The impeachment hearings before the House Judiciary Committee in 1974 illustrate the important role the staff play in committee proceedings. The range of staff activities is extremely broad, depending upon the committee and the nature of its chairman. It is not unusual for the staff to have the responsibility for scheduling and arranging meetings, preparing agenda, selecting and scheduling witnesses and related activities. In addition, the staff frequently prepare questions for members, conduct briefings for members, draft amendments and bills and in some cases conduct the interrogation of witnesses. On occasion, hearings may be conducted entirely by the staff, though this is rather unusual. As a general rule, committee reports are almost entirely a staff product, a fact that sometimes causes a bit of consternation on the part of some members. In the 82nd Congress, when the Social Security Act Amendment was under consideration, Representative Thomas A. Jenkins commented:

> When the bill was reported out, it was accompanied by a beautiful big report. I daresay that nobody on the Ways and Means Committee wrote a line of that report, . . . and nobody saw that report as far as I know: I know I did not see it.[10]

Such reports drafted by committee staff may have considerable impact as they are read by other members, by those in administrative agencies, by judges, by the General Accounting Office and others.

Because of their tenure, expertise and the nature of the services they provide, some staff members occupy positions as rather significant "powers behind the scenes." Richard Bolling, writing of veteran House parliamentarian, Lew Deschler, said he had a "large-sized influence growing out of encyclopedic knowledge . . . a virtual monopoly on current precedents in the House." "It is he," wrote Bolling, "not really the Speaker, who decides in practice to which committee a bill is sent."[11] The significant twenty-one day rule for removing bills from the House Rules Committee was drafted by Deschler at Sam Rayburn's request. Another prime example of a staff member who became a powerful figure in his own right was John Blandford, counsel to the House Armed Services Committee. Given virtual carte blanche by Mendel Rivers when he was chairman, Blandford, a Marine Corps reserve general, frequently chastised high-ranking cabinet officials testifying before the committee. It was also commonplace for Blandford to scold congressmen who criticized Rivers, who remarked of his chief counsel, "I find it hard to imagine the Armed Services Committee operating without him."

Since they are sometimes thrust into positions of speaking or acting for their bosses, it is very important for staff members to understand their true role. Don Nicoll, an aide to Senator Edmund Muskie, observes:

> I have to commit him sometimes without talking to him, but there's no question about who casts the votes and who's got the best political judgment.[12]

Some staffers come to enjoy the power and influence of the offices in which they work and are inclined to confuse their own roles. A young female aide on the staff of Senator Gaylord Nelson introduced in his name a bill to make Catalina Island into a national park. When former California Senator Tom Kuchel learned of the bill, he threatened to introduce legislation to make the entire state of Wisconsin into a national park. Other cases such as those involving congressional staffers Bobby Baker and Martin Sweig take on a more serious nature. Sweig even resorted to impersonating his boss, Speaker John McCormack, over the phone. Such abuses of power by congressional staff members take on added significance because they are responsible to no electoral constituency. A patent reply from John Blandford to newsmen's questions was, "I answer to Mr. Rivers, not to the public." So it becomes the task of a harried and oftentimes overworked boss to make sure that staff members do not abuse the powers which inevitably become theirs as a result of the system. Insuring the appropriate accountability of staff members under these circumstances becomes a significant problem.

In addition to accountability, Congress faces a number of other serious questions relative to staffing. For one thing, Congress has allowed a serious imbalance to develop between itself and the executive branch in terms of the sources of information and expertise available. Congress now has ten to fifteen thousand people working directly for it, but the President has half this number working in White House offices alone. Congress now has two or three computers; the executive has warehouses full of computers and whole platoons of specialists to interpret data. The increasing complexity and technical nature of much legislation has forced the lawmakers to turn more and more to specialists and experts for help. Since their own retinue and the committee staffs have only a few technical experts, they have had to rely heavily on the executive branch for this type of assistance. This is not always a healthy situation, as it may reduce Congress' independence and its ability to serve as a check on the executive.

John Kennedy in the Bay of Pigs fiasco relied heavily on the "experts" in the CIA and Pentagon and largely ignored the advice of Senator Fulbright who was opposed to the adventure. The Watergate Affair apparently was conceived and carried out within the executive branch. Had congressional advice been sought, the results might have been different. The point is that over-reliance on "experts" in policy-making may not always produce the best results. On some issues the "feel" of the politician with years of practical experience may be more reliable than all the fact-filled dossiers of the technical experts.

Simply expanding the staff of the Congress is not the solution to all the problems, however. In fact, what staff is available has not been used in the most effective fashion. Many congressmen's staffs presently spend 80-90 percent of their time on the mail and such matters as veterans affairs and lost social security checks. These are worthwhile tasks, but probably shouldn't warrant this lion's share of staff time. Political scientist Thomas Cronin says Congress already has too many committees and too much staff. Give them more staff, he says, and they will simply use it to get re-elected.[13] No doubt overstaffing is as undesirable as understaffing. Too large a staff could become a buffer between the elected representative and his constituents, making effective contact and communication difficult. The Congress must seek to strike the proper balance between inadequate staff support and an unwieldy and unresponsive bureaucracy.

Congress might well be tempted to go overboard on staffing in an effort match the executive branch. This is a temptation to be resisted, because while Congress can take steps to alleviate the present imbalance, the members could not realistically hope to match the executive branch employee for employee or computer for computer. To offset the imbalance, Congress must take steps to improve its staff by reducing the patronage jobs and hiring more experts and modernizing its information services. Its members and committees must also develop more effective means of tapping outside sources of information and expertise. The restoration of Congress as a co-equal branch in the governmental system is a prime argument for up-dating and improving its staffing research facilities.

Conclusion

In Congress the press of the routine is insistent and the pressures to which the member is subjected are constant and intense. Fletcher Thompson (R. Ga.) says, "We're on the run all the time and there's always something more to do." That the pressures on members are growing is attested to by the fact that an unusually large number of incumbents, several with considerable tenure, decided not to seek re-election in 1974. Several of them observed that being in Congress "wasn't any fun any more." For many the legislature may become a frustrating place. The work is difficult, demanding great concentration and requiring the patience of Job. Its results are often extremely slow in coming, then often piecemeal and partial, far less than perfection. Legislative work is complicated, requiring specialization, experience, organizational skill and the ability and inclination to compromise. Many find it quite difficult to adjust to the congressional atmosphere: personal abuse, constant jockeying for position, back-biting, petty jealousies, constant tension and the disrupted personal life. Especially for the young, ambitious and impatient, Congress is a most frustrating place. Don Riegle writes:

> My initial enthusiasm and idealism have long since been tempered by the frustrating realities of day-to-day existence. The constraints are hard and mean and making the right thing happen is damn near impossible.
> . . . I encounter frustrations daily that make me want to scream or lash out. Sometimes I feel I *have* to blow, but I almost never do that anymore. It's wasted effort.[14]

He adds resignedly, "There's damn little you can get your hands on, make happen or influence." Individual personality becomes a substantial factor in how one adapts to Congress and what he accomplishes.

The types of people attracted to run for Congress become a key factor in how the institution functions. Through its history all types of individuals have been seated as members of the Congress, including those guilty of fraud, other felonies and all manner of irregularities. Because it is usually the most exceptional and flamboyant members who attract the attention of outsiders and their actions reflect on the entire institution, legislatures frequently acquire a public image not wholly deserved. One observer opined, "Now an' then an innocent man is sent t' th' legislature." Members themselves are frequently among the harshest critics of their colleagues. Ron Dellums (D. Calif.) has charged that congressmen on the whole "are mediocre prima donnas who pass legislation," and Representative Dewey Short of Missouri has described the House as a body of "supine, subservient, soporific, supercilious, pusillanimous nitwits." The Congress is very much a group of individuals whose personal talents are quite unevenly distributed. All things considered, the calibre of the Congress is probably about as good as could be expected. The elections and campaigns do serve as a weeding-out process to a certain degree, and to reach the Congress one does have to possess some degree of ability. Also the "Chester Arthur Syndrome" is evident in Congress as many tend to grow into the jobs as they serve.

Still a major problem faced in an electorally staffed representative democracy is how to attract and elect those best qualified for the offices. The quality and character of the government depend heavily on the character of those who fill the key positions as Watergate has so profoundly illustrated. Yet a democratic system provides no guarantee that the best will even choose to run, or if they do, that they will be elected. A key question that must be answered is how to attract the best talents available and to retain them in government service. How can public offices best be made prizes to be sought rather than burdens to be avoided by the most honest and able citizen?

Our present system for electing the Congress falls short of these objectives in several respects. In the first place, few voters really understand and appreciate the jobs which they perfunctorily decide by their ballots. Their decisions on personnel to fill the vital positions are made in a haphazard and poorly informed manner. Our style of campaigns and the coverage of Congress by the news media don't do a lot to alleviate this. As news broadcaster Sander Vanocur has pointed out, how much do the media cover the House? To what extent do they go into depth and point out to the voters who the real wielders of power are? How many people knew who Wayne Hays was? Vanocur says the first decent article about his powerful committee chairman appeared in *Playboy* magazine. The irony of this process is that in all too many instances it appears that those members displaying the greatest capabilities for growth are the ones defeated, while those cautious and often less-able, safe-district spokesmen are returned election after election to build up seniority and forward their prejudices. It frequently seems that those who survive the longest, are those who say and do the least. Senator Robert Packwood (R. Ore.) notes:

> If you're non-controversial and unobtrusive, you'll be re-elected many times and then go into that marvel of congressional operation, the seniority system. And ten years after you're dead they'll name a dam after you.[15]

There is some evidence that politics and the attitude toward politicians are changing. As the voters show some indications of becoming more issue-oriented and more sophisticated in their choices, the time is ripe for the first-rate unknown to knock off the entrenched, old-style politician. This has already happened to such powerful figures as William Fulbright, Emanuel Celler, Wayne Aspinall and Mendel Rivers, and the prospect of such an occurrence has caused a number of other old-timers to decide not to seek re-election. One hopes that Watergate and its aftermath will make the voters even more determined to return first-rate candidates to office rather than to ignore their responsibility and turn their backs on the electoral process. As Don Riegle says, "If we lose this generation through cynicism and loss of faith, then we'll probably have lost the chance for meaningful democracy in the years ahead."[16]

Notes

1. *The Federalist*, p. 371.
2. Charles Clapp, *The Congressman*, pp. 397–414.
3. Julius Duscha, "An exodus from Congress: 'No longer any fun,'" *Courier-Journal* (September 15, 1974).

 4. *Ibid.*
 5. *Ibid.*
 6. Frank Smith, *Congressman From Mississippi*, p. 38.
 7. Fairborz Fatemi, "Can The Incumbent Be Defeated?" in Groennings and Hawley, p. 229.
 8. Joe Martin, *My First Fifty Years in Politics* (New York: McGraw-Hill, Inc., 1960), p. 78.
 9. Kenneth Kofmehl, *Professional Staffs of Congress* (West Lafayette, Ind.: Purdue Research Foundation, 1962), p. 96.
10. Thomas A. Jenkins as quoted by Kofmehl, *Ibid.*, p. 122.
11. Richard Bolling, "The House," *Playboy Magazine* (November, 1969), 256.
12. Don Nicoll as quoted by Robert Sherrill in "The Shadow Congress," *Courier-Journal & Times Magazine* (January 24, 1971), p. 14.
13. Thomas Cronin, "Congress's Responsibility," *The Center Magazine* 7 (September/October, 1974), p. 50.
14. Don Riegle, *O Congress* (Garden City, N.Y.: Doubleday & Co., Inc., 1972), pp. 90, 62.
15. Robert Packwood, "Congress's Responsibility," *The Center Magazine* 7 (September/October, 1974), p. 44.
16. Don Riegle, *O Congress*, p. 104.

Chapter III

Structure, Organization, Rules, and Procedures

THOUGH OFTEN TAKEN for granted, the structure, organizational machinery, rules and procedures of our legislative bodies are a not insignificant element in the legislative process. Far from being neutral, these elements can frequently be used by those who understand and control them to work their will. *How* things are done may well affect *what* is done in the United States Congress. The rules and procedures may have a significant bearing on the final outcome either by impeding or facilitating the success of the various participants in the legislative process. The competing forces in the legislative arena must constantly keep the rules and procedures in mind as they map out their strategies and tactics. The legislator who knows the rules of the game is in a better position to influence outcomes more in his favor and to successfully counter the strategies and tactics of his opponents.

Structure

As a whole, Congress is an intricate and complex institution, but its formal structure is relatively uncomplicated and remains substantially unaltered from the time of its creation 187 years ago. The seventeenth amendment adopted in 1913 provided for senators to be elected by direct popular vote rather than by state legislatures, and members of the House are now elected from districts within their states rather than at-large. However, the bicameral system, one of the numerous compromises reached at the Philadelphia Convention, is still intact, and the federal courts, while ruling that representation in both houses of the state legislatures must be based on population, have refused to apply the same requirement to the United States Senate.

While the formal structure remains essentially the same, the relationship and respective roles of the two houses of Congress have deviated considerably from that envisioned by the Founding Fathers. Though they finally agreed to a lower house of popularly-elected representatives, many of the delegates to the Philadelphia Convention had grave misgivings about mass democracy. They accepted a popularly-elected lower house because they envisioned the Senate, elected by the state legislatures, as a more elite and conservative body that could restrain the more radical House. Changes in the methods for selecting the membership of the two houses have tended to cause the reverse to be true today. Senators, elected to represent more diverse statewide constituencies, tend to be the moderates, while House members, many of whom come from safe districts whose populace frequently share rather narrow interests and prejudices, are the more conservative influence in Congress. Thus, contrary to what the framers expected, it is the popularly-elected Senate that may today legislate out of current passions and the House that is often more inclined to be more cautious and deliberative in its approach to many matters.

One of the arguments for having a two-house legislature is that such a system will produce better legislation because one house can act as a check on the other and correct its legislative mistakes. In actual practice bicameralism may encourage poor legislation because on occasion one house may pass a poor bill, assuming that the other will get it off the hook by acting more responsibly. The other house, however, may or may not prevent such a measure from becoming law. Bicameralism does have a number of other implications that are significant for the legislative process. Since a measure must pass both houses in identical form to go to the President for his signature, House-Senate conferences to iron out differences on legislative proposals are frequent. The conference committee emphasizes the art of compromise, results in policy by a small number of participants, and tends to obscure legislative decision-making even further. Having two houses and frequently using conference committees makes it considerably more difficult for the electorate to understand and follow what goes on in Congress. The two-house arrangement and the widespread use of legislative committees enhance the access of special interest spokesmen to the legislative process. The special interests favor this arrangement because they have a better chance of finding some point along the legislative route where they can bring substantial influence to bear.

Probably most significant for legislative action is that with the two-house arrangement it is inevitable that there will be differences and occasional friction between the two. In the Congress a feud between the two houses smolders constantly and the slightest provocation of latent jealousies may bring open conflict. A bone of contention for a number of years has been the relative role of the two houses on appropriations measures. The Constitution says all revenue bills must originate in the House. The House has successfully maintained a similar prerogative over appropriation measures as well, but not without protest from the Senate. In 1962 these differences were manifested in a dispute between Carl Hayden (D. Ariz.), chairman of the Senate Appropriations Committee, and Clarence Cannon (D. Mo.), chairman of the House Appropriations Committee, as to whether a conference committee should meet on the Senate or House side of the Hill. Extremely sensitive to Senate dominance of conference action, Cannon demanded that a House member alternate as chairman of appropriation conferences and that committtees meet on the House side. Hayden indicated he would agree to this *if* the Senate was allowed to originate one-half of the appropriation measures. Cannon, of course, was not about to agree to this. So, while these two aging patriarchs (Hayden was 84, Cannon, 83) argued over a meeting place, the federal government had to borrow money to pay some of its employees.

Because of our bicameral system, there are two distinct classes of citizens in Congress: senators and representatives. Some real differences in the membership and functions of the two houses tend to emphasize rather than ameliorate their innate jealousies. The fact that the Senate has only 100 members and they are elected for six-year terms makes it a more select and prestigious group than the 435-member House. The smaller membership and greater attention from the news media give senators more visibility than representatives. In the much larger House there is little individual identity and unless one chairs a powerful committee, not much feeling of individual power. Many House members feel that senators get too much undeserved publicity. They feel they work harder and do a more thorough job, but get less credit and attention. The fact that the Senate is a prime recruiting ground for Presidential candidates while the House is not also rankles. Only James Garfield has been elected directly from the House to the Presidency.

The United States Senate is unique among the upper houses of legislatures around the world. While in other countries the upper bodies have been declining in importance and power, the U.S. Senate has grown more powerful and prominent. In recent decades its powers of confirmation and foreign policy debate have given it added significance. This increased Senate role and influence has contributed to an inferiority complex on the part of the House. Many House members harbor a strong antagonism toward the Senate and this is sometimes used to stir up opposition to measures coming from the Senate. House members are particularly sensitive to references to the Senate as the "upper house" and to themselves as the "lower house." In the House the Senate is "the other body," and a rather over-rated one in the members' opinion. Most House members feel they are closer to the people, work harder and do a more thorough job of legislating.

In performing their legislative functions, both bodies have their strengths and weaknesses. The short tenure of House members tends to limit the foresight of the body, while the six-year, overlapping terms of senators provide an element of continuity and stability lacking in the House. Further, the unwieldy size of the House has virtually ruled out any real debate of issues, and the Senate is clearly superior in public debate. Consequently the news media tend to gravitate to the Senate. On the other hand, the House is probably still more truly the "peoples' branch" of the Congress. As Stewart Udall noted in the *Congressional Record*:

> Those who complain that House members spend too much time running errands for home folks, or respond too readily to the demands of pressure groups, are really making the charge that they are preoccupied with the next election—which is precisely what the founders intended.[1]

The two-year term imposed by the Constitution means that representatives must be constantly in touch with their constituents. Election is always just around the corner, and they don't have the time that a senator might to recover from a blunder. Members of the House must keep their fences mended at all times. Also, because of their smaller constituencies and smaller districts, House members frequently have deeper roots and a greater rapport with their constituents than do senators.

One area in which the House definitely excels is that of committee work. Because House members are limited to service on only one "major" committee, though they may serve on a second minor committee, while a senator may serve on several major committees, House members become specialists and they have more time to devote to their committees. Often a House committee will spend five, six, seven times as much time on a particular measure as its Senate counterpart. Also the senator, who because he holds seats on several major committees has to be a generalist, is sometimes at a disadvantage in conference committees. Commenting on this point, Congressman Chet Holifield (D. Calif.), said,

> When we go into conference on a bill with a group of Senators, they are unable to comprehend the scope of the bill. They always have to have administrative aides behind them whispering in their ears telling them what the answer is to anything that is said.[2]

Congresswoman Edith Green (D. Ore.) adds,

> I have just been appalled at every conference I have ever gone to that a senator has no idea what's in a bill. Unless he has an aide standing at his left ear telling him what to say, he wouldn't know.[3]

Despite their lack of the representative's first-hand familiarity with specific legislative measures, a factor somewhat off-set by the senator's larger staff, the senators usually pretty well hold their own in conferences. In fact the House is inclined to be overly sensitive at times and tries hard to avoid appearances of conceding to the Senate on measures.

Though a House member may occasionally ask to be allowed to testify before a Senate committee, House members have not felt welcome on the Senate floor since Representative Preston Brooks beat Senator Charles Sumner senseless with his cane in 1856. Senators would not sully their dignity by appearing in the House, and on the whole they simply ignore its existence. Few senators really understand the House and its operations unless they previously have served in the House. The consequence of these attitudes is to magnify rather than reduce frictions between the two houses. What we have in Congress is two separate systems operating side by side, each with its own lunchrooms, barbershop, gyms, and even different bell calls to maintain their distinctions. These differences between the two houses are so pronounced that even the cause of black solidarity has not bridged the gap. Senator Edward Brooke has not been embraced by his black colleagues in the House.

Thus the two houses meet jointly for ceremonial functions and indirectly through the joint and conference committees, but beyond this they maintain a stubborn independence of one another. Because of their petty jealousies, there is generally a woeful lack of communication and coordination between the two houses on legislative matters. Consultation and exchange of information are virtually nonexistent, even at the leadership level, and parallel committees operate almost totally independently of one another. In fact, the chairmen of parallel committees frequently may be barely on speaking terms. Differences between the two houses may be more difficult to bridge than differences between Democrats and Republicans.

Until the conference stage, each house tends to legislate in a vacuum, too proud and too stubborn to acknowledge what is going on on the other side of the Capitol. Such jealousies and lack of cooperation may cause good ideas and sound legislation to suffer. In 1969 a House subcommittee chaired by Representative Joe Waggonner (D. La.) undertook a study to determine potential computer uses in Congress. An invitation from the chairman to Senate leaders to contribute personnel to a working group was not even acknowledged. It was later reported that Majority Leader Mike Mansfield felt the offer should have come from the House leaders rather than from a mere subcommittee chairman. Waggonner later led a fight to kill a proposal for a Joint Committee on Legislative Data Processing, an area where the Congress already lags far behind. Such petty bickering between the two houses serves no constructive purpose when what is needed is more coordination and cooperation in developing and enacting sound legislative proposals. The innate hostility of the two houses needs to be transformed into healthy competition contributing to sounder legislative activity.

Formal Organization

A key to the operations of any legislative body is the organizational machinery and the type of leadership provided in the body. The Constitution states that the Vice-President shall preside over the Senate and that the House shall elect a Speaker; beyond this the internal organization is left up to the respective houses. In this area, the political parties have once again come to play a key role in the legislative process, as they have developed and staffed the key leadership positions which make the Congress work.

While the House and Senate are similar in some respects, there are differences in their organization and leadership. The big, rather unwieldy House functions effectively only under strong leadership; consequently it is considerably more hierarchical and formal in its organization than the Senate. While the formal leadership positions in each house are significant, much of the leadership is, in the final analysis, personal rather than institutional. The formal political organization within the Congress is not really emphasized; the *Congressional Directory* doesn't even describe it fully.

In early Congresses, leadership was conferred by the President upon selected members. Jefferson in particular used this method to promote his programs in Congress. During Madison's administration, however, Congress began to display more independence and developed its own leadership machinery and internal power structure. Today, at the opening of each Congress, the parties meet in their respective caucuses or conferences and choose those who will fill the key leadership positions. More and more, leadership within the Congress, especially in the Democratic party, has become incompatible with party leadership outside the Congress. Those qualities which make one an effective public leader outside the Congress may actually work against internal leadership. In the contest for the majority whip position in the Senate between Robert Byrd and Ted Kennedy, Byrd's supporters suggested that Kennedy was a spokesman for the national Democratic party rather than a party leader within the Congress. Some of his colleagues obviously felt that Kennedy's national party status disqualified him for congressional leadership.

In addition to the ability to survive elections and a considerable amount of good luck, becoming a leader in Congress demands hard work, shrewd political acumen, legislative skill, and the ability to earn the confidence and respect of one's colleagues. A prime example of how one rises to a leadership position in Congress is Robert Byrd, majority leader in the Senate. Byrd, a rather colorless and relatively unknown legislative technician, is a master of Senate internal politics. Possessing great capacity for hard, sustained work on dull and routine legislative detail, Byrd spent more time on the floor than most of his colleagues. He congratulated them on their birthdays, kept an eye on their pet legislation, and helped them with legislative and parliamentary details. When he challenged Humphrey for the majority leader's spot, he had a lot of IOU's out among colleagues and Humphrey decided to withdraw without a vote showdown. Byrd is not a prominent figure in his party nationally, but he knows the internal politics of the United States Senate.

Really effective leadership, a key to the successful functioning of Congress, demands considerable talent. The number of medio-cre to totally ineffective leaders outnumbers the really effective ones by far. Effective leadership in the Congress involves overcoming cleavages within the leader's own party and bridging the gap be-tween the two parties to build the necessary majorities. The leader must be flexible and creative; he must be able to foresee problems that may arise, and he must be able to differentiate between what is critical and what is less important. Compromise is the name of the game in the legislative process, and the leader must know when to stand firm and when to give a little, Above all, the effective leg-islative leader must have the ability to pull together from a variety of small sources a considerable amount of power and influence. He will be successful to the extent that he is capable of lining up the votes of members, several of whom may feel they are voting against the desires of their constituents. The leader must be able to demonstrate that the member's influence and standing with his constituents will not be jeopardized.

Leadership Selection

On the whole the system for selecting those to fill leadership positions in Congress is a closed and rather rigid process. Some-times an incumbent leader is forced out, but challenges to tradi-tional patterns and customs for filling these positions are usually doomed to failure. Once in a leadership post, the member is in a good position to maintain his support by determining who gets the favors. As one observer said, the tie that binds is "boodle." The careful leader sees to it that he is better informed than the rank-and-file member. His superior information places him in a position of power relative to his less-informed colleagues. Also the leaders are in a position to make things happen or not happen. A word from the leadership to a key committee chairman can be a determining factor on the inclusion of an important amendment to a measure or its prompt handling and reporting out of committee. The leaders play a key role in scheduling, timing of votes and other matters important to the success or failure of the member's legislation. Thus the leadership positions confer upon certain members substantial resources for maintaining their positions once elected.

However, the leadership must be careful in performing their roles. They lead only because they win rather consistently. Should the leadership lose too often, then the power and influence would quickly wane. This tends to make the leadership extremely cautious. If they aren't certain of victory, they prefer that a matter not be brought up. Most leaders don't enter a struggle just for the sake of a contest; they are usually most patient and prefer not to act before they are sure the votes are there for victory. As a consequence, the leadership may defer action on an issue for years while the pressures necessary to produce the votes build. For some members outside the leadership, this is extremely frustrating. Also, the leaders usually prefer to operate through traditional channels and harbor a strong distaste for legislative short-cuts.

Though members are elected to leadership positions in the caucuses of each of the parties, the process, for all practical purposes, is not completely open nor highly democratic. Because of various factors that come into play in such elections, the results are often foregone conclusions. The single most important consideration in these choices is usually seniority, especially in the House. This is not to say that the top position always goes automatically to the most senior member, but the likelihood of a Henry Clay being chosen Speaker in his first term is slim indeed. As a general rule, leadership positions go to those with several years of service and legislative experience. Sam Rayburn had served in the House for twenty-seven years when he was elected Speaker; John Mc-Cormack, thirty-five years; and Carl Albert, twenty-five years. No Speaker in this century has come to the job with less than fifteen years in the House. The normal pattern is for the leaders to move progressively toward the top; that is, when the Speakership becomes vacant, the majority floor leader moves up to fill the Speakership and the majority whip becomes floor leader, etc. Should the majority party become the minority party, then the former Speaker becomes the minority floor leader, the majority leader becomes minority whip, etc. The same general pattern is followed in the Senate also, though seniority is not quite so strong in leadership choices there. Lyndon Johnson became majority floor leader during his first term, four years after his election.

Other factors also come into play in the filling of party leadership posts. Incumbent leaders, the President, and interest groups may exert influence on those choices. Former Senate Majority Leader Mike Mansfield reportedly was not enthusiastic about Russell Long as majority whip, but he stayed quiet on the matter. Had he spoken out he probably could have blocked Long's election. In so doing, however, he would have antagonized a powerful committee chairman. In 1959 a well-organized drive resulted in Charles Halleck defeating incumbent Joe Martin for the position of minority leader in the House. Martin said auto, business and beef interests helped Halleck beat him, and he also felt that Eisenhower and Nixon failed to come to his aid as they should have. He indicated that he felt that John Tabor of New York voted against him for personal reasons, something that happens more frequently in these contests than many realize. Carl Albert apparently was opposed to the selection of Dan Rostenkowski as majority whip in the House in 1972, and this was largely a personal matter. Rostenkowski was a member of the late Mayor Daley's Chicago organization, and Albert held Daley largely responsible for the riotous Democratic Convention in 1968 which embarrassed Albert as the presiding officer. Albert's antagonism toward Daley apparently carried over to Rostenkowski as well and was a key factor in his defeat.

In another recent contest for Democratic House leadership, the late Hale Boggs won the majority leader position from several challengers. A key element in his victory apparently was the support he received from Wilbur Mills and other colleagues with whom he served on the Ways and Means Committee. They supported Boggs for the floor leader position because he had advocated reducing the 27 percent oil depletion allowance and they wanted him off the committee.

In filling the leadership positions there is considerable wheeling-and-dealing and vote trading. Sometimes a key element can be the method of voting used. The secret ballot may produce quite different results than voice voting. When he was seeking the majority leader position in the House, Morris Udall noted that he had obtained eighty-five commitments, but in a secret ballot got only fifty-eight votes. Another factor may be that younger members may anticipate personal advancement for themselves through a change in leadership.

In the final analysis, the formal leadership in the houses of Congress is a closed structure to which access is quite limited. Writing in his syndicated column, Russell Baker states,

> The Congress of the United States consists of approximately thirty old men, most of whom are alive most of the time. They are referred to as "the leadership," . . . Almost anyone can become a member of "the leadership" except for women, Negroes, city dwellers, members who face opposition when they stand for re-election, and persons under 70.[4]

While the leadership may not be quite so exclusive as Baker implies, it is certainly a rather elite, and in many ways unrepresentative, group when compared to the national electorate or the total membership of Congress.

Some leadership positions such as the president pro tem of the Senate are token rewards for senior members of the party or for those working diligently on the party's behalf. They have little real influence in and of themselves; though they may serve as stepping stones to positions of much greater influence and power, such as those of whip, floor leader or even Speaker.

House Leadership

The leadership hierarchy in the House and Senate differ somewhat and their powers and methods of operation are not the same. The House leadership consists of the Speaker and whomever else he may decide to include in his inner circle. This usually includes the majority floor leader, the majority whip and his assistants and a few key committee chairmen. The minority floor leader may be consulted frequently on matters of scheduling and procedures. The real leader and the man who sets the tone for the entire body, however, is the Speaker. In the large and unwieldy House, he is a crucial figure and his leadership is indispensable to the effective functioning of the body. His role in the House is threefold—he is the House's presiding officer; he is the political leader of the majority party; and he is a voting member and the representative of his home district.

As a political leader, the Speaker of the House is a powerful figure, ranking second only to the President, and even the President is usually quite careful about offending a Speaker unnecessarily. Powerful Republican Speaker Joe Cannon once declined to attend a White House dinner because he was to be seated protocolwise lower than the attorney general. President Theodore Roosevelt quickly proceeded to give another dinner with the Speaker as guest of honor. This tradition of a dinner honoring the Speaker is still observed by Presidents. Other Speakers also have expressed their awareness of the prestige and power of their office. Thomas B. Reed once remarked that the Speaker had but one superior and no peer. By the one superior, he may well have meant the Almighty, rather than the President. Sam Rayburn was noted to observe that he never served *under* any President, but had served *with* eight.

While the Constitution provides for the position of Speaker of the House, it has nothing to say about his duties, responsibilities or authority. Consequently the political powers of the office have depended to a marked degree upon the personality and ability of the man occupying the office. Early Speakers functioned primarily as presiding officers and did not exercise a strong leadership role in the House. During his tenure as Speaker, however, Henry Clay expanded both the power and prestige of the office; and through Clay the Speaker became the leader of his party in the House. The powers of the office continued to grow until during the Speakerships of Thomas B. Reed (1889–91 and 1895–99) and Joseph G. Cannon (1903–1911), the Speaker ruled with almost unlimited power.

Finally, the House had had enough and in 1910–11 the members revolted and stripped the Speaker of much of his power. With the Speaker's power reduced, party caucuses were revived. Gradually, however, the Speakers regained their power and control, and today the Speaker is again a paramount figure in the legislative process. As the presiding officer of the House and the leader of the majority party, he is in a position to wield considerable power and influence. He presides over sessions of the House, puts questions to a vote and announces the vote, appoints chairmen of the Committee of the Whole and members of conference and select committees, chooses Speakers *pro tem* and exercises control of the floor through the power of recognition. He exercises considerable influence and control over the fate of legislative measures through his power to refer bills and reports to committees and his ability to sidetrack or pigeonhole a measure through the various scheduling and calendar devices which he controls. The chasm between the committees and the House floor is bridged by the Speaker, who is responsible for the flow and scheduling of legislation for floor action. If the Speaker doesn't want a measure considered, its chances of coming to a vote are indeed slim. On the other hand, he can pave the way for easy passage through his control of the time when a measure is considered. On at least one occasion, John McCormack facilitated consideration of the appropriation for the House Un-American Activities Committee while potential objectors were out of the chamber, several being out of town. The whole matter was considered and passed in about thirty seconds. Such a move would be impossible without the acquiescence of the Speaker. The Speaker, with the aid of the parliamentarian, interprets and applies the rules of the House; he is the final authority on every action in the House. He, as well as the President, must sign every bill before it becomes law. As the leader of his party in the House, he wields considerable influence on committee and other appointments. He is in a position to be privy to information that may be most useful to colleagues, and he dispenses various personal favors which may be judiciously used to build up obligations that can be cashed in later. While he is a symbol of the House, he also remains a voting member who can participate in discussion. Though used rather infrequently, when the Speaker does exercise his privilege to the floor to speak, the House listens. The ultimate power and influence of the Speaker depend upon the man himself, his view of the job, the support of his colleagues and the finesse and skill with which he uses those tools at his disposal.

Probably one of the most effective Speakers ever to operate in the House was Sam Rayburn of Texas. Rayburn's was largely a personal leadership. He believed that leadership could best be exercised through "personal friendship" and "reasonable persuasion." According to Rayburn, he led "by persuasion and kindness and the best reason." However, Rayburn's kindliness and friendliness in no way indicated a softness on his part. He served in positions of legislative leadership much of his life—he was speaker of the Texas House at age twenty-nine—and it was a role he liked and and exercised with gentle firmness. He noted, "I like responsibility because I enjoy the power responsibility brings." As Speaker, Rayburn was motivated by a strong instinct to win. He once told a friend, "I hate like hell to be licked. It almost kills me." With this attitude he developed an acute sense for assessing his strength on specific issues. Measures were not brought up for a vote until he knew he had the necessary numbers. Because of his success rate and extensive power, a myth of invincibility developed about "Mister Sam" which worked to the benefit of his leadership.

Short (5'6"), stocky, and bald, Rayburn shunned publicity, wielding his vast power quietly, almost invisibly. But behind the scenes, his voice was often a decisive one. Dressed in dark suits and black hats, he would never have been picked from among a crowd as one of the most powerful political figures in America; yet during his tenure, he built the Speakership into a position of its greatest influence since the days of Reed and Cannon. In running the House, Rayburn relied more on his immense personal influence than on the structural power of the Speakership. His close friend and fellow Texan, Lyndon Johnson, said Rayburn ran the House out of his hip pocket.

Actually Rayburn used all of the various tools at his disposal to pull together and wield his vast influence. He dominated his own party in the House. He had been Speaker longer than most had served, and he had performed so many personal favors for members that there were few in either party who didn't owe him something. His office door was always open and he took a personal interest in his colleagues; he was especially kind and helpful to new members, something not soon forgotten on their part. Rayburn was able to identify personally with virtually every member of the House and he was much more than just "Mister Speaker"; he was one of the boys. Mister Sam also possessed unequalled legislative skills and knew the ins and outs of the House better than any other member. He devoted twelve to fourteen hours a day to House operations, and he literally soaked up information like a sponge. When the House was in session, it was his whole life, and as a leader he was always on top of what was going on. His rather casual style and light touch tended to belie his awareness and his ability to anticipate legislative difficulties. His "feel" for the mood of the House was so acute that he could read the body as most people read their daily papers. He could sense the most subtle changes in House atmosphere and adapt his timing and strategy accordingly. He once confided to close friend Richard Bolling, "Dick, if you can't feel things you can neither see nor hear, you don't belong in this business." His feel for the House was really nothing mystical; he had cultivated it through years of experience in legislative bodies.

Because of his great sense of the House, Rayburn was able to adapt his tactics to the mood of the House. He knew when to resort to bargain and compromise and when to be firm. He was able to anticipate instances when he might be challenged and when he would not. In 1941 the House passed the Draft Extension bill, 203 to 202. Rayburn as Speaker announced the outcome and added, "Without objection, a motion to reconsider is laid on the table." No such motion had actually been made, and Representative Carl Anderson of Minnesota questioned the action. The Speaker snapped, "The chair does not intend to have his word questioned by the gentleman from Minnesota or anybody else." End of discussion. Four months later the Japanese attacked Pearl Harbor.

Not a long-range planner, Rayburn ran the House on a day-to-day basis, adapting his strategy and tactics to suit the immediate situation. He knew when to descend from the Speaker's chair to exercise his right to address the floor or to offer an amendment to a pending measure. He knew the individual members and how to appeal to each of them. Rayburn was a great Speaker because of his ability, through his tremendous legislative skills and immense personal popularity, to put together, vote by vote, a majority. "Mister Sam" would have to rank as one of the most, if not the most, influential of all House leaders.

Recent Speakers have not been the stabilizing force in the

House that Rayburn was, and many members have experienced considerable frustration under the less dynamic and less forceful leadership of John McCormack and Carl Albert. James Reston of the *New York Times* said Speaker McCormack was "an amiable and industrious old gentleman whose outstanding quality is durability." McCormack, referred to by some of his colleagues as "The Archbishop" because of his staunch Catholicism, was quite accommodating and adept at corraling individual votes on issues. However, he lacked both the legislative skill and feel for the House possessed by Rayburn, and he frequently failed on strategy and tactics. The Adam Clayton Powell case is a prime example of McCormack's inability as a leader to anticipate and head off trouble. McCormack refused to face up to this issue which kept festering and growing. Eventually Powell was stripped of his seniority and chairmanship, but the move snowballed further into an effort to deny him his seat in the House. More vigorous leadership could have headed off this misguided effort which resulted in the Harlem constituency being unrepresented for two years.

Though a shade more dynamic than his predecessor, John McCormack, former Rhodes Scholar Carl Albert was frequently a reluctant leader who failed to demonstrate the qualities necessary to lead the House in a really effective manner. One colleague said, "Carl Albert is a nice man, but as a leader he leaves something to be desired." Several members saw Albert as being too much a "nice guy" who sought to be friends with everyone. They felt he was overly cautious, a fence straddler who frequently lacked any overall plan of action. Defeated in his first test of strength as Speaker, an effort to revive the twenty-one day-rule, Albert got off to a questionable start. When the Emergency Employment Act of 1971 came to the floor in May, Albert and his co-leaders suddenly found themselves outflanked and had to pull the bill off the floor to avoid defeat. It took them two weeks to regroup their forces and beat the conservative coalition. Such performances led several colleagues to suggest that Albert needed to "get tough" and provide more forceful leadership for his party in the House. After all, the Speaker is expected to be a housekeeper, a conciliator, a skilled legislative tactician, a master politician, and, above all, a leader. On the whole, Albert did not demonstrate a really strong inclination to provide the House the forceful leadership it must have to operate effectively.

Across the Capitol on the Senate side, the power of the leaders is both greater and less than that of the House leadership. In the Senate, the leadership has less control over debate, over who speaks, and has fewer sanctions over individual members on voting. On the other hand, members of the Senate leadership do not share their power with so many other groups as do their counterparts in the House. Though not mentioned in the Constitution or in the Senate rules, the key figure in the Senate leadership is the majority leader. The Senate's majority leader plans the legislative program and controls the legislative schedule, devises his party's strategy, serves as the party's principal spokesman, plays a key role in the selection of other party leaders, and generally oversees the way in which the Senate goes about its business. Once again, as in the case of the House Speaker, much of the majority leader's power is personal rather than structural and institutional. The overall power and influence depend to a great extent upon the individual in the position.

Probably the most effective person ever to serve as Senate majority leader was Lyndon Johnson. Elected to the floor leader's position in only his fourth year in the Senate, Johnson became the consummate artist in getting the votes he needed from his colleagues. Under him the majority leadership became a position of enormous power, and from it he wielded tremendous influence. Writing of Johnson's role in in the Senate, columnists Evans and Novak said, "The House was unwieldy, but in the Senate a leader could work miracles if he knew how to trade. Johnson was a born trader."[5]

When Johnson came to the Senate as a freshman, Richard Russell (D. Ga.), was the power in that body. Russell accepted Johnson for the top leadership post and got a real leader whether he anticipated it or not. Somewhat later, he described Johnson in these terms:

> Lyndon Johnson hasn't got the best mind in the Senate. He isn't the best orator. He isn't the best parliamentarian. But he's the best combination of all those qualities.[6]

The effective Senate majority leader must be a skillful compromiser, a nimble position shifter, able to quickly change course without losing his balance, and a persuasive diplomat capable of welding rebellious senators into some semblance of unity. Another essential quality for the effective majority leader is the ability to sense the mood of the Senate and to know when its members are ready to get on with the business at hand. Like his fellow Texan in the House, Sam Rayburn, Johnson possessed a keen "feel" for the Senate, and his sense of timing was superb. He seldom wasted his time and energies on lost causes, and if he was ever caught off-guard as floor leader, no one ever knew about it.

Also, as was the case with his close friend, Rayburn, much of Johnson's leadership and influence was of a personal nature. LBJ was a consummate public relations man and an astute student of human nature. He had an instinct enabling him to find every small pressure point, either personal or political, which could be used in lining up the necessary support for a measure. The tools available for insuring the loyalty of members on party programs are quite limited, but LBJ was an artist at using every available resource to accomplish his task.

Frequently pictured as being a sort of sleight-of-hand legislative Houdini, Johnson's success really stemmed from his superb knowledge of the Senate and its members. He was a master at using all sorts of ploys to achieve his legislative objectives. He used parliamentary maneuvers to gain time when needed; he resorted to lengthy all-night sessions when he felt he could capitalize on the fatigue of the opposition. Much of his success derived from his considerable skills as a legislative tactician. His head counts were unerringly accurate and his sense of timing was precise. Like Rayburn, he began to develop a legend of invincibility which enhanced his influence with colleagues. Those who supported the majority leader were not unrewarded for their efforts. Every means available, from choice committee assignments, better office space, junkets, campaign funds and aid, to such personal courtesies as Johnson's attendance at funerals, weddings, etc. were used as rewards. Johnson preferred to talk and cajole members into his camp, but when the situation demanded he could be rough as well. In lining up the necessary support, LBJ frequently resorted to what was known as the "treatment," ranging from supplication, accusation, cajolery, exuberance, scorn, tears and complaint to outright threat.

About nine-tenths psychological, Johnson's treatment was said by some to have an almost hypnotic effect. Whatever the effect, it often meant the necessary votes to get a measure approved.

Of his role as majority leader, Johnson said in 1953:

> I don't believe the sole duty of an opposition party is to oppose; I believe the United States Senate has a duty to have its own programs, too. Now that the Republicans are in the White House, I am not interested in running a party that can *only* attack Eisenhower.[7]

Following this philosophy, Johnson frequently found it easier to work across the aisle with Senate Republicans than with the liberal colleagues in his own party. For this he incurred their frequent criticism and his influence began to decline. His leadership was further weakened in 1958 with the election of a group of younger, more independent freshman Democratic senators.

Johnson was succeeded as majority leader by a man almost totally his opposite in character and style. Mike Mansfield, whom political writer Saul Pett described as being "as dynamic as a celery stick," did not, unlike his predecessor, relish his position of power and leadership. He was much happier in his role as just the senator from Montana. As a leader, Mansfield was extremely low profile, exercising his power and authority with utmost care. One of the least combative men in the Senate, he preferred to lead through gentle persuasion, accommodation and mutual understanding. He lacked almost totally Johnson's capacity for getting tough. Because he was so fair, honest and humble in his role, Mansfield became somewhat of an "untouchable" among his Senate colleagues. His across-the-aisle counterpart, Everett Dirksen, praised Mansfield as a leader who led "through sheer force of character and gentility." He added to please not ask him to campaign for a Republican senator from Montana. Dirksen's successor, Hugh Scott (R. Pa.), said Mansfield was "the most decent man I've ever met in public life." While his manners were unusually gentle, Mansfield was extremely tough-minded. He was far more familiar with the substance of issues than LBJ ever was, but he lacked many of the qualities of the really effective leader. One observer remarked that Mansfield would have made a much better priest than majority leader.

While the Speaker of the House and the majority floor leader in the Senate fill the dominant leadership roles, others share this function. The minority floor leaders in each house provide the leadership for their legislative parties and stand ready to assume the top leadership positions should their party become the majority. In nominating Joe Martin for minority leader of the House, Allen Treadway, (R. Mass.) said, "We are doing more than electing a floor leader. We are choosing a symbol of the Republican Party in this House." The role of the minority leader varies significantly with the different occupants of the position. Some leaders see their role as a sort of "loyal opposition," constantly challenging the majority, while others, like Everett Dirksen, are more inclined to cooperate whenever possible. For a number of years, Republican leaders in the Senate, Robert Taft, Kenneth Wherry, and William Knowland, appeared to have little appreciation for the leadership potential of their positions. Knowland in particular ran a "one-man show" as minority leader. When Everett Dirksen, a much more practical politician, came to the position he took a much more pragmatic approach. According to Dirksen, he was a "legislator," not a "moralist." Contrasting Dirksen's leadership to Knowland's, one senator noted, "Dirksen doesn't stand on principle so much; he gets on the phone and lines up the votes for our side." Dirksen and Johnson operated a lot alike and they frequently cooperated closely as leaders of the opposing parties in the Senate. Their completely honest and open relationship enabled them to disagree vigorously but without rancor. This type of leadership enabled them to get things done that otherwise would not have been possible. Such a relationship between the leaders, however, depends heavily on the individuals involved.

Also sharing in the leadership function in both houses are the majority and minority party whips. This term as applied to these functionaries in the Congress is a misnomer. It implies that the function of these leaders is to apply pressure and to bring reluctant party members into line. In practice the whip organizations are more a communicataions network between the rank-and-file members and the leadership. Their attitude generally is "vote with us if you can, but don't go against your district." The whips check key votes in advance and then try to get their supporters to the floor and keep them there for the right moment. The key to an effectively functioning whip organization is timing. The whips must have their maximum voting strength on the floor at exactly the right moment. If a call is made too soon and the members enter the chamber to find nothing happening, many will wander away before the vote is taken. On the other hand, the whips must not be caught with their guard down by an unexpected vote. They must work closely with the floor leaders and be on their toes at all times.

There are various other positions of leadership and party organization in the Congress such as the caucus chairman, the party conference or caucus, the campaign committees, the patronage committees and others. These, however, are relatively minor leadership positions which normally play only marginal roles in the day-to-day functioning of the Congress.

Informal Organization

Oftentimes just as significant as the formal structure and written rules are the informal structure and unwritten rules of the Congress, those which have become well-established through years of customary and traditional usage. In the final analysis, these informal arrangements may have even more far-reaching effect on legislative processes than do the formal machinery and organization. Over the years various informal groups and practices have appeared in the Congress, some of considerable legislative import. During his years as Speaker, Sam Rayburn developed an informal and somewhat fluid, personal advisory group that came to be known as his "Board of Education." Being invited to meet and share a drink with Mister Sam's "Board" was quite a status symbol in the House. With their spirit of compromise, primed with bourbon and branch water, the "Board" was able to work out solutions to numerous difficult legislative issues. The "Board" fell into disuse under John McCormack

In the House a variety of informal groupings have developed, some much more structured than others. Some are primarily social systems, while others have definite legislative objectives. One of the most active and prominent of the informal organizations in the House is the Democratic Study Group (DSG). Although not a single line appeared in the press when the liberal Democrats of the House organized the DSG in 1959, it has become a significant factor among House Democrats. Though its membership is open, the primary objective of the DSG has been to organize the more moderate Democratic representatives. Its membership usually constitutes about one-half of the House Democrats. The DSG has its own offices, an executive committee, its own whip system, a full-time staff and fund-raisers. It researches issues, helps members in their campaign efforts and helps raise funds in their behalf.

Other informal groupings, such as the Wednesday Club (House liberal Republicans), the Chowder and Marching Club, S.O.S., Acorns, the Prayer Breakfast Group, the Gym Group, etc., are not so highly structured as the DSG. They do, nonetheless, serve a number of functions in the larger, more formal House ranging from providing colleagues the opportunity to get to know one another better, to serving as potential sources of assistance on legislation. While the influence of such groups would be difficult to assess, they serve as a mechanism for the exchanging of information, for educating one's colleagues on issues, for indoctrinating freshmen members, for the developing of closer rapport among members, and for increasing confidence in one another's political judgment. Over a period of time, feelings of fellowship develop among the members of particular groups, and in some instances such informal relationships may exert considerable influence on the legislative process.

While one can gain a relatively satisfactory understanding of the formal organization of Congress quite readily, understanding the system as it actually functions is much more difficult. The picture is complicated by the existence of many informal as well as formal centers of power in the Congress, and by the highly personal nature of much of the power wielded. As one member observes:

> Here, more than in any other situation in which I have found myself, things are not what they seem. There are subcurrents and subscenes which don't strike the naked eye, but which play important roles in determining the final outcome of legislation and all magnitudes of decisions.[8]

Though theoretically the powers of all seats in each house of Congress are equal, it quickly becomes clear that some members wield substantially more power and influence than others. As a Senate staff member once observed, "All senators are equal, but some senators are more equal than others." The author of Federalist Number 53 proved a pretty good prophet when he wrote:

> A few members, as happens in all such assemblies, will possess superior talents; will, by frequent re-elections, become members of long standing; will be thoroughly masters of the public business, and perhaps not unwilling to avail themselves of those advantages.[9]

This has certainly proved the case, as seniority coupled with the committee system has become the hallmark of the distribution of power among the members of Congress. Roland Young in his book, *This Is Congress,* says the key to power in Congress is seniority, since this is the primary consideration in dispensing favors and appointments. Because of this almost ironclad tradition, the interior lines of communication and strength are concentrated largely in the hands of those who have been there for many years. In fact, many suggest that a member may have to be on the Congressional scene for ten, fifteen to twenty years before he has a voice in what goes on, and even longevity is no guarantee of influence if he lands on the wrong committee or somehow gets crosswise with the internal power structure of his house.

This rather rigid system of control by a select group of the more senior members is often quite difficult for the newcomer to accept. He arrives on the Washington scene all starry-eyed and full of bright ideas for legislation that will solve the problems of his district and the nation, only to discover that there is really very little he can do as an individual member. If he attempts to challenge the system, he runs the risk of alienating those who might become allies and help him achieve some of his goals down the road. The freshman who dares to challenge the system usually finds there are numerous effective ways in which he can be put down. His bills get bottled up in committee; he gets little or no patronage; and on the whole his life as a legislator can become quite miserable. The internal power structure in Congress is based on quietude and getting along with one's colleagues and the leadership. Freshmen who are too vocal, who draw too much attention to themselves, who do not show the proper deference to their seniors are courting trouble. The internal power system provides few advantages to the new-comers, the independents, the gadflies, the impatient, the innovators and those who challenge the traditions and customs of the Congress.

In this system, committee chairmen, who will be discussed more thoroughly in the next chapter, have come to play a paramount role. They have become virtually autonomous centers of power who may or may not be receptive to the formal leadership of the legislature. While Speaker, Carl Albert said, "The leadership doesn't have the power to force committees to do things. There is no way a Speaker can get a chairman to do something he is firmly committed not to do. . . ." Because of the powers committee chairmen wield over legislation, few members are willing to openly challenge these oligarchs of the committee system.

What this all boils down to is that unless a member is a part of the formal leadership, belongs to the informal power structure, or is chairman of an important committee, he isn't going to influence normal legislative operations a whole lot. Since the informal power structure within the Congress is not clearly defined and often not easily identifiable, it is possible for a member to serve in Congress for many years, be very close to a position of real power, and yet remain virtually unknown to the nation at large. Consider for example, the former representative from Kentucky, John Watts, who was second ranking Democrat on the Ways and Means Committee. How many Americans ever heard of John Watts? The ultimate result of the informal power arrangements within the Congress is to almost totally obscure and confuse the real decision-making process and make it virtually impossible to fix responsibility for the fate of much legislation. No readily identifiable man or group of men are responsible for action taken in Congress. The actual wielders of power are so well concealed by the informal and diffused power structure that it becomes next to impossible for the average voter to know whom to hold responsible for a particular action.

Rules and Procedures

In addition to organization, both formal and informal, a most important consideration, as far as our legislative bodies and their operations are concerned, is the rules and procedures under which the bodies function. If a deliberative body is to function at all, particularly with any degree of efficiency and harmony, it must be guided by some rules of procedure. This is particularly true of legislative bodies where differences of opinion and conflicts of interest, which must be resolved, abound. Under the Constitution, each house of Congress is charged with establishing its own rules of procedure. Both houses have adopted numerous and often complex and involved rules of procedure. For example, the House rules fill 538 pages and precedents and rulings interpreting and applying these rules fill eleven bound volumes. The presiding officers and the parliamentarians are key figures in the interpretation and application of these rules. In early 1900, when a constituent asked his representative for a copy of the rules of the House, perhaps as an astute comment, he was sent a photograph of Speaker Joe Cannon.

A major concern with the rules of Congress has been that, according to numerous critics, they are hopelessly outdated and cumbersome. Both houses continue to operate under rules as set forth in *Jefferson's Manual,* with various amendments which have been added over the years. In spite of rather widespread and repeated criticism, Congress has revealed extreme reluctance to change its rules and procedures. Internally the House and Senate are among the most conservative institutions in the nation. In Congress, tradition and custom frequently overshadow logic, and when in doubt, Congress acts on precedent. This reluctance to tamper with rules is reinforced by the leadership and by those with a vested interest in the *status quo.* Even some of those calling loudest for reform secretly enjoy the benefits and prestige which derive from existing rules and traditions. Those in positions of power have spent considerable time and effort working their way up through the existing structure and rules and they view with apprehension any efforts at change which might undermine their positions. The leadership generally prefers to conduct business through normal procedures, since this tends to maximize the chances of success and helps to reduce the chances for defeat which tend to erode the power of the leadership. Also, the leadership may use key votes on procedural issues to enhance their control and influence. They may be able to line up more votes more easily on a key parliamentary or procedural question than on a substantive one. Thus, in Congress, a member may undertake about anything he desires so long as he observes the proper form. There is a very strong reluctance, however, to bypass normal channels and to depart from past precedents and tradition. In a most interesting exchange on the floor of the Senate in the 91st Congress, Senator Fulbright (D. Ark.), a strong critic of the Viet Nam war, opposed a move by

Senator Robert Dole (R. Kan.) to repeal the Tonkin Gulf Resolution. Fulbright favored repeal, but contended Dole's move was improper procedure; he felt the motion for repeal should come from the Senate Foreign Relations Committee of which he was chairman.

In recent Congresses there have been some indications that the power of the long-entrenched oligarchs who oppose change is beginning to erode somewhat. There have been some modifications in the rules and procedures which indicate an increasing strength among the reform elements. Though seniority has not been abandoned, the way has been opened for challenging seniority as the method of selecting committee chairmen. Committee meetings have been opened up more; secret voting has been reduced; some chairmen have been deposed and others have had their powers and discretion trimmed; and the procedure for ending a Senate filibuster has been made a little easier. That the power of the conservative establishment has not become completely dissipated, however, has been illustrated on several recent occasions. At the start of the 94th Congress, when Wilbur Mills was deposed as chairman of Ways and Means and the committee's membership enlarged, the House leadership relented and allowed the senior members to go ahead and organize the committee and its subcommittee before the new members were appointed. This meant the senior members could claim the choice positions, making the reform somewhat less than complete. In the 92nd Congress, the House rejected a proposal made by a special committee headed by Richard Bolling for wholesale committee reform in favor of a proposal from another committee headed by Julia Butler Hansen which recommended only minor changes in the House committee structure; and though the procedure has been opened up considerably, a majority of committee chairmen are still those with the most seniority. Thus far the impetus toward large-scale reform has not become overwhelming in either house of Congress.

Another facet of legislative rules is the application and enforcement as they pertain to the members. Again, Congress has been most conservative, displaying strong reluctance and inconsistency when it comes to applying the rules to its own membership. In its entire history, the House has censured eighteen members and expelled three; the Senate has censured seven and expelled fifteen. The last expulsions were in 1861 in the House and 1862 in the Senate. The infrequency of actions against members is more a commentary on congressional aversion to self-discipline than the high level of ethical conduct of its members. Normal procedure is to quietly and quickly clamp the lid on any reports of wrongdoing by members, so the scandal won't become public and taint all members. When there is any other option available, members rarely are disciplined by their colleagues.

In a couple of recent cases the House and Senate each took action against a member for wrongdoing. In 1967 the Senate censured Thomas Dodd (D. Conn.) and the House, in action later held improper by the Supreme Court, denied Adam Clayton Powell (D. N.Y.) his seat. In these cases, as in the earlier, more prominent case of the Senate censure of Joe McCarthy (R. Wis.), the houses acted largely out of self-defense; i.e., they called the errant members to account only after their actions began to reflect unfavorably on the entire Congress. In pushing for action against Powell in the House, Clark MacGregor, later a staunch defender of Richard Nixon before the House Judiciary Committee, as campaign director of the committee to re-elect the President, observed, ". . . he has repeatedly insulted the members of this body and the House of Representatives as an institution."[10] In regard to the enforcement of the rules as applied to its members, Congress is vulnerable to criticism as the home of the double standard. Prospective appointees to high level federal positions are examined carefully in Congress and expected to make full and complete disclosures of all outside investments and financial interests. Congress has yet to adopt rules requiring full and complete disclosures for its own members. The member who is careful not to step on the toes of his colleagues and conducts his activities so as not to reflect unfavorably on the Congress, has little to fear from his house in the way of rules enforcement. This rather casual attitude toward its own rules and the behavior of its members does not enhance the image of Congress with the average voter, and the behavior of members is only little influenced by fear of punishment within the Congress.

Summary

A strong natural curiosity exists among most observers as to the how and why of congressional rules and procedures. To fully understand the Congress and its operations, one must also appreciate that organization, structure, and procedure are not neutral; they serve the purposes of those who best understand and control them. There is considerable room in either house for those who know and understand and can use the rules and procedures to out-maneuver those who don't.

Also there is much about legislative organization and proced-ures that does not readily meet the eye, even of an experienced ob-server. The complex legislative process involves many areas of compromise, negotiation, horse-trading and behind-the-scenes ma-neuvering and informal arrangements which are not evident in the formal structures and procedures through which bills are enacted.

On the whole, the U.S. Congress is a group of followers, not leaders; thus, one of the most important keys to an effectively functioning Congress is vigorous and forceful leadership. Many of the problems experienced in Congress in recent years stem from a rather flaccid and unambitious leadership that backs away from pushing for the changes necessary to make Congress more effective. The task of the political leaders in a democracy is challenging and tough; the political leader is constantly faced with difficult choices as to what course of action will best serve society's needs. In the last decades there has been an increasing gap between the aging leadership in Congress and the increasingly young populace of the country, and the leadership has not displayed any strong in-clination to push for much-needed programs. The House leaders stood by and let Wilbur Mills bottle up important Medicare legisla-tion for six years. It has often been necessary to develop an over-whelming public mandate before the Congress will act.

In all fairness, it must be said that Lyndon Johnson and Sam Rayburn led their houses in easier times, but none of their succes-sors have demonstrated either their capacity or desire for really ef-fective leadership. As a consequence, the Congress has declined even further as an effective partner in the national government. There is a growing need for reform and modernization of the rules and organization if the Congress is to exercise its share of political leadership in our society. However, the existing power structure— especially the committee chairmen and those who aspire to chair-manships—fear change, and the tendency when institutional au-thority is challenged, is for all members to close ranks and rally to defend the integrity of Congress. In the absence of strong and effective leadership pressures for change, chances for structural and procedural reforms are slim indeed.

Notes

1. Stewart Udall, "A Congressman Defends the House," *Congressional Record* (January 13, 1958).
2. Chet Holifield as quoted by Julius Duscha in "An Exodus from Congress: 'No longer any fun,'" *Courier-Journal* (September 15, 1974).
3. Edith Green as quoted by Julius Duscha, *Ibid.*
4. Russell Baker, "Modern Saga: The Old Man and Capitol Hill," *Courier-Journal* (November 18, 1968).
5. Rowland Evans and Robert Novak, *Lyndon B. Johnson: The Exercise of Power* (1966).
6. Richard Russell as quoted by Frank Smith in *Congressman From Mississippi*, p. 188.
7. Lyndon Johnson as quoted in "Lyndon Johnson: A Presidency Tempered in Congress," *Congressional Quarterly* (January 27, 1973), p. 127.
8. As quoted by Charles Clapp, *The Congressman*, p. 25.
9. *The Federalist*, p. 352.
10. Clark MacGregor as quoted by Richard Lyons in "The Irony of Adam," *The New Leader* (March 13, 1967), p. 3.

Chapter IV

The Committees
of Congress

THOUGH NOT MENTIONED in the Constitution and used on a limited
scale in early Congresses, committees have become the very heart
of the legislative process. They are the embodiment of the political
struggle and the key to the distribution of power within the legislature. Individually, members of Congress, with the exception of
a small elite guard, have very little influence. By developing expertise as members of particular committees, they can enhance their
influence. Thus most members today have come to place a lot of
import on their functions as members of congressional committees.
Though some members find their committee assignments provide
only marginal benefits and therefore spend little time there, most
members spend more time in committee work than on the floor.
This generally pays good dividends in that the members who command the most respect and wield the most influence in Congress
are those who do their committee work and become experts on
those legislative programs in which their committees specialize.

Today committees constitute the core of the legislative process
in Congress, as the whole function of law making centers around
the idea of committee expertise. The committee system has enabled the members to specialize and develop expertise in particular
areas of legislation, and it is only in this way that Congress has
been able to cope with the increasing complexity of legislative issues. The committee system is significant also in that it is only
through its committees that Congress can develop the centers of
expertise that can counter the ever-increasing specialization within

the executive branch. Because the committees are regarded as the sources of legislative expertise, deference to the authority of committees has become extremely strong in Congress.

The committee system has also played a significant role in enabling the Congress to handle its voluminous work load with some semblance of order. The 1st Congress had no standing committees, but used the Committee of the Whole for handling measures. In the 6th Congress only 161 bills and resolutions were considered; whereas, today approximately 20,000 items are processed by each Congress. Only through the committee system could the Congress cope with this tremendous volume of legislative proposals.

Because of their vital role, committees have come to dominate the legislative process. All congressional action springs from one committee or another; and as former Representative Clem Miller observed, Congress is really a collection of committees that come together in the chambers periodically to approve one another's actions.

Types of Committees

Today the Congress uses a variety of committees, but the workhorses of the legislative process are the standing committees of the two houses. Standing, or permanent, committees are those congressional committees provided for in the rules to carry over from one Congress to the next. These committees provide an element of continuity to the legislative process and enable members to build expertise in a particular legislative field. Normally only standing committees have the authority to report bills and resolutions.

Not used extensively in early Congresses, standing committees had by 1825 emerged as the primary tools for handling legislation in Congress. From that point until 1946 the number of committees in use proliferated considerably. The Legislative Reorganization Act of 1946, the first major overhaul of congressional machinery in decades, reduced the number of standing committees in Congress to fifteen in the Senate and eighteen in the House. Since this time, Congress has been rather conservative about adding standing committees, adding only two in the last twenty-five years—on aeronautical and space sciences and on ethics. A major objection to creation of new standing committees is not so much philosophical as the lack of adequate space to house them.

The standing committees of Congress come in considerable variety and operate in diverse manners. The committees range in size from the District of Columbia Committee with fewer than ten members to the House Committee on International Relations with fifty members. The work load and method of operations of the committees also vary considerably. Some committees conduct almost all sessions openly while others, such as the Appropriations Committees, conduct most of their business behind closed doors. Some committees operate quite democratically while others are dominated by rather autocratic chairmen. Standing committees also vary considerably in their prestige and influence in the legislative process, ranging from the highly prestigious and powerful bodies, such as Appropriations, Ways and Means, and Rules in the House and Foreign Relations, Finance, and Appropriations in the Senate, to the less prestigious committees on veterans affairs, post office and the District of Columbia. Without its system of standing committees the work of Congress would come to a grinding halt.

Along with its standing committees, Congress also makes use of a number of select committees. Select, or special, committees are units set up for a particular task, and once their job is done they are disbanded; i.e., unless like the former House Committee on Un-American Activities,* they manage to gain approval as permanent panels. Though they do not normally have the authority to report legislation, select committees may focus on significant issues and command a good deal of attention. Consequently such committees may provide ample opportunity for their leaders to gain public exposure and forward their careers. Harry Truman's activities as chairman of the select committee investigating waste and inefficiency in war materiel helped him to a Vice-Presidential nomination; Estes Kefauver's televised investigations into organized crime made him a TV hero and potential presidential candidate;

---

*This committee's name was changed to the House Internal Security Committee. This committee was disbanded by the House at the start of the 94th Congress, a rather unusual action.

and George McGovern's role as chairman of the Senate Select Committee on Nutrition and Human Needs has provided him considerable publicity. Such committees also help to focus attention on crucial social issues and generate public demand for legislative action.

The Congress also has made limited use of joint committees. These are committees made up of an equal number of members from each house, and the chairmanship rotates between the senior Senate and House member. For years the chairman of joint committees was a senator, but the House finally prevailed and got a rotating arrangement. Currently Congress has nine working joint committees, but their legislative functions are limited in most cases. Though there are numerous obstacles to the use of joint committees in the Congress, there is a pressing need for more interaction and collaboration between the two houses and a reduction in duplication of effort and unnecessary waste of time. More use of joint committees appears to be a prime method for moving toward these objectives.

A special type of joint committee frequently used by Congress is the conference committee. The Constitution requires that all measures to become law must pass both houses of Congress in identical versions. Since many measures pass each house in somewhat different form, it becomes the function of the conference committee to formulate a compromise bill acceptable to both houses. The conference committee is composed of members selected by the presiding officer of each house and is usually dominated by the more senior members from each body. Usually meeting behind closed doors and operating with considerable anonymity, the conference committee plays a paramount role in the legislative process.* While each house must concur in the conference report for it to become law, the conference committee has sufficient flexibility and discretion as to what course it takes when it meets to consider differing House and Senate versions of a measure. The impact of the conference action is further enhanced by the fact

---

*Congress did move at the start of the 94th Congress (1974) to open up conference committee sessions more than in the past. A majority can still vote for executive sessions, however. The full effect of this move remains to be seen.

that conference reports must be accepted or rejected as reported; they cannot be amended. This gives a small number of conferees from each house a tremendous amount of power and influence in the shaping of national policy. Because they do operate largely behind the scenes, most observers are unaware of the role and influence of conference committees in the legislative process.

Adding a further element of obscurity to the legislative process are the myriad subcommittees of the Congress. Most of the standing committees of Congress use a system of smaller subunits to expedite the handling of measures referred to them. These subcommittees present an even more confusing diversity to the average observer than their parent permanent committees. Though some major committees, such as Ways and Means, have been reluctant in the past to use subcommittees, others such as Appropriations become virtual holding companies, with the subcommittees doing much of the work and exerting much influence. A powerful subcommittee chairman, such as Dan Flood or Jamie Whitten, can certainly make his weight felt. The committee reform plan adopted by the House in the 92nd Congress requires each standing committee to have at least four subcommittees. While they tend to fragment and further obscure legislative decision-making, the subcommittees do offer several advantages. They enable the full committees to consider and dispose of more legislation than would otherwise be possible. They enable committee members to specialize and become expert in particular areas of legislation. And they provide leadership and effective participation opportunities for many more members, especially the newer and younger members. While they may be almost completely overshadowed by the more senior members in full committee and on the floor, the more junior members may have their day in subcommittee work.

Though their roles will vary considerably from committee to committee, subcommittees exert substantial influence on the legislative process. A small subunit of three to five members headed by a powerful chairman can play a key role in determining national policy. Because of the deference in Congress to committee expertise in a particular area, subcommittee recommendations may have undue influence in determining the final form a measure takes. It is not unusual for the full committee to ratify subcommittee recommendations, report to the floor and have the action again rubber-stamped at that stage. Thus, policy is really being molded by a small handful of members. Of course, the full body can raise questions, offer amendments and make changes, but it frequently doesn't. Thus men like Dan Flood, Jamie Whitten, William Natcher, and Joe Waggonner wield tremendous power and influence in those areas over which their subcommittees have jurisdiction.

Committee Functions

In carrying out their legislative role, the committees of Congress engage in a variety of functions. Paramount among these, of course, is that of law making. The role of the committees in this respect has been magnified by the increasingly technical and complex nature of legislation. Through their specialization, the committees provide the expertise in Congress for handling the highly complex and technical issues. The committees also facilitate the discussion of substantive policy content, clarification of issues and resolution of conflicts so necessary for effective law making.

Every measure enacted into law is a product of the committee process. The committees shape the measures they ultimately report for action in "marking-up" sessions. These sessions usually occur behind closed doors and the end product is frequently the result of extensive haggling, horse-trading, compromise and careful consideration of what the committee thinks will succeed on the floor. The reception of a bill on the floor reflects how accurately a committee has anticipated the preferences of the chamber. The committees usually try to put together a bill in such a way as to prevent adverse reaction to any one portion from defeating the whole measure. By functioning in this manner, the committees resolve many of the conflicts surrounding particular issues and smooth the way to passage once the measure reaches the floor.

Another function of the committees is to conduct hearings on bills referred to them. Committee hearings range from perfunctory appearances of routine witnesses to lengthy and involved efforts to gather information needed to legislate soundly. On one recent measure, the House Education and Labor Committee held seventy-five days of hearings, heard 275 expert witnesses, and considered thirty-one different formulae for allocating federal school aid funds. All testimony before the committees is included in the record and published. This may be quite voluminous; recent hearings before the

Defense Appropriations Subcommittee filled nine volumes and 8296 pages. Another 5924 pages were "classified" and removed from the record.

Usually, depending on the time available, congressional committees are willing to hear about anyone who desires to testify. Normal procedure is to start by hearing witnesses from the executive agencies most directly interested in a pending measure. When a bill is referred to committee, a copy is forwarded immediately to the agency that will have the responsibility for administering the law if it is enacted. The agency witnesses are usually followed by the spokesmen for various special interest groups desiring to be heard. The session continues until all those requesting to appear have been heard.

Actually the role of committee hearings as a means for informing members and gathering useful information probably is overestimated. Much of the prepared committee testimony is routine and not very informative for most members. Commenting on Secretary of State William Rogers' appearances before the House Appropriations Foreign Operations Subcommittee, one representative said, "He nodded and smiled for nearly two hours and offered generalities that provided us less insight than this morning's *Washington Post*." In many instances most committee members have heard essentially the same testimony from the same witnesses before. New members may hear a new viewpoint presented, but for most of the old-timers it's all rehashed material.

If they don't inform the members, what worthwhile purpose do committee hearings serve? While the benefits may be limited, the hearings do serve a communications function. They provide a means for transmitting information between members and executive agencies, interest groups, policy experts and the general public. As a channel of communication between Congress and the electorate, hearings can provide an effective means for building public support. The hearings on Viet Nam before the Senate Foreign Relations Committee are a prime example. Committee hearings also may serve as a safety valve by providing those with axes to grind and those who feel they must speak out, a chance to be heard. For some elements all that is necessary to satisfy them is the opportunity to let off steam. Finally, the hearings help members establish a public record which may be helpful in a number of ways. Members frequently ask witnesses leading questions in an effort to get their own positions written into the record. Hearings also may serve as a record to which the voters can refer. And the courts may on occasion look at committee hearings in an effort to determine legislative intent. Thus, in the final analysis, committee hearings are probably much more valuable as channels of communication than as a method of informing members of Congress on legislative issues.

Similar in purpose to hearings are committee investigations designed to help the Congress perform its law-making function. Investigations differ primarily from hearings in that witnesses testifying at hearings ask to be heard and appear voluntarily; whereas, those appearing at investigations are invited to appear or are subpoenaed. Committee investigations are a traditional tool of the Congress and have been used almost from its beginning. The investigative process has been held by the courts to be a legitimate function of Congress as long as the subject under investigation is related to Congress' law-making function. The expanded use of investigative committees and the over-zealousness of some chairmen in recent decades have raised a number of questions relative to the procedures of congressional investigative committees. Witnesses appearing before these committees do not have guaranteed to them the same rights as those appearing in the courts. The actions of such units as Joe McCarthy's Senate investigative subcommittee and the House Un-American Activities Committee in the 1950's raised serious questions relative to the procedural rights of witnesses appearing before congressional committees.

A number of members, among them Harry Truman, Estes Kefauver, and John McClellan, have made substantial reputations as investigators.

Committee investigations are vital to the legislative function, providing information necessary for sound laws. However, care must be taken to insure that these committees operate within the bounds established by the courts in conducting their investigations. While the legislative need-to-know must be served, it must not be served at the undue expense of individual freedom and privacy.

Closely related to the investigative function is the oversight function of congressional committees. The most effective legislative oversight of the executive branch comes through the work of congressional committees. Realizing this, Congress has made an attempt to have its committees parallel the administrative organization. This helps facilitate committee oversight of executive operations. Executive agencies are extremely sensitive to the possibility of investigation by congressional committees and they try to conduct their activities in a way that will head this off. Frequently all that is necessary to bring an agency into line is for a member of Congress to raise the threat of a committee inquiry. Likewise, when agency officials appear before legislative committees, members may offer suggestions on what they consider should be the proper operation of the agencies. Often, though such suggestions don't go into the law, they are all that is necessary to get the desired action from an agency. Were it not for its committees, Congress could not begin to cope with the challenging task of oversight of executive operations.

Committee Members

For most members of Congress, committee activity takes most of their time, and for most it will be through their work on their respective committees that their legislative reputations are made. Thus, the most immediate task facing the newly elected member is to get himself appointed to a choice committee, a matter that can be most important in shaping his future career in Congress. Unless a kindly, veteran colleague takes him under his wing, the freshman is left largely on his own in this task, and, as Clem Miller observed, unless some unusual political circumstance or personal qualification exists, the newcomer may very well find himself assigned to a committee that hasn't the remotest connection to his major interest or that of his district. In 1969 both Shirley Chisholm and Allard Lowenstein, liberal freshmen Democrats from metropolitan New York, found themselves assigned to seats on the House Agriculture Committee. Mrs. Chisholm objected vigorously and was reassigned to Veterans Affairs, also a low interest committee. She later moved to Education and Labor, which was more to her liking. While a member who is extremely dissatisfied with his assignment may appeal to his party's caucus, most hesitate to do so as this may brand them as "mavericks" and "troublemakers," reputations that are sometimes costly and hard to shake.

For some new members, being assigned to an undesirable

committee may mean a long delay before they can work on those things that are of primary interest to them and their districts. On the other hand, winning assignment to a committee whose work is interesting to the member and relevant to his state or district, maximizes his opportunity for providing useful service and succeeding as a congressman. Thus personal and district interests are frequently the major consideration in determining the committee assignments members seek. Former Representative Frank Smith (D. Miss.) points out in his autobiography how his interest in flood control and water resources, matters of direct concern to his constituents, led him to seek membership on the House Public Works Committee.

The process through which members are assigned is an intricate and highly personal process, frequently involving considerable jockeying for choice seats. Personal popularity and careful bargaining are key factors in getting desired assignments. In some instances a member may sacrifice substantial seniority on a committee to block another member from gaining a key committee assignment. In the early 1950's George Aiken gave up thirteen years' seniority on the Senate Labor and Public Welfare committee to take a seat on Foreign Relations. A major reason for his change was to block the red-baiting Joe McCarthy from getting the seat. In 1951, William Fulbright (D. Ark.) gave up his number-two position on the Senate Banking and Currency Committee to block the liberal William Proxmire (D. Wis.) from a seat on the Senate Finance Committee, and in 1973, Senator Robert Griffin moved from the Finance Committee to Foreign Relations to block Senator Edward Brooke from a seat on the committee, primarily because of Brooke's dovish position on Viet Nam. Sometimes the long-range effects of these personal considerations on assignments may not be as originally intended. In 1959 when Ed Muskie (D. Me.) entered the Senate, he rubbed Senate Majority Leader Lyndon Johnson the wrong way and was assigned a seat on the Senate Committee on Public Works. However, over the years as air and water pollution emerged as substantial public issues, Muskie's seat on that committee became more and more important and valuable to his career.

Assignments to the standing committees are made by each party's committee on committees in the respective houses. The method of selecting the committee on committees differs for the two parties. In the House, the Democrats, until the opening of the 94th Congress, used their members on the Ways and Means Committee as a committee on committees. With the opening of the 94th Congress this function was transferred to the House Steering and Policy Committee in line with the practice of using the Senate Steering Committee in this role. Transferral of the appointive function from the Ways and Means members, a role they had held since 1911, was a result of the infusion of an unusually large number of liberal, freshman Democrats into the caucus and the decline and fall of Wilbur Mills as the powerful chairman of Ways and Means. The Steering and Policy Committee in carrying out the appointing role will be both more liberal and more responsive to the party leadership than were the members of Ways and Means. The Republicans appoint a committee on committees in each house. In both parties vacancies on the committees on committees are filled by the party caucus, except in the Senate, where members of the Democratic Steering Committee are appointed by the majority floor leader subject to approval by the party caucus. The Republican committees on committees, especially the House committee, tend to be much larger and more complex in their operations than are their Democratic counterparts. The Republican committee in the House in the 93rd Congress had forty-five members. A smaller, sixteen-member executive committee really made committee assignments. The executive committee is composed of one member from each state having at least seven Republicans in its House delegation plus one member selected by the minority leader to represent the other states with Republican representation in the House, and two members elected to represent the two most recent "classes" of Republican freshmen. On the executive committee a system of weighted voting is used with members voting in proportion to their respective states' Republican strength. This provision gives greater power to those members representing states with large Republican delegations. In 1973, four executive committee members, Del Clawson (Cal.), Howard Robison (N.Y.), William Minshall (Ohio), and Leslie Arends (Ill.) controlled sixty-seven votes; only sixty-five were needed for appointment to a seat. In both parties some members use their positions on the committees on committees as bargaining tools, collecting obligations which they can cash in later.

In making assignments to committees many factors come into play, the most important of which is politics. Unlike the House, in the much smaller Senate, committee seats are well spread around and each member usually has at least one choice assignment. Lyndon Johnson as majority leader adopted the practice of trying to give each Democrat at least one choice seat, and each party has generally followed this practice. Senators may hold assignments on two "major" committees and one "minor" committee. However, in the House there is much more competition for seats on the most desirable committees while seats on the less important committees may go begging. In the House, the committees on Rules, Appropriations, and Ways and Means have been designated as exclusive committees and members serving on any one of these may serve on no other committee. The committees on Agriculture, Armed Services, and Banking and Currency, Education and Labor, International Relations, Interstate and Foreign Commerce, Judiciary and Public Works are "Major" committees. Each member is to be assigned to at least one "major" committee, but may not serve on two "major" committees. He can serve on one "major" and one "minor" committee.

When the new member arrives, he is asked to express his committee preferences in priority order. Depending on a variety of factors, these preferences may or may not be a prime consideration in the assignment he ultimately receives. In some cases these lists may not reflect the true interests of the freshman member anyway. Some freshmen tend to shy away from seats on those committees handling highly controversial legislative matters that they fear might raise questions jeopardizing their re-election chances. Others may not ask for their first choice in committee assignments, but for one they feel realistically they are more likely to get. Some of the more exclusive committees, such as Foreign Relations in the Senate and Rules, Appropriations, and Ways and Means in the House, are usually out of reach for the freshman member. The leadership generally prefers to fill the more exclusive seats with "responsible" members who are likely to be around for a while. A "responsible" member is one who will not rock the boat and whose behavior and actions will reflect favorably on the House. These "responsible" members are from safe districts and have the necessary "independence" (from their districts' desires) to go down the line with the leadership on certain policy matters. Thus, most members on Appropriations are "insiders" and over fifty years of age. In 1966, David Pryor (D. Ark.) was named to Appropriations in an almost unprecedented action, but this was largely with the aid of Wilbur Mills, chairman of Ways and Means and the Democratic committee on committees. More recently, however, Mills was unsuccessful in an effort to get an Arkansas freshman, Ray Thornton, on Appropriations. There is a very strong hesitancy to appoint freshman members to such prominent and powerful committees. In the 94th Congress, with an unusually large freshman class of Democrats, two freshmen, Joseph L. Fisher (D. Va.) and Martha Keys (D. Kan.), were named to Ways and Means in a most unusual action. Fisher's predecessor, Joel T. Broyhill, had held a seat on the committee, and Mrs. Keys had campaigned hard, contacting every member of the caucus and telling them that her region was unrepresented on the committee and that the committee needed a woman.

In their efforts to gain good committee seats, especially the most attractive ones, freshmen are frequently pitted against colleagues seeking to improve their own assignments. While there is some hesitancy to move from committee to committee and lose one's seniority, especially if one has been on a committee for several years, some members do choose to change. Birch Bayh (D. Ind.) sacrificed ten years' seniority on the Senate Public Works Committee for a seat on Appropriations. Edith Green (D. Ore.) gave up her ranking position on the House Education and Labor Committee to take a seat on the powerful House Appropriations Committee. While seniority has become less and less a factor in the making of committee assignments, it remains difficult for a freshman or even a less senior member to successfully challenge a more senior member. In 1971 a contest for a vacant seat on Ways and Means developed between Joe Waggonner (D. La.) and Donald Fraser (D. Minn.). When Fraser took his case to the Democratic caucus, Hale Boggs, Carl Albert and Wilbur Mills all supported Waggonner, the more senior member.

A major consideration in assigning members to committees is geography. Careful attention is given to maintaining the proper regional balance on important national committees such as Appropriations, Ways and Means, and Rules. The most qualified candidate may be denied a seat because his state or region already has a full quota on the committee, or because the seat to be filled is regarded as the property of a particular state. A 1969 vacancy on Ways and Means by tradition belonged to Pennsylvania; therefore, the selection of a member to fill the vacancy was made within the Pennsylvania delegation. In cases such as this the zone representative on the committee on committees and the dean of the state's delegation will pack a lot of weight on the choice. Appeals for assignment of seats on this basis are generally quite effective, though not always. In seeking a vacant seat on Appropriations, Bill Burlison (D. Mo.) wrote the committee on committees, "Missouri feels it is entitled to continued membership on this committee, in view of its large Democratic delegation." He got the assignment. On the other hand, Texas had historically had a member on Ways and Means, primarily to protect the oil depletion allowance and assure ample contributions from the petroleum industry to Democratic coffers, but in 1971 Omar Burleson (D. Tex.) was defeated for a seat on the committee by Jack Gilbert, a liberal from New York. Interestingly, the Republicans decided to name George Bush, a Texan, to the committee in an effort to tap some of the oil money. In 1973 the southern Democrats' effort to fill one of three vacancies on the Rules Committee also failed as all three seats were assigned to moderate-to-liberal members. Thus, while regionalism is a prime consideration, it is not an iron-clad rule. Some effort is also made to balance committee memberships ideologically, but this is extremely difficult and not generally a primary concern.

On occasion the parties may try to help a member improve his job security or enhance his chances for re-election by giving him a choice committee assignment. When John Watts (D. Ky.), a member of the powerful House Ways and Means Committee, died, he was replaced on the committee by Joseph Karth (D. Minn.). This was probably an effort by the Democratic leadership to strengthen Karth in a marginal district. How much assignment to a prestigious committee can help a member with his constituents and improve his chances of re-election is difficult to assess.

While committee assignments are customarily regarded as exclusively an in-house operation, outside influences may come into play. The oil industry with its concern for maintaining the depletion allowance has consistently exerted a potent influence on appointments to the House Ways and Means Committee, which handles tax legislation. Though, as noted earlier, Omar Burleson was defeated for a seat on the committee in 1971, fellow Texan Bill Archer, with the help of the oil interests, gained a seat on Ways and Means in the 93rd Congress. Outside interests may be particularly active in efforts to influence appointments to the committees on committees as this may lead to more influence on appointments to other standing committees.

Though they are not in a position to dictate selections, the chairmen of congressional committees, especially the more exclusive ones, may have a lot to say as to who serves on their committees. Most chairmen do not hesitate to make their preferences known and their expressions of choice may pack considerable weight with the committees on committees. Chairman of the House Judiciary Committee, Peter W. Rodino, Jr. (D. N.J.), indicated his preferences for Democrats to serve on his committee at the opening of the 93rd Congress and all were honored. But chairman of the House Armed Services Committee, Edward Hebert (D. La.), was not as successful. Hebert indicated that he would accept any black other than Ronald Dellums (D. Cal.), to serve on his committee. Dellums was selected anyway. A powerful chairman's objection certainly makes attaining a desired seat more difficult, however.

Many other factors may also enter the picture as the party committees decide which members to place on which committees. Such factors as background and expertise, ideology and policy orientation, personality, and party regularity may be considered. Republicans appear a bit more inclined to look at a member's party loyalty and past voting record in making choice assignments than do the Democrats. A Don Riegle or a Paul McCloskey (R. Cal.) may be passed over for top assignments. The role a member is expected to play on a particular committee may also be a consideration. One member of the Democratic committee on committes in the House said of assignments to the Rules Committee:

> A majority of us feel the Speaker has to have control of the Rules Committee. I resented the way Smith and Colmer ran the Rules Committee. All McSpadden* has to do is go along

---

*Clem Rogers McSpadden, Democratic Representative from Oklahoma, named to the House Rules Committee in 1973.

> when Albert calls him up on something. We didn't put him
> on there to exercise independent judgment on substantive
> questions of legislation.[1]

Thus, getting on the "right" committee, a matter that can either
greatly facilitate or handicap one's career in Congress, hinges on
a variety of factors, not the least of which is the highly political
process through which appointment decisions are reached.

Committee Chairman

The committee a member is assigned to becomes of paramount importance because it is his committee membership which
enables the lawmaker to specialize in one area of legislation and
become an "expert." And it is this "expertise" coupled with seniority that becomes the power base for most members of Congress.
Without such a base from which to operate, the power and influence of most individual members would amount to little. This is
doubly true for committee chairmen in Congress. Morris Udall
says,

> The committee member who has served twenty years is not
> just 5 percent more powerful than the member who has
> served nineteen years. If he is chairman he is 1,000 percent
> more powerful.[2]

Committee chairmen, especially those who head certain key committees, play a commanding role in Congress. Being the ranking
member around Congress doesn't mean that much relative to what
being chairman means. It is the chairmen who frequently dominate the Congressional scene, albeit with a certain degree of
anonymity.

How have the committee chairmen come to be such dominant
figures in the legislative process? We have already noted how expertise in a particular legislative field serves as a source of power,
but to fully understand the role and influence of the chairmen, one
must also understand the implications of the seniority system in
Congress. Chairmen are usually characterized as having acquired
their significant positions under the "seniority rule." In reality, seniority is not a rule at all, but rather a practice of long standing in
both houses which grew out of a desire for expediency and independence. In the Senate, a dispute between party leaders and the
Vice-President in 1846 led to the use of seniority for selecting

chairmen; and the House, though it had on occasion used the practice earlier, adopted the custom in 1911 following the revolt against Speaker Joe Cannon. So the custom of assigning chairmen on the basis of seniority was adopted as an antidote to autocratic leadership.

Prior to the adoption of the custom of seniority, the leader in each house had designated committee chairmen, and under this practice even minority members occasionally were given a chairmanship. Under the tradition of seniority, the member of the majority party having the longest period of uninterrupted service on each committee automatically becomes the chairman of that committee. The rules do prohibit a member from chairing more than one standing committee. Though not a part of the formal rules of the two houses, the custom of seniority has been extremely durable and has become self-perpetuating. With seniority steadily increasing in acceptance and importance, it wasn't long before committee chairmen had developed strong and relatively autonomous centers of power in the Congress. The chairmen owed their positions, not to their party or the leadership, but to their own ability to be re-elected and to accumulate uninterrupted service on their respective committees.

With the committees becoming independent centers of power and with their ever-increasing importance in the legislative process, the chairmen took on an entirely new role in the Congress, emerging as powerful figures with whom the President and the party leaders had to deal. Probably no other single feature has affected the Congress so much as the seniority system, which has become more than just a convenient method for designating committee chairmen. It is today a spirit that permeates the whole operation of the Congress. An increasingly important factor in the distribution of authority in Congress, seniority has made longevity and the ability to get re-elected prime determinants of power and influence in the national legislative process.

Under the custom of seniority, the person who can get to Congress, win re-election, and outlive colleagues on his committee, automatically becomes a figure of some power and influence, presiding over major policy decisions in such significant areas as taxes, appropriations, social security, air and water pollution, and foreign affairs. Even though his committee assignment may not have been

the one he most desired, as the member gains in seniority he becomes more and more aware of the implications a change to another committee would have on his expertise and influence. Thus,
as former Senator Joe Clark observed, "Once a member is appointed to a major committee he tends to dig his feet in and wait
for death, defeat or resignation of his seniors to bring him out at
the top of the list."[3] The result is that at an age when most corporation and business leaders have long since been retired, a member
of Congress may just be attaining a position of leadership. It was
thirty years before George Mahon (D. Tex.) reached his position
as chairman of the powerful House Appropriations Committee and
John McCormack and Ray Madden were both over eighty on becoming Speaker and chairman of the House Rules Committee
respectively.

The fact that the system tends to penalize the younger and
more vigorous members while elevating the elderly and often atypical members results in much criticism of the seniority custom. Opponents of the practice maintain that leadershp in Congress should
go to the fittest, not to those who have been able simply to hang
on the longest. They insist that the practice stifles the ambitions
of the younger and frequently more able members while elevating
the mediocre. It requires only longevity and re-election, thus encouraging some members to be overly cautious and follow courses
of action that minimize their chances for defeat. Lose once and
you start over at the bottom of the list. For this reason, seniority
favors those who come from one-party, noncompetitive and often
atypical states and districts. Along these lines, since the members
come from safe districts and since their positions derive from their
ability to be re-elected, seniority tends to reduce party responsibi-
ity. The practice also results in an unevenness in members' abilities
to represent their constituencies with equal effectiveness. And, finally, the system results in leadership that is often elderly, sometimes
verging on senility. According to Don Riegle, some chairmen can't
hear very well, can't see very well, and have difficulty working a
full day. He notes that there are so many old people in the Congress that an ambulance is kept parked behind the Capitol and
stretchers and oxygen tanks are kept in the cloakrooms.[4]

On the other side, the seniority system has its defenders,
many of them, of course, in the Congress. An old saw around Cap-

itol Hill is that seniority really isn't so bad, "and the longer you're here, the better you'll like it." Some valid points can be made in defense of the system, and a major difficulty facing the reformers has been to come up with an alternative system that would work better. Defenders of the system point out that it insures committee chairmen who are veteran legislators with long experience and who know the ins and outs of the committee and the Congress. They add that the system has produced as many or more chairmen of real stature and ability than it has poor ones. It is also pointed out that this process of selecting chairmen provides a degree of insulation from the President, the parties and interest groups that could be lacking under other methods. The current method also accommodates the rise to power and prominence of members from small states, something that might not occur were chairmen elected. It is also emphasized that the election of chairmen could lead to disruptive competition, intrigues and bargaining, and deadlocks within the parties that would waste time and destroy party unity and cooperation. Many members are reluctant to give up the seniority approach for one of electing chairmen because they feel that the present system promotes senior members who know what is going on and some fear outright election could lead to vote-trading and electioneering by those wanting to be chairman.

The reluctance to make any real changes is reflected in the recent "reforms" which have occurred in the system. The 1970 Legislative Reorganization Act has no references at all to seniority in spite of a long battle by liberal elements to get some changes. The party caucuses have made some changes which, on paper at least, reduce the reliance on seniority in making appointments. In 1970 the House Republican Conference adopted a resolution stating that ranking Republicans on committees would be elected in the conference by secret ballot after recommendations from the committee on committees. The candidate recommended need not be first in seniority on his committee. In 1971 House Democrats changed their rules to provide that any ten members of a committee could force a record vote in the caucus on a committee chairman, and in 1973 they approved a requirement of voting on all chairmen in the party's caucus.

Commenting on these "reforms," one observer wrote, "No longer will chairmen rule without fear of retaliation by rank-and-file members. A new responsiveness to colleagues' concerns should follow these reforms." He went on to say, "If seniority continues to dominate leadership selection, at least it will be by consent of the party caucuses." Viewing the "reforms" somewhat more realistically, this observer concludes, "Its successes have been incremental rather than sweeping and thus far have yielded no revolutionary upheavals in the congressional power structure."[5] This is really a rather roundabout way of saying that the efforts at reforming the seniority system in Congress have moved forward but without producing any dramatic results. Simply requiring that powerful chairmen who have dominated the legislative process for years be voted on in caucus is not likely, under normal circumstances, to produce any sweeping reforms. The party caucuses have always had the option of rejecting a more senior member for chairman, just as they could strip any member of his seniority if they so chose. Having such authority and exercising it are two different matters, and unless the parties show more inclination to break with tradition than they have to date, sweeping changes are not likely. Neither party has demonstrated overwhelming tendencies for such action. When John N. Erlenborn (R. Ill.), a more junior member, challenged Frank Horton (R. N.Y.) for the ranking Republican seat on the House Committee on Government Operations, Horton won 100 votes to 36. On the Democratic side, disgruntled party members led by Jerome Waldie of California launched an effort in 1971 to unseat senior committee member John L. McMillan (D. S.C.) as chairman of the House District of Columbia Committee. Defeated in the party caucus, the members took their case to the floor of the House where they were defeated 258 to 32. Even more significant was that 100 members abstained from voting and 42 voted "present," indicating their strong reluctance to break with precedent. In 1973 when the Democrats voted on all chairmen in their party caucus, the largest tally against any chairman was only 49 votes. Chet Holifield, (D. Calif.) object of an ouster effort, was elected 172–46, better than 3 to 1. In 1974 with the infusion of an unusually large contingent of seventy-five freshmen into their caucus, the Democrats did produce some cracks in the foundation of the seniority structure. In caucus action three chairmen, Edward Hebert of Armed Services; W. R. Poage of Agriculture; and Wright Patman of Banking and Currency, were voted out of their chairmanships. When Hebert threatened to challenge the caucus action by taking his case to the floor of the House, he was discouraged by the party leadership. In fact, Democratic Majority Leader Tip O'Neill observed that in his opinion anybody in the Democratic caucus who joined a coalition with Republicans to restore Hebert's chairmanship "should be stripped of his seniority and maybe ejected from the caucus."

In spite of the tremors created by the 1974 caucus actions, neither house appears inclined at this point to depart totally from seniority. The three chairmen who were deposed were replaced in each case by the next ranking member on the committee, and except in matters of personality, the changes were not really that drastic. Also, even the reform-minded caucus failed to follow Steering Committee recommendations to replace chairman Wayne Hays (D. Ohio), who as head of both the House Administration Committee and the Democratic Campaign Committee doled out favors and money to his fellow caucus members. Thus at this stage neither party shows any real inclination to break completely with the time-honored custom of seniority in selecting committee chairmen and ranking members.

What it all boils down to really is the question of what is to be the proper role of the committee chairman. And this, as with most other positions of leadership, hinges to a marked degree upon the individual in the position. A number of factors work together to make the committee chairman a powerful figure in Congress: the necessity of delegating substantial legislative authority to the committees; the traditions of seniority and of younger members acquiescing to their elders; and the methods used for the distribution of favors, patronage and other privileges. The chairmen become the focal point of the committee system because they control the organization and procedures, the staff and personnel policies, the subcommittee assignments, the referral of bills to subcommittees, the agenda, the scheduling of hearings, and other functions of their committees. The chairman usually knows legislation handled by his committee about as well as anyone, as he usually has the responsibility for managing bills from his committee on the floor. Also, the chairman is largely responsible for determining whether disputes are ironed out within the committee or go to the floor. Many chairmen go to great lengths to try to achieve an accommodation with the minority because they don't like committee differences to be aired on the floor. Because of his role in the legislative process, the committee chairman is in a position of power and influence in the Congress.

The standing committees of Congress are characterized by complex and shifting patterns of influence, but to a marked degree the individual style and personality of the chairman sets the tone of each committee's operations. The extent to which the chairman dominates his committee will vary greatly, but many committees take on the character of a powerful chairman. Committees range in method of operation from highly democratic to virtual dictatorships, as some chairmen exercise their power as arbitrary and heavy-handed autocrats while others operate with a soft touch and a high degree of finesse.

Chairmen operate with various degrees of success and employ a variety of methods to control and influence their colleagues. Adolph Sabath (D. Ill.), a rather ineffective chairman of the House Rules Committee, was sometimes mocked by some of the more powerful members of his committee. When he felt he was losing control, Sabath would resort to fainting spells. On one occasion he cautiously opened one eye and inquired of Clarence Brown (R. Ohio), "Have they all gone, Clarence?" Clarence Cannon (D. Mo.), former chairman of the powerful House Appropriations Committee, frequently assigned to insignificant subcommittees, members who refused to cooperate, an effective reprimand in a committee where subcommittees play a very important role. Chairmen may also pass over certain members for subcommittee chairmanships, as Graham Barden, chairman of the House Education and Labor Committee, did in by-passing Adam Clayton Powell in the 1950's. Some chairmen have elected not to set up a system of subject matter subunits within their committees, but rather to use a system of general subcommittees. In this manner the chairman retains more flexibility as to which subcommittee gets a particular bill. Some chairmen also tend to give newcomers a hard time in committee. Long-time chairman of the House Armed Services Committee, Carl Vinson (D. Ga.), put junior members of his committee at the rear of the committee rostrum where they were seldom recognized for questions. One young member infuriated the chairman by making the glass chandelier above him tinkle to attract the chairman's attention.

Probably the model of the powerful committee chairmen in Congress, until his troubles with a Washington stripper embarrassed his colleagues, undermined his power base and forced his resignation as chairman, was Wilbur Mills (D. Ark.), who chaired the highly significant House Ways and Means Committee, or as Russell Baker referred to it, the "Wilbur D. Mills Committee," which is responsible for originating all tax law. Speaking of his powerful colleague, Don Riegle wrote, "The man whose power within the Congress probably counts for more than all the other members put together is Wilbur Mills of Arkansas." He went on to add that Mills wrote the tax bills the way he wanted them or they just didn't come out of committee.[6] Even President Lyndon Johnson had to strike a bargain with Chairman Mills in 1964 before he would move the tax cut bill pending in his committee. Yet Mills wielded his power and influence with such finesse that other members were seldom rankled. One colleague said,

> Mills uses power with the softest touch of anybody I've ever seen. When he manhandles you, you think he's been using velvet. You don't feel offended a bit. Sometimes you don't even know it happened.[7]

A fellow committee member, James C. Corman (D. Cal.) said, "I've opposed Wilbur on lots of bills, and he's never retaliated. He's never done anything to me on the Committee on Committees."[8]

With their own bases of power securely fixed in their home states and districts, and their positions of leadership virtually assured by seniority, the committee chairmen may move away from the party leadership and other elements in the policy system to reign in their own individual styles over particular areas of public policy. Other members may be most reluctant to buck powerful chairmen who have life or death control over their legislative measures and other favors they depend upon as legislators. Thus, only a stern and vigorous leadership is able to deal effectively with the experienced and savvy old hands who head the committees. Not since the Texas team of "Mister Sam" and LBJ have the two houses had the strong leadership necessary to deal effectively with the chairmen; and even in the latter years of their leadership, Johnson and Rayburn experienced set-backs more frequently. Under the present leadership, Congress is dominated by the committee chairmen and their handpicked "consultants."

Committee Staffs

An element frequently overlooked when discussing congressional committees is the role and influence of the committee staffs. Except for the chairmen and ranking members, turnover on the committees of Congress is surprisingly high, causing the complexion of the committees to constantly change. Thus it is frequently the staffs that provide an element of continuity and stability to the committee system. This rather rapid rate of turnover also tends to enhance the influence of the staff in committee functions. It is the staff that provides the element of expertise necessary for handling the legislation coming before the committees.

The role of the staff will depend a lot on the individual chairman, but much of the work of the congressional committees must be borne by the professional staffs. Many chairmen virtually turn over to the staff the matters of scheduling hearings, setting the agendas, scheduling witnesses and handling the day-to-day routine operations of the committees. Most committee reports are largely the work of the staff, and much of the legislation introduced by members has its origin with committee staff. When it appeared that a committee headed by Richard Bolling to study committee reform in the House would recommend that the House Education and Labor Committee be split, chairman Carl Perkins decided it was time to counterattack. Another committee headed by Julia Butler Hansen was also charged with looking at committee reform in the House. Bill Cable, a top staff member on the Education and Labor Committee, was assigned to work with the Hansen committee. The plan eventually reported by the Hansen committee and adopted by the House over the Bolling committee proposals was largely the work of Bill Cable.

The growing complexity and technicality of much legislation coupled with the pressing demands on his available time mean the congressman must of necessity rely heavily on committee staff to help with his legislative tasks. This inevitably means that committee staffs, responsible to no electorate, exercise some influence

over national legislation. Key staff members on powerful committees who have the confidence and support of their chairmen may
wield considerably more influence than some junior members of
the Congress.

Committee Powers and Influence

In the words of Representative Dave Martin (R. Neb.), the
committees "are the heart and soul of the legislative process" in
Congress. While there are methods through which the committees
can be by-passed, there is great reluctance to resort to these procedures. Committee chairmen are powerful figures in the Congress
and for most members they are not persons with whom to trifle.
Consequently the committees exercise virtual life or death control
over those measures referred to them. In modern Congresses there
will be 15,000 to 20,000 bills introduced; of this number between
10 and 15 percent will be reported for floor action. The remainder
die in committee. A chairman's decision not to report a bill poses
a major obstacle to its passage. Though the rules of both houses
provide a discharge procedure, resort to this method has not been
very successful. Since the adoption of the discharge rule in the
House in 1910, more than 800 discharge petitions have been filed.
Of this number, fewer than twenty-five have succeeded and only
a couple of measures discharged have been enacted into law. Many
members vote against a bill brought out under the discharge procedure as a matter of principle.

In addition to their filtering function, the committees of
Congress also enjoy a broad discretion when it comes to the treatment they give bills referred to them. They may report a bill unchanged; they may substitute their own version. If a bill is to be
gutted, it usually takes place at the committee stage behind closed
doors and out of the public eye. It is at this point frequently that
provisions are inserted or deleted to satisfy powerful members of
the body or powerful special interests. Because many of the committees and their subcommittees tend to be special interest oriented, it is often at this stage that the policy objectives of Congress
get distorted. Frequently alliances or relationships develop between
agencies and committees or special interests and committees which
make it extremely difficult to bring about effective change in certain areas of policy. For example, the favor with which the De-

fense Appropriations Subcommittees look upon Pentagon requests makes any effective reduction of the budget in this area extremely difficult. Or, take the case of the federal food programs which have been developed largely by the U.S. Department of Agriculture and the Agriculture Committees of Congress. These programs have had as their primary objective, not the feeding of the poor and hungry, but rather the use of farm surpluses and the protection of the market interests of certain farmers. No effective lobbies look out for the poor and hungry, but the farmers have their lobbies and their spokesmen on the Agriculture Committees. Only after a number of books and articles and a public outcry over the revelations of "hunger in America" did the Congress finally react. Committees may come under the domination or influence of special interests and because of the tendency of the Congress to acquiesce in committee decisions, the result may be unchecked influence for such special interests.

The action taken in committee has a tremendous bearing on the fate of a bill when it reaches the floor. If a committee reports a bill unanimously, recommending its passage, ratification by the full chamber is virtually assured. A committee may also report a bill recommending that it not be passed. This, however, is unusual because if a committee opposes passage of a measure, the bill simply is not reported out. When a bill comes from committee to the floor, there is usually little an individual member can do to alter the work of the committee. Unless the chairman is willing to accept it, amending a committee bill on the floor is extremely difficult. Thus committee recommendations and reports carry an inordinate amount of weight when it comes to action taken on the floor of both houses of Congress. Members hard-pressed for both time and information tend to rely heavily on committee actions and committee members when it comes to voting. A southern Democrat says, "Often there's little time to consider how to vote; you must rely on people who can be trusted who are on the appropriate committee. . . ."[9]

The committees also may exert influence on voting in yet another way. Committee members often are much like the members of a large, closely knit family, developing feelings of close comradeship. One member described the results this way:

You tend to go along with your fellow committee members on bills in which they are particularly interested. I find myself going along sometimes even with members on the other side, although for some that principle works in reverse: they irritate you so much that you are against anything they are for.[10]

Committees also may have considerable impact upon public policy through their investigations and reports. Most agencies and organizations are understandably averse to being hauled before a congressional committee to answer questions about their operations. Considering that telecasting of a hearing can reach millions of viewers immediately, the effect on the public can be dramatic. Though much of the information and opinion that comes out of a committee hearing, or is incorporated into a committee report, may not be enacted as law, it can still have significant impact. Take, for example, the budget hearings of the various agencies before the appropriations subcommittees of Congress. Though they are not written into the law, these agencies frequently operate with copies of the subcommittee's reports as their bible, because they don't want to face embarrassing questions when they go back to defend next year's budget request. Thus the congressional committees make their presence felt in many ways.

Committee Reform

It is difficult to overstate the role and influence of committees and their chairmen in the Congress. Because of the traditional reliance upon the committees to provide the necessary legislative specialization and expertise, they have become independent and separate centers of power in the legislative process. A powerful leader like former Speaker Sam Rayburn was able to impose his will upon some committee chairmen, but most of the chairmen owed "Mister Sam" a debt and he could call these in when need be. Other less forceful and vigorous leaders may stand virtually powerless before the potent committee heads in Congress when they decide to oppose a particular policy.

Because the seniority system has in the past tended to bring to the chairmanships members who frequently have been atypical of their national party leadership, clashes between committee chairmen and the majority in the party have not been unusual. In both parties, but especially in the Democratic party, the custom of seniority has worked to the advantage of the more conservative elements. For two generations Southern Democrats held the key chairmanships and dominated congressional committees. Until recent Congresses, though Southern Democrats accounted for a smaller proportion of the total Democratic membership in Congress, they retained a disproportionately large number of the chairmanships. In the Senate in 1949, for example, they controlled eight of fifteen chairmanships and as late as 1959 they held ten of sixteen. Thus, though the number of nonsouthern, more moderate Democrats has been steadily increasing, while the Southern bloc in the Senate has shrunk over the last twenty-five years from 26 to 16, the moderates have had great difficulty in getting much of their legislation through the Congress because the committees have remained under the domination of their more conservative colleagues.

The custom of seniority also has had another significant impact relative to chairmen and the representativeness of Congress. Because seniority accrues to those from safe, noncompetitive districts, many of the most able members of the Congress representing areas with the most vigorous party competition have the least political clout, while those representing the atypical and least competitive districts have the most power and influence. Reapportionment has made Congress overall more representative of urban and suburban America, but so far it has had only minor effect on committee chairmanships. Consequently, a nation whose population is young, urban, mobile and geographically dispersed, is represented by a legislature whose committees are dominated by chairmen who are elderly, rural and frequently highly parochial in their views. The old are legislating more and more for the young; the average age in the United States is under thirty while the average age of committee chairmen is sixty. At the last census the U.S. population was about 70 percent urban, but only a handful of chairmen represent districts with more than 50 percent urban populations. In the 92nd Congress, eight of twelve subcommittees of the House Appropriations Committee were chaired by Southerners. The *Washington Post* editorialized, "The result is an outrageous concentration of power over government spending within a few states that are not representative of the nation as a whole."[11] The major problem arises from the fact that these powerful figures in the legislative process frequently do not see eye to eye with their leaders and a majority of their party, and are in a position to stifle majority action. Wilbur Mills, Democratic chairman of the House Ways and Means Committee for more than a decade, signed the "Southern Manifesto" in 1956, and in the 90th Congress voted with the conservative coalition* 74 percent of the time. Yet Mills faced his first opponent for re-election in eight years in 1974 and won in spite of an embarrassing incident involving his actions with a Washington stripper known as the "Argentine Firecracker" and questions raised about illegal campaign contributions from the milk industry. William Colmer, former chairman of the powerful House Rules Committee, whom Richard Bolling described as "slightly to the left of Ivan the Terrible," voted with the conservative coalition 85 percent of the time in the 90th Congress. These are the men who determine whether or not much-needed policies, such as tax reform, medicare, and aid to education, ever reach the floor for a vote.

Because of the obstructionist tactics of a number of these chairmen, the seniority system has become one of the most criticized aspects of Congress and a prime target for the reformers. Actually, the reformers have not focused on the real problems stemming from the seniority custom. The real issue here is not "effective leadership" as the reformers frequently insist, but rather *too effective* leadership, or at least, domination of the processes by a sometimes unresponsive and irresponsible leadership. The solution is not necessarily to change the method for selection, but to alter the authority of the chairmen. The bad thing about seniority has been the excesses allowed under the system which have made the chairmen autonomous, independent little barons ruling over their exclusive legislative domains. Some members recognize the problem for what it is. Representative Ben Blackburn (R. Ga.) says,

> Where I do feel considerable evil is done is in granting to the

*A combination of conservative Republicans and Southern Democrats in the Congress.

> Chairman such broad discretionary power that he can be un-
> responsive to the will of the Congress or even to the will of
> a majority of his own committee.[12]

Even with the seniority tradition, the worst abuses of the
committee system can be remedied, but only if the members themselves decide to make the necessary changes. Here again is a case
where the majority has frittered away much of its power in a manner very similar to the way the legislative branch has defaulted to
the executive. The problems arise not so much from power-hungry
chairmen grasping power as from other elements in Congress, including the leadership, allowing chairmen to exercise an unwar-
ranted amount of control and influence over legislation. Undeni-
ably, seniority brings to power an occasional chairman who should
never have been placed in such a position, but no alternative approach guarantees against this happening. What is needed is a
stronger determination on the part of both the leadership and the
majority that they will not allow a few in key positions to stifle the
whole legislative process. When enough members decide to revolt
against the chairmen as the House did against the Speaker in 1910,
then the stranglehold of committee chairmen will be broken and
they will be made more responsive to the will of the majority. This is the direction the reform efforts need to take to be really
effective. The changes at the opening of the 94th Congress were
a step in the right direction, but both houses still have a way to go
before the reform is complete.

While some reforms have been accomplished, indications are
that a majority have not yet reached the point where they are ready
to undertake the necessary action to make committees and their
chairmen responsive to the majority. Minor skirmishes have resulted in limited successes. For two decades Howard Smith (D. Va.)
as chairman of the House Rules Committee was a thorn in the
side of the liberal Democrats. Finally in 1961 the party leadership decided to dilute his power, not by taking away his chairmanship, but by enlarging the liberal membership on his committee, a move that proved less than a total success. When William
Colmer succeeded Smith, his colleagues forced him to agree to
written rules of procedure for the Rules Committee and to regular
weekly meetings. A favorite tactic of Smith's had been to simply

refuse to schedule hearings. Some minor revolts have also occurred in other committees, but in most cases these have simply made it a bit more difficult for chairmen to thwart the will of the majority on the committee.

Though there is much lip service to reform in the Congress and some window-dressing in both houses, indications are that any real changes will probably come through evolutionary rather than revolutionary processes. In 1973 Senate Republicans adopted a plan providing that members of each standing committee would elect the ranking Republican member. However, most Senate Republicans indicated they did not foresee drastic changes as a result, but hoped for a gradual moving away from the system whereby seniority is the sole qualifying factor. Also in 1973, House Democrats adopted a requirement that all committee chairmen had to be approved by a majority vote of the full party caucus, an apparent victory for the liberals opposed to the seniority system. The Democratic caucus then proceeded to vote in all senior members as committee chairmen with the largest vote against any chairman being only 49 votes. In 1975, again voting on all chairmen in the House, the Democratic caucus did depose three aging and dictatorial chairmen, but a majority of the House's chairmen were reelected by sizable margins, though several have frequently been criticized by their colleagues.

All too typical of reform efforts in Congress was the House's attempt to accomplish some meaningful committee reforms in 1973–74. First a committee headed by Richard Bolling, a strong reform advocate and a somewhat abrasive individual, was established. However, as Bolling's committee began to get into its task, it began to invade the "territorial imperative" of some other committees. Education and Labor would have been split and some other powerful committees, including Ways and Means, which each year gets about 20 percent of the bills introduced in the House assigned to it, would have had their committee domains threatened by the sweeping overhauls being considered by the Bolling committee; the chairmen counterattacked. At their urging, the House leadership established another committee headed by Julia Butler Hansen (D. Wash.) to also study the issue of committee reform. The proposal produced by the Hansen committee emphasized rela-

tively minor procedural changes, leaving existing committee juris-
dictions largely intact. The Hansen committee report was adopted
203 to 165 and the Bolling plan never got to a vote.

In voting against the Hansen proposal, freshman Representative Romano Mazzoli (D. Ky.) said he favored the Bolling plan's
proposal to limit each member to one major committee because
he saw this as a chance "to let some of us junior members have
some influence, to spread the action a little bit, to let the power
percolate down through the ranks."[13] Indications are that those now
in positions of power will share their authority only with great reluctance. Any changes in this direction will come gradually and
without their blessing. However, indications are that such changes
are in the offing. Time may do more than anything else to change
the impact of seniority and committee chairmen on the Congress.
Probably one of the most significant, but least noticed, trends in
national politics is the accrual of seniority by a number of more
liberal members in both houses of Congress. A new era in congressional leadership is slowly dawning. As the conservative members
who built up seniority during the 1950's have died, retired, or in
some instances, been defeated, more moderate colleagues have
moved up the seniority ladder. Now many of these members are
in line to move into key chairmanships which were once the bas-
tions of power for their conservative colleagues. Because of this
trend, David Broder, noted political writer for the *Washington
Post,* predicts that in the next decade Senate politics, as long as the
Democrats are in the majority, will have an increasingly Northern
and liberal tone. Only a generation ago, Southerners accounted
for about one-half of the Democratic caucus in the Senate and
dominated most committees because of their seniority. Today
there are fewer than twenty Southerners and more than forty non-
Southerners, as the moderate to liberal wing has grown substantially over the last decade at the expense of the Southern conservative wing. Added to this is the fact that several newcomers,
such as Lloyd Bentsen (Tex.) and Wendell Ford (Ky.) and Walter
"Dee" Huddelston (Ky.) are really only nominal Southerners.
Though Southerners still head almost half the Senate committees,
their control is gradually withering. Already Sam Ervin has been
succeeded by Ed Muskie and John Sparkman by William Proxmire,
and indications are that by 1980 Southern chairmen will be down

to only two or three. Similar trends also are evident in the House. Thus time will gradually accomplish what the reformers have failed to do for decades, i.e., bring to the chairmanships of the powerful congressional committees members who are more responsive and whose thinking is more in line with that of their national party leadership.

Notes

1. Congressional Quarterly, "Politics of House Committees: The Path to Power" (February 10, 1973), p. 281.
2. Morris Udall, as quoted by Larry King, "Inside Capitol Hill: How the House Really Works," *Harper's* (October, 1968), p. 67.
3. Joseph Clark, *Congress the Sapless Branch* (New York: Harper and Row, 1965), p. 178.
4. Don Riegle, *O Congress*, p. 163.
5. Groennings-Hawley, *To Be A Congressman*, pp. 147–48.
6. Don Riegle, *O Congress*, p. 64.
7. As quoted in *Congressional Quarterly* (February 10, 1973), p. 280.
8. *Ibid.*
9. As quoted by Roger Davidson, *The Role of the Congressman* (New York: Pegasus, 1969), p. 83.
10. Charles Clapp, *The Congressman*, p. 16.
11. "Sweep Out the Seniority System," *Washington Post* (January 19, 1971).
12. Ben Blackburn as quoted by Jonathan-Hawley, *To Be A Congressman*, p. 134.
13. Romano Mazzoli as quoted by Charles R. Babcock in "Office cheers Perkins' aide for 'protecting committee.'" *Courier-Journal* (October, 1974).

Chapter V

Debate and
Floor Action

THOUGH MUCH OF the significant action in the formulation and enactment of a law occurs somewhere other than on the floor, it is
here that much of the attention is focused. The task of getting a
measure through the Congress is intricate and involved, demanding
a lot of planning, groundwork and strategy. The legislative process
in Congress is not unlike an iceberg in that only a small portion of
what is there appears above the surface. Much of the really important action has occurred in the committees and cloakrooms before
measures reach the floor.

While the House and Senate chambers are not the great for-
ums of debate and conflict pictured by many, they are still impressive places, full of drama and conflict and steeped in history and
tradition. The chambers become a meeting place for the members
who come there to catch up on the latest news and share a few
stories with their colleagues. And even though floor action may
generally be confined to ratifying and amending committee actions,
no description of the congressman's world would be complete which
failed to capture at least some of the atmosphere and mood of the
chambers.

An observer of floor activity in the U.S. Congress sees a
blending of unique dignity and often disconcerting disorder. In the
House in particular, where there are no assigned seats, conversation frequently overshadows debate, and the situation often appears
to be one of disorder and confusion. In earlier days, the chambers
were at times most disorderly places with canings, fistfights, shoot-

ings and various assaults occurring there. John Randolph of Virginia delighted in bringing his unruly hounds into the House chamber until Henry Clay, as Speaker, put a stop to it. On one occasion, when Speaker Reed ordered the chamber doors locked to prevent the disappearance of a quorum, a Texas representative kicked out the door panels so he could escape. "Kicking Buck" Kilgore became a tourist attraction in the House chamber.

For these and other reasons many observers have been quite critical of Congress and its actions. Ralph Waldo Emerson once referred to the Congress as "a standing insurrection." In 1831, visiting Frenchman Alexis de Tocqueville wrote that he was struck with the "vulgar demeanor" of the House and described its members as almost all "obscure individuals." Tocqueville was a bit more impressed with the somewhat more elite Senate. Augustus Foster, secretary of the British legation, also describing the House in the early nineteenth century, wrote:

> This undoubtedly is a miserable place, but the elect of all the states are assembled in it, and really such a gang to have the affairs of an empire wanting little of the size of Russia entrusted to them, makes one shudder.[1]

While the Congress still operates today much as it has throughout its history, decorum has improved considerably. Serious fights are now very rare, and the Congress is one of the best-behaved legislative bodies in the world. The turbulence so often displayed in the *Chambre des Députés* in Paris, the House of the People in New Delhi, or the *Knesset* in Tel Aviv is largely absent. Members normally treat one another with formal respect and maintain a high degree of decorum.

Debate

The rather widespread popular concept of the Congress as a great forum for public discussion of legislative issues is largely a fiction. Though one of the things Congress does best is talk, it is rare for congressional debate to display real technical excellence. Much of the floor action is only window-dressing and the speeches are more for the gallery or the *Congressional Record* than for one's colleagues. Action on the floor often proceeds rather lamely and much of the discussion is not real debate at all, but a series of set speeches. Commenting on the so-called "Great Debate" on Vietnam, one senator observed, "We haven't had any real debate yet. One day the hawks come in and make their pitch, and then a few days later the doves flock in together. It's only an accident when there's any cross-examination or argument."

The quality of the speeches in Congress come in as many varieties as Heinz has soups, ranging from frightful to fascinating. The word "bunk" or "buncombe" had its origin in Congress with Representative Felix Walker of North Carolina, who informed his colleagues they needn't listen as he was going to deliver a speech for his constituents in Buncombe County. In his autobiography, Don Riegle warns that "bullshit is an occupational hazard" around Congress. As to the intellectual and educational quality of many speeches, Speaker Reed once observed that two colleagues "never open up their mouths without subtracting from the sum of human knowledge."

All of this is to say that much of what passes for debate in the Congress is not actual debate at all, but rather speech-making and sometimes grandstanding for the public and especially the constituents back home. Consequently, few observers feel today that debate still serves its historic function of defining and clarifying the issues so members can vote intelligently. Though some members have considerable ability as orators, most veteran legislators feel that as a general rule oratory changes few votes. Usually as issues mount in importance and pressures become more intense, the ability of one side or the other to influence votes on the chamber floor is reduced. On occasion members do change the votes of other members, but this is more by quiet persuasion and subtle pressures applied behind the scenes rather than through the impassioned debate in full assembly. Such changes only rarely affect the final outcome on an issue and would be decisive only in a few borderline cases.

Members of Congress are essentially "feeling" people. They are influenced by the prevailing moods of the chambers, and for debate to have much impact, the mood must be receptive. It is difficult to take to the floor and inform people who aren't really interested in listening. One factor that reduces the impact of debate in Congress is the poor attendance on the floor. Because so much of what transpires on the floor is routine, many members don't feel compelled to attend. Closing debate on a measure usually finds

10–25 percent of the members absent and it is quite clear their votes aren't based on these concluding arguments.

While some members are recognized as authorities on particular subjects and may have measurable influence, they usually exercise restraint and limit their speech-making on the floor, realizing that reputations are seldom made through debate, but frequently tarnished. The advice of most veterans regarding the question of speaking out is, "If you feel strongly, then speak out; if you don't, let it pass." Newcomers are frequently reminded that, "The speech you didn't make can't defeat you." While a talking senator may exert some influence in molding public opinion that a House member seldom achieves, most members of both houses must be careful, especially the more junior members, about diluting their influence by speaking too frequently and indiscriminately. One member observed of a colleague:

> _____ was one of the most able speakers on almost any subject that came up, and he usually spoke on every subject before us. Yet members resented the fact that he was in on every discussion.[2]

Thus the member who wields the most influence in debate may be the one who confines his speaking to those topics on which he speaks with some degree of expertise. Some of the most able members in the Congress never gain much real influence because they feel compelled to speak their minds and are frequently resented by their colleagues. Many members might be well advised to follow Sam Rayburn's advice to a freshman colleague. The newcomer asked the Speaker if he was doing too much talking on the House floor. "Yes," responded Rayburn. "Well," said the freshman, "what should I do about it?" "Quit it," replied Mister Sam.

One reason debate in Congress is not more significant and is not of higher quality is that it is poorly reported and attracts little attention. As a general rule, the news media pay scant attention to floor debate, and if reporters should cover discussion of some issue, they tend to focus only on the more influential and best-known members. Because most debate isn't even covered by the news media, it is a rather fruitless exercise for either informing or appealing to the public. Most members feel they can spend their time better in other pursuits.

Though the discussion in the chambers is dutifully recorded by batteries of stenographers and printed daily, few people make the *Congressional Record* a part of their daily reading. As a vital and reliable record of what transpires on the floors of Congress, the *Congressional Record* leaves much to be desired. Two practices in particular make the *Record* a less than dependable account of what actually was said on the floor of Congress. In the House, members are allowed to "revise and extend their remarks," thereby inserting into the record matter which never was delivered on the floor at all. Secondly, members are allowed to proofread and edit their remarks before they are finally printed as a part of the *Record*. Though this is supposedly simply for the purpose of making corrections, members frequently rewrite their remarks so that what finally goes into the *Record* hardly resembles what was actually said on the floor. Consequently the historian looking for a complete and accurate record of what was said on a particular issue in the Congress may be on a futile search. Televised coverage of House and Senate debate would help to reduce some of the deviousness now accompanying the recording of actual debate on the floor.

The Calendar System

The passage of a bill in Congress is an intricate and complex process and bringing a bill to the floor and to a final vote requires skillful negotiation and careful maneuvering. The legislative decision-making process involves numerous stages and there are many points along the way where a bill can be sidetracked or defeated. Consequently the major portion of the bills introduced in each session never reach the floor for consideration. The procedures in both houses for bringing a bill to a final vote can be lengthy and time-consuming. Considerable criticism of both houses centers around the obstacles and delays hampering the passage of much legislation.

Floor procedures in the two houses are substantially different, with the much larger House using an intricate system of calendars, special days and procedures. In the Senate, a bill may be tied up interminably or even killed by a filibuster. In the House, debate is strictly limited, and though there are ample opportunities for delay, once on the floor, a measure usually moves inexorably toward a final vote. In fact, it is rare for the House to spend more than a day on one particular bill, though on occasion various delaying tactics may be employed for a variety of reasons. Sometimes opponents may resort to a whole series of quorum calls and roll-call votes to delay action on a measure. In 1974, Craig Hosmer (R. Calif.) called for nine quorum calls on a strip mine bill to which he was opposed. This was an effort to give the mining lobbyists an opportunity to influence more votes. A substitute bill favored by the mining interests eventually was defeated anyway, 255 to 156. In 1968 the House was in session 726 hours, 196 of which were spent on quorum calls and roll-call votes. So quorum calls and roll calls, which normally take from twenty-five to thirty-five minutes each, can consume considerable time. On at least one occasion, a Democratic clerk in the House consumed fifty minutes in a roll call while the Democratic leaders tried to round up more votes. Thus, while there are various means for putting off a decision, sooner or later a measure on the floor of the House is voted either up or down.

To expedite the handling of its legislative business the House has developed an elaborate system of calendars for the posting of various types of bills. All revenue and appropriations bills are posted on the *Union* calendar. These are privileged* bills and all items on this calendar are considered in the Committee of the Whole.** All other public bills, other than money bills, go on the *House* calendar. Most of these bills must go through the Rules Committee before being brought up for consideration on the floor. All private bills, such as measures involving individual claims against the government, go on the *Private* calendar. These measures are passed routinely unless objected to. Objection by two or more members recommits a measure to the committee reporting it. Minor, noncontroversial measures are placed on the *Consent* calendar, a special calendar for expediting the handling of rela-

---

*Privileged bills are measures which do not have to go through the House Rules Committee before being considered on the floor.

**The Committee of the Whole House on the State of the Union is a special procedure used in the House which requires only 100 (as opposed to 218 normally) for a quorum. Debate is limited to five minutes per member and no recorded votes are kept. This method is used to expedite handling of certain bills.

tively routine and noncontroversial items. The representative who places an item on the Consent calendar is expected to clear the posting of the item with its opponents. Measures on the Consent calendar pass automatically when called up unless some member objects. If a member objects, the item is returned to the calendar until the next call. On the next call, the item passes unless at least three members object; if three or more members object, the item is removed from the Consent calendar. Both parties have officially designated "objectors" who have the responsibility of watching the Private and Consent calendars to see that items don't slip through unnoticed. The final House calendar is the *Discharge* calendar on which are posted measures that have been removed from committee by a discharge petition.

The House also has an established schedule for transacting business on certain calendars and a number of so-called special days. Bills on the Private calendar are called up on the first and third Tuesdays of each month. Consent bills are considered on the first and third Mondays, and items on the Discharge calendar are considered on the second and fourth Mondays. The second and fourth Mondays of each month also are District of Columbia days when measures dealing with the District are brought up for consideration.

Another special procedure is Calendar Wednesday, when the roll of House committees is called alphabetically and any member of a committee may call up for consideration any measure, other than a privileged bill, which has been reported by the committee and posted on the House calendar. Measures called up under Calendar Wednesday may be debated a maximum of two hours with the time equally divided. Obviously, not many bills could be heard on any one day under these conditions. Calendar Wednesday was adopted in 1910 as a means of by-passing the autocratic leadership of the House. Actually Calendar Wednesday has proved to be a most ineffectual procedure for bringing measures to the floor and is used infrequently. Shortly after its adoption, George Norris (R. Nebr.) said it was "the most comical parliamentary joke that ever came down the legislative pike . . . a homeopathic dose of nothingness." Representative Richard Bolling (D. Mo.) has described Calendar Wednesday as "a form of masochism, akin to volunteering for the medieval rack." Normal procedure is for the House to dispense with Calendar Wednesday by unanimous consent and proceed to other matters.

Under normal procedures the calendars are considered at the designated times. The House and Union Calendars must be considered each day unless the House recesses, rather than adjourns, or unless the call of the calendars is dispensed with by formal action. In addition to the calendar system, measures may be called up by unanimous consent, or on the first and third Mondays, the Speaker may entertain motions to consider items under suspension of the rules. Suspension of the rules limits debate to forty minutes and measures to pass require a two-thirds vote. Neither unanimous consent nor suspension of the rules is used frequently in the House.

By contrast, most business in the Senate is conducted by unanimous consent. The Senate has only two calendars—a Calendar of General Bills and an Executive Calendar on which treaties and Presidential nominations requiring Senate approval are posted. The actual scheduling of measures for floor consideration is done by the majority floor leader in consultation with the majority policy committee. Because measures can be brought up only if no one objects, the majority leader usually works closely with the minority floor leader also to keep him abreast of what action is anticipated. Since a simple objection can prevent action, this procedure works to the advantage of those seeking to block action on a particular measure. As long as the majority leader is careful to keep others informed of his anticipated actions, however, he usually doesn't encounter too much difficulty getting measures to the floor.

The House Rules Committee

In the House, because of the unique role of the Rules Committee, problems may arise in getting a measure to the floor for consideration. As major public bills are reported by the committees they are posted on the appropriate House calendar. Items placed on the Union calendar are privileged and pose no problem. However, most measures on the House calendar can only be brought to the floor under a rule issued by the Rules Committee. Thus the Rules Committee takes on a vital function in determining what comes up for discussion and under what conditions.

First founded as a select committee in 1789, Rules was elevated to permanent status in 1880 and in 1883 was given its traffic-cop role. Once it became the place where bills were given precedence and the ground rules laid for their floor consideration, Rules became one of the most powerful committees in the Congress. From 1880 to 1910 the Rules Committee was the tool of the Speaker of the House. The revolt against the Speaker in 1910 resulted in his removal from Rules and established the committee as a separate center of power, not necessarily controlled by the leadership. As the committee asserted its independence it went beyond what some members saw as its proper role. Not only did the committee determine when bills should come up for consideration, but also the length of time they could be debated, the number and type of amendments that could be offered, and whether points of order could be raised. The committee's procedural judgments became substantive judgments, as it weighed the merits of bills and decided whether they should be considered at all. Defending the committee and its role against its critics, Howard Smith (D. Va.) said, "My people didn't send me to Congress to be a traffic cop." He believed firmly that his committee should carefully weigh the merits of a bill before sending it to the floor. As a consequence of its expanded role, the Rules Committee frequently presented the House with some tough choices, or on the other hand, no choice at all.

By 1937, as a result of appointments to the Rules Committee, a conservative coalition had gained control of the body and for thirty years the Democrats had almost continuous trouble getting any sort of liberal legislation through the committee. In this period the Rules Committee became a sort of "third branch," a policy committee unto itself, ruled, in the words of one observer, by a group of "political primitives." Asserting its independence from the leadership, Rules, from 1947 through 1959, denied eighty-three leadership requests for rules while reporting to the floor for consideration over forty bills which had been held up in other committees, a prerogative the committee has.

John O'Connor (D. N.Y.), one-time member of the committee said, ". . . the Rules Committee has a pigeonhole . . . and the cobwebs are so thick over that pigeonhole you can hardly see it is a pigeonhole." Speaker Rayburn had a good working relationship with Judge Smith and if he really wanted something, he could usually get it out. However, he sometimes became exasperated and attacked the committee, as he did in 1945 when he took to the floor and said:

> I take this time to warn the members of this House . . . the Committee on Rules was never set up to be a legislative committee. It is a committee on procedure to make it possible that the majority of the House of Representatives may have the opportunity to work its will. . . .[3]

However, the majority could not always act because Rules was not controlled by the majority. So in 1949, Rayburn had the Twenty-one-day Rule adopted. This procedure provided that the Speaker or a committee chairman could, after a measure had been held in Rules for twenty-one days, call up the measure for floor action. The rule was in effect for the sessions of 1949–50 and was revived in 1965–66. It was used with some success, but many members are reluctant to use such procedures which by-pass traditional channels. In 1971, when Speaker Carl Albert proposed that he be given the authority to remove a bill from Rules after thirty-one days, he was beaten 233 to 152.

Efforts to change the Rules Committee usually encounter unusual difficulty. However, in 1960 the committee went too far in its treatment of liberal measures, and the Democratic leadership decided it was time something had to be done. After considering various alternatives, Rayburn committed himself to a proposal to enlarge the Rules Committee from twelve to fifteen members. This would allow for the appointment of two moderate Democrats to the committee, thus providing a one-vote margin for the moderates. The proposal passed on an extremely close vote and the moderate members were appointed. The one-vote margin proved too tenuous, however, as one moderate was ill in the hospital for several months and another refused to support a liberal aid to education bill because it failed to provide aid for parochial schools.

Finally in the 89th Congress (1965–66) the powers of the committee were modified somewhat when its authority to grant or refuse a rule sending House-approved bills to conference was taken from the committee and given to a majority in the House. Also in 1966, when Smith departed Congress and William Colmer succeeded him as chairman, Colmer was forced to agree to regularly scheduled meetings for the committee. With Colmer's retirement at the end of the 92nd Congress, the appointment of several new liberal or moderate members, and the Democratic caucus' granting to the Speaker at the start of the 94th Congress the power to nominate all Democratic members of the Rules Committee, the Committee has become more of an arm of the House leadership. There is still, however, the possibility that the Committee may challenge the leadership on occasion. Certainly the powers are still there should the committee again decide to assert its independence.

In reality the Rules Committee behaves arbitrarily on only a relatively small number of measures. It denies rules on only about a dozen bills per Congress and most rules granted are open rules. From 1939 to 1960, 1215 rules were granted; 1128 were open rules, only eighty-seven were closed.* However, many of the bills blocked in Rules have been major pieces of legislation, and the fact is that eight members of the House sitting on the Rules Committee can, if they choose, block action by the entire body. Nonetheless, the House has been most reluctant to reform the committee and to reduce its powers substantially. Many feel the committee serves a useful purpose by slowing down and spacing out the legislative process. Furthermore, the committee provides a needed burial ground for measures that could not conveniently be allowed to come to the floor for a vote. Many members have on occasion been saved from having to cast a potentially embarrassing vote when the Rules Committee sat on a particular measure. And finally, the committee has from time to time been a convenient scapegoat for the House leadership. Since they don't control the committee, they cannot be held responsible for the failure of measures killed there. All of these factors, coupled with the strong sense of tradition in the Congress, make it difficult to get substantial changes even in a committee which frequently has been a thorn in the side of the majority.

The Filibuster

While the Senate does not have a Rules Committee that blocks action, it does have an equally effective means of frustrating majority rule. That means is uncontrolled debate, or the filibuster.

---

*Open rules are rules which impose no limits relative to floor debate and amendment while closed rules prescribe quite precisely the amount of time for debate and the types of amendments, if any, which are in order.

The Senate does not impose limits on debate as does the House, nor does it effectively enforce a rule of germaneness. The result is that a minority may on occasion thwart majority will on a measure by engaging in lengthy debate which prevents the measure from being brought to a vote.

In the Senate all other rules give way to that of unlimited debate because in 1806 the Senate struck from its rules the motion for the previous question. The filibuster was not actually used until 1841, but since has been used on numerous occasions, often quite successfully. It was not until 1917, after President Woodrow Wilson had publicly criticized a "little group of willful men reflecting no opinion but their own" in the Senate for blocking legislation to arm American merchant vessels, that the Senate finally adopted Rule 22 providing for cloture. Under Rule 22 a filibuster can be broken, but the procedure is difficult. First, sixteen senators must sign a petition to end the filibuster; the petition is then voted on after two days, and if three-fifths of the Senate membership vote for the motion, debate is terminated. That is, debate is ended after each Senator desiring to speak is allowed up to one hour of speaking time.

In the years since its adoption, Rule 22 has been the object of much discussion and reform effort. A 1949 effort to liberalize the rule backfired and the Senate actually ended up making cloture more difficult by requiring that the motion for cloture be approved by two-thirds of the Senate membership rather than two-thirds of those voting. The 1949 rules also provided that cloture could not be invoked on motions to change the rules. This made it even more difficult for the moderates to even get consideration for changing Rule 22. In 1959, when another effort was made by the antifilibuster elements to moderate Rule 22, then majority leader Lyndon Johnson worked out a compromise plan. Under the Johnson compromise, the vote necessary for invoking cloture was restored to two-thirds of those present and voting and cloture could be invoked on motions to change the rules. However, the Senate was designated as a "continuing body," which meant that its rules carried over from one session to the next. This made it more difficult for the antifilibuster forces to bring up Rule 22 for consideration. In 1969, Vice-President Hubert Humphrey as presiding officer in the Senate ruled that a simple majority vote was sufficient to invoke cloture, but Senator Spessard Holland (D. Fla.) appealed the decision and Humphrey was overruled 45–53. Recent reform efforts have focused primarily on trying to get the two-thirds vote requirement reduced to a simple majority, or at least to a three-fifths majority. Twenty-one additional cloture votes since 1917 would have succeeded had the requirement been only a three-fifths majority. The reform elements were finally successful in their efforts to reduce the required vote on cloture to three-fifths at the beginning of the 94th Congress in 1975, but only after a real struggle with those seeking to protect the filibuster as an instrument of the minority.

Under the previous system, cloture efforts were not often successful. Since the adoption of Rule 22 in 1917, more than ninety cloture votes have been taken and fewer than twenty have been successful. For the period 1927 to 1962, cloture was not invoked successfully a single time. Many significant pieces of legislation were delayed or killed by filibuster. Probably more significant than the formal procedures for invoking cloture is the way in which the Senate leadership chooses to handle filibusters. As majority leader, Lyndon Johnson was inclined to go with round-the-clock sessions in an effort to exhaust the filibusterers. His successor, Mike Mansfield, devised a "two-track" system which devoted one-half day to the filibustered measure and one-half day for other Senate business. This approach took a lot of pressure off those conducting a filibuster.

Mansfield's refusal to hold twenty-four-hour sessions has radically altered the filibuster. The long-winded harangues of the Huey Longs and Strom Thurmonds have been replaced by a "new style" filibuster. Under the "new style" the member does not have to talk and hold the floor for twenty hours at a time, but he and one or two colleagues simply are on hand to indicate that they will object if anyone tries to force a vote on the issue they oppose. In the hands of a determined minority the "new style" filibuster is no less effective than the old. In fact it may be even more effective because it imposes much less strain on those conducting it, and may be less frustrating to their colleagues, thus reducing their inclination to vote for cloture.

While the filibuster has been used by determined minorities more to delay and to hinder than to inform and educate (as frequently proclaimed) and to thwart the majority in Congress more often than the President, efforts at easing the rules for limiting debate in the Senate have met with determined opposition. Once considered as primarily a tool of the conservative, Southern Democrats in the Senate, the filibuster has its supporters among other elements as well. In recent years, many moderates have decided that the filibuster is a tool to which they, as well as the conservatives, can resort on occasion to protect their interests. Here again, efforts at reform also run into the strong element of precedent and tradition. Many senators will vote against cloture even though they may favor the measure being debated because they feel the filibuster protects minority rights and therefore should be retained. This sentiment makes it extremely difficult not only to invoke cloture but also to bring about any extensive changes in the rules which would make ending a filibuster a simple majority decision.

Voting

On those measures that somehow survive the labyrinthine legislative process, members must make some judgments and cast their votes. How do members arrive at the decision on how they should vote on a particular measure? What factors influence the legislator's ultimate decision most? How does he get the information he needs to make up his mind? All of this, of course, will vary from issue to issue and from legislator to legislator. But these are all-important factors bearing on the process of legislative decision-making.

A few decades ago the legislator's task of making up his mind how to vote was probably not quite as difficult as today, at least in some respects. In earlier sessions the member was faced with decisions on maybe three or four major issues, and on the whole his life was much less complicated than today. All of Congress' business could be wrapped up in a nine-month session. As the volume and complexity of the member's work have grown tremendously, tensions have also been increased by a multitude of outside pressures. More and more districts have become competitive, making tenure less certain; his constituents don't understand and appreciate his job; and his individual power and ability to influence the legislative process are limited.

Today so much time is demanded by attention to the personal demands of constituents that many members are becoming more and more convinced that they do not have sufficient time to study, understand and vote wisely on important measures. The sheer volume (5,000 to 20,000 bills introduced and 1,000 acted upon in each Congress) and the press of time make it almost impossible for even the most conscientious lawmaker to keep up and be informed on all the major issues. Most members have neither the time, the inclination, nor the means to cope with the huge volume of material continuously thrown at them. The member may be buried under volumes of information and reports, but much of it is irrelevant and what he needs is not readily retrievable. Hearings, investigations and reports provide the Congress with huge amounts of material, but frequently these are so poorly organized that even with the best of intentions, members have a difficult time making much use of the material. For example, public hearings on the 1964 tax reform bill alone filled 4,000 pages in seven volumes. In most cases neither the member nor his staff, which spends much of its time on constituent and district matters, has the time to wade through all the material and conduct its own research.

Consequently the legislator is under extreme pressures in his effort to perform his official tasks responsibly. The sheer volume of information and overwhelming complexity of issues on which he must make decisions force him to act time after time on the basis of incomplete information and to rely heavily on others for counsel and advice. This situation enhances the influence of special interest groups, executive agencies and other forces outside the Congress. More often than they would like to admit, members find themselves in a position of voting on an issue about which they know little or nothing. In these cases they must rely heavily on the committee reporting the bill, a trusted colleague, an agency spokesman, a lobbyist, or someone in a position to be informed on the measure. When he hurries to the floor to answer a roll-call vote, the member may not even know what is under discussion, much less be in a position to make an informed judgment. Under such circumstances, he may on occasion cast his vote on the basis of last-minute whispered instructions or a signal from a trusted colleague or, perhaps, as he hurries into the chamber a party aide or doorkeeper indicates, "committee voting aye."

As a consequence of such circumstances, many members feel increasingly that they are unable to vote intelligently and rationally

on many of the issues that come to the floor. Members are forced
to live with the feeling that they may be making wrong decisions
which might be avoided if they had more time, more selective information and greater capabilities for informing themselves and
weighing the alternatives more carefully. If they are to perform
more effectively, the members must develop better and more dependable sources of information and counsel, both inside and outside the Congress, and must continue to apply their powers of observation and judgment to the best of their ability.

The matter of deciding how to cast one's vote on a difficult
issue is no easy task. Frequently the legislator is subject to many
cross-pressures when it comes to casting his vote on a particular
issue. His party may want one thing; his constituents may want another; and powerful groups in his district may be lined up on both
sides. All of these are factors he must consider as he tries to decide
what is best for his state or district, for his own political future,
and for the nation as a whole.

On many issues brought to the floor, the voting lines are
pretty well set by the committee chairman, the leadership and the
senior members. The political party, a most significant force in the
organization and leadership of the Congress, is also a factor on
many votes. Interest groups are another potent influence in many
instances. Probably the factor taking precedence over all others,
however, is constituent interest and pressure. Congressmen vary,
of course, in their responses to their constituents. There are in
Congress those who lead their districts and there are those who
are led by them. Many members, because their constituents hold
their future in their hands, are hypersensitive to anticipated constituent reactions. These members tend to vote almost entirely on
the basis of the reaction they expect from the voters in their states
or districts. Other members are inclined to show more independence
and to ignore constituent pressures on occasion.

Even those who are prone to function as rubber stamps for
their constituents encounter problems in this role, however. How
do they effectively discover the will of a majority of their constituents? Many of the issues on which they must reach a decision don't
affect their constituents a whole lot one way or another. Simply
reading the mail and the local papers and talking to a few people

can give one a distorted view of what constitutes the general will. John Kennedy once observed:

> In Washington I frequently find myself believing that forty or fifty letters, six visits from professional politicians and lobbyists, and three editorials in Massachusetts newspapers constitute public opinion on a given issue. Yet in truth I rarely know how the great majority of the voters feel, or even how much they know of the issues that seem so burning in Washington.[4]

Some members send a questionnaire to their constituents asking their advice on various issues. Since everyone is prone to be flattered to be asked his opinion on great issues, this is as much, or more, a publicity gimmick as an effort to learn what one's constituents really think. A recipient of one congressman's questionnaire responded, "We sent you up there to answer these!"

In the final analysis most members approach the question issue by issue and vote by vote. When they can, they will support the leadership and the party; on other occasions they may vote for a particular interest in the state or district. Sometimes they may vote a certain way to help a good friend or to repay a debt owed from a previous vote. These actions generally occur on those issues where serious conflicts with constituent interests will not result. On those issues where constituent interests are strong and fairly clear, most members are inclined to lend a receptive ear. Even the party leaders accept this as a legitimate claim on the member's vote.

Another factor which may enter into the picture is the method of voting used. Voting on a legislative measure can become quite involved, making accurate analysis difficult. Oftentimes various amendments and procedural motions are offered in an effort to confuse the issue and possibly defeat a measure. Members must be extremely careful to keep track of the effect all these motions have on the measure under consideration. An "aye" vote on a particular amendment or on a procedural motion may in effect be a "no" vote on the measure being debated. Frequently the vote on a key amendment or a procedural motion is a better indicator of members' true positions than are their votes on final passage. Astute observers will catch such inconsistency in the voting of members, but most of the general public will be misled by looking only at the vote on final passage. The National Council of Senior Citizens rated members of Congress in 1973 on the basis of ten key votes on issues of concern to the elderly. Philip Guarino of the staff of the Republican National Committee was very critical of the ratings, saying that twenty-seven votes, rather than ten, should have been considered. He wanted to include seventeen votes on final passage of bills or approval of conference reports while the National Council of Senior Citizens maintained that these did not necessarily reflect the members' true positions on the issues.

The method by which votes are taken may be a factor in the final outcome. Congress uses four methods of voting. By far the most common method in both houses is *viva voce*—the voice vote, with the presiding officer announcing the verdict. When votes are so close as to be questionable, one of the other methods may be used. On a division of the house, all those favoring the bill stand and are counted, then those opposed stand and are counted. On a teller vote, the members form lines of those for and against a measure and march past the tellers (counters) who tally the votes on each side. Until recently none of these types resulted in the recording of individual votes; however, the Congressional Reorganization Act of 1970 requires the recording of teller votes. This may bring some changed results when this procedure, which is not used very frequently, is resorted to. Previously, only the fourth method, the roll-call vote, recorded the vote of each member individually. On occasion close observers were able to change the outcome on a particular measure by demanding a roll-call vote rather than allowing the verdict to be made by one of the other voting methods. It is well-known that some members vote differently on a measure when they know their vote is a matter of record, which constituents and potential opponents can check on later.

Interpersonal Relationships

Probably the two most important components of the legislator's environment are his external public and the colleagues with whom he must function day-to-day. Interpersonal relationships among the individual members become a prime factor for consideration in analyzing the legislative process. The actual mechanics of the process itself are not difficult; it is the vitally important human element that frequently makes the process so unpredictable and uncertain. While personalities and personal feelings are certainly not the only factor at work, accounts of the legislative process which overlook the fact that the Congress is a body of real people, displaying all sorts of human likes, dislikes, flaws and appetites, leaves out an important aspect. Who sits next to whom on the House floor or who is up roaming the chamber talking to which member may be most revealing about what is developing on a particular measure. Probably the most effective lobby in Washington is one congressman lobbying another.

The member of Congress interacts with many persons and groups and there are many arenas in which impresssions of colleagues are formed. Most of the scenes of interaction are informal: cloakrooms, dining rooms, gymnasia, swimming pool, barbershops, social functions, etc. Any type of activity—social, political, religious, recreational—that brings members into close association with one another may promote feelings of comradeship and friendship that may be carried over into the law-making process. There is a natural tendency for one to be influenced by what his friends think and to want to help them when he can. Thus personal friendships may become an important factor, especially on measures such as private and noncontroversial bills which may be personal pet projects. One member, explaining the passage of a particular bill, observed:

> _____'s reclamation project carried by just a few votes. One thing that broke the liberal and big city line against it was the fact that all the boys who played poker and gin rummy with him voted for it. And they took some of the rest of us with them. They said he wasn't going to be so difficult in the future.[5]

On the other hand, such personal feelings can have exactly the opposite effect, and a particular individual's name on a measure can automatically cost it several votes. While it is hard to determine why some members are successful and others are not, it remains a fact that some members simply have a knack for rubbing many colleagues the wrong way and this substantially limits their influence. A prime example of this type was Congresswoman Bella Abzug (D. N.Y.), who represented a district including Greenwich Village and the West Side of Manhattan. A loud, outspoken, opinionated, sometimes profane gadfly, and a Northern radical in a body controlled largely by conservatives and moderates, Bella displayed a rare penchant for treading on toes. Preparing to enter the House chamber to be sworn in, Ms. Abzug was told by House doorkeeper Fishbait Miller that she must, in keeping with House tradition, remove her hat. Her tart response was that Mr, Miller could "go --- himself." Bella told one reporter, ". . . I want to ruffle them. They want everybody to feel they're always playing the game. That's the way it is, elitism of this club. That's not my style."[6] Bella and her outspoken melodramatics didn't set well with many colleagues, and after only a few months in the House, she had succeeded in alienating not only her natural enemies but many of her potential allies as well. The Nader group's study of Congress estimated that Ms. Abzug's support could automatically cost a bill up to twenty to thirty votes. Another member who also frequently antagonized his fellow members with his independent and some-times irreverent attitude was Congressman Don Riegle now Demo-cratic Senator from Michigan. Riegle commented on his standing with colleagues with this observation on a conversation with Jim Harvey, who was a candidate for vice-chairman of the Republican Conference:

> I was a little sensitive about standing with him too long; I didn't want any antagonisms that other members feel toward me to rub off on him.[7]

As a general rule members of both houses still subscribe ra-ther strongly to Sam Rayburn's maxim that "The way to get along is to go along." Congress operates with a strong tradition of mutual respect and expressions of disrespect for one's fellow members are out of order. While members may occasionally chop one another up rather badly on the floor, then proceed to the cloakroom for a drink together, the onslaughts are not usually direct personal at-tacks, which are frowned upon. Most congressmen feel that they have much better ways to spend their time than in chastising or maligning their colleagues. Besides, airing dirty linen publicly is discouraged because it is bad for the legislative image. Members who make it a practice to attack and criticize their associates fre-quently get the freeze treatment. They find their colleagues most uncooperative on projects for their districts; their bills get bottled up in committee; they are passed over for patronage and other fa-vors, and they are often personally ignored. Colleagues are not inclined to forget such indiscretions quickly. Sam Steiger, a conservative Republican from Arizona, appearing on the Joe Pyne TV show, commented that some of his House colleagues were so stupid that he wouldn't hire them to push a wheelbarrow. It was nearly four years before Steiger finnally got back in the good graces of several of his more senior colleagues. Don Riegle noted that Julia Butler Hansen (D. Wash.), chairman of a House Interior Committee subcommittee, was still miffed at him five years later for challenging "her bill" on the House floor. The member who attacks fellow members or impugns the reputation of Congress probably is only hurting himself. Regardless of how he feels, he would probably be better off to respond as did John McCormack when asked about a particular member: "I have a minimum high regard for the gentleman," responded the Speaker.

Tendencies toward showmanship or excessive aggressiveness, especially on the part of newcomers, are most unwelcome in Congress. Those displaying the qualities of public show, open defiance of customs and traditions, unnecessary bravado, are looked at askance. Members who feel compelled to speak on every issue can quickly undermine their influence. The snow jobs are to be saved for the home folks, not imposed upon one's colleagues. A cardinal rule is, "Thou shalt not demagogue thy colleagues." One member, describing another said, "He talks all the time, asks stupid questions, and seldom contributes anything. He just rubs people the wrong way."[8] A member who openly criticizes associates or the Congress, who demonstrates impatience or dissatisfaction with the established customs and procedures, and who simply has a hard time accepting the Congress as it is, may find his aspirations for leadership and influence facing serious trouble. A good example of a member who frequently feels compelled to speak out on issues is Richard Bolling (D. Mo.). This characteristic sometimes gets Bolling into trouble and causes many of his colleagues to consider him as "abrasive" and not " a member of the team." Being a member of the team has different meanings for different members. Don Reigle says,

> In Congress, being a team player means acquiescing without a fight. It means staying silent while the wrong things are done. Being a team player in the House means throwing the game.[9]

But, back to Bolling. When the House was discussing questions of ethics and conduct, William Colmer designated Richard Bolling to head a subcommittee of the House Rules Committee to report out a resolution to create a House Committee on Standards of Official Conduct. The normal procedure in Congress is to name the chairman of the unit reporting such a resolution as chairman of the committee to be created. Because Bolling in his book *House Out of Order* had been rather critical of John McCormack's leadership as Speaker, McCormack made it clear that any resolution for creating a Committee on Standards of Official Conduct was not to bear Bolling's name when it came to the floor. Thus Bolling's opportunity to become chairman of the Committee on Standards of Official Conduct went out the window with his criticism of the leadership.

It is frequently those who work quietly but diligently behind the scenes who wield the most influence and command the respect of their colleagues. What really counts toward getting ahead in Congress is working in committees to establish oneself as an expert, being well-informed, dedicated, fair and honest. There is great respect among legislators for expertise and integrity. Members come to rely on certain individuals as being "experts" in a particular area and this gives them great influence. The legislators also admire the skilled technicians among their ranks. In his autobiography, Don Riegle observes how impressed he is with the legislative skills of Bill Natcher (D. Ky.), a member of whom most citizens have never heard. Yet, because of his skill and his membership on the House Appropriations Committee, Natcher is a powerful figure in Congress. Because much of the legislative business involves unofficial, unrecorded commitments worked out in conversations among members, integrity becomes an important element in members' estimations of one another. A member's spoken word becomes his bond, and those who cannot be trusted soon become known and their influence virtually destroyed.

The new member, arriving freshly on the Washington scene, is in for some cultural shocks. Fresh from an electoral victory, it may be rather difficult for him to accept the status bestowed upon freshmen members in the Congress. In a setting where prestige and power are everything, he is low man on the totem pole. He is a newcomer in a body where, to a considerable degree, personal relationships among members are conditioned by seniority. Though the elder statesmen of the Congress have mellowed somewhat from earlier days when they did not hesitate to let the new arrival know in no uncertain terms that it was they who ran the show, seniority still packs a lot of weight and many old-timers make it clear that the newcomers are to demonstrate the proper deference. As former congressman Everett Burkhalter noted, they are not "vicious or vindictive people in most cases." They are simply asserting their customary prerogatives.

As a consequence, the freshman legislator rarely feels completely at ease with his elders, and many newcomers chafe at having to take a backseat to colleagues who seem less than able and articulate policy-makers. Everett Burkhalter, who became frustrated and quit after one term, wrote:

> I could see I wasn't going to get anyplace. Nobody listens to what you have to say until you've been here ten or twelve years. These old men have got everything so tied down that you can't do anything.[10]

Another disgruntled young member stated:

> This damned place is a plenary of Rotarians. The house acts, thinks, and reacts in terms of some stodgy old Philadelphia club. It's over-polite and phony and nothing much gets done. Nobody listens to my speeches. New ideas scare these old-timers to death.[11]

William Saxbe stated publicly while still in the Senate that the job really wasn't what he had expected. He said it failed to give him the satisfaction he'd been seeking. As a consequence, some, like Burkhalter, quit. Most however, though frequently with considerable reluctance, gradually come to accept the system. John Breckinridge (D. Ky.) observed that Congress really wasn't much fun when he first arrived, but he added that he found himself "disliking it less all the time." This is the experience of most members who stick around for any length of time. They find initially that the Congress, in the words of former Representative Charles Weltner (D. Ga.) "allows for precious little ingenuity." But as they remain on the scene and gain in seniority and influence, their youthful visions of what was "best" become more and more tempered by practical considerations of what is possible. This is not to say that men of vision are not needed, but simply to point out that the key to the legislative process is compromise, and the longer a member is around the more he comes to appreciate that fact.

Summary

The rules, traditions, and customs of the Congress are at times terribly frustrating to those who want quick and vigorous responses to issues and are discouraging to many an able and ambitious newcomer. On occasion the rules and traditions work to the advantage of a determined minority over the majority, but they do, nonetheless, serve a useful purpose. The decorum in debate and the deference with which members treat one another, though it frequently appears a big "put-on" make it possible for today's opponents to be tomorrow's allies. The approach removes disagreement on issues from the personal level and permits members to disagree vigorously over issues and programs without injuring personal relationships. Members as different in their political philosophies as Pete McCloskey and John Rousselot can remain close friends. This is a key element in the successful functioning of a legislative body such as the United States Congress.

With all the recent advances in voter science and technologies, the growth of opinion polling, and the increasing reliance on the television and radio media for campaigning and communicating with the voters, many have tended to lose sight of, or at least downgrade, the traditional role of the Congress. Advances in polling and opinion sampling have prompted news commentator David Brinkley to suggest that we establish a system for direct referendum on some issues. This suggestion overlooks the fact that it is through daily meetings and working together in the halls of Congress that our elected representatives really demonstrate the true spirit of the republican form of government—something quite different from direct democracy. It is here that the elected representatives, through justifying the interests of particular constituents to their colleagues and the consideration of competing and alternative courses of action, provide some insurance against the excesses of democracy and provide a buffer against mob rule and decision-making based solely on popular passions of the moment. We must not ignore the reality that members of Congress serve a broader function than simply to register the sentiments of constituents on the issues.

Through the aggregation of interests, compromise and conflict resolution, and providing a degree of legitimacy for policies adopted, Congress performs a vital function in our system. Without this role of the Congress, decisions would likely be much more difficult to attain and once arrived at, might well polarize the public. It is to Congress' credit that most measures win general acceptance by the public.

On the other hand, the traditions and customs and the strong feeling of institutional loyalty among the members do make much-needed changes and reforms more difficult to achieve. Because members all share the threat of defeat at the polls and many of the same tensions and uncertainties of office, a sense of unity develops and they are inclined to sympathize with one another's problems. Strong bonds may develop between those who arrive on the scene at the same time regardless of party, and the members tend to develop a desk clerk's ability not to ask embarrassing questions about a colleague's behavior. This tendency frequently causes the Congress to try to ignore or sweep under the rug wrongdoing by its members and to be extremely reluctant about exercising its own disciplinary responsibilities. Cases must involve flagrant abuses which tend to tarnish the image of the whole body, such as the actions of Joe McCarthy, Thomas Dodd, or Adam Powell, before the Congress feels compelled to act. One member wrote:

> One of the problems here is that of cronyism. All kinds of strange alliances develop and people just don't like to hurt one another. Part of the problem is that the men who might well bring about reform in our system are so much a part of the cronyism that you really cannot count on them.[12]

Another aspect that irritates many about the present operation of the inner power structure in Congress is that the rewards tend to go to those who keep quiet, avoid risks, and don't rock the boat, while those who are conscientious, but outspoken, and who challenge the system, may find their roles and influence substantially reduced. Because the distribution of power within the Congress becomes such a highly personal matter, public awareness of who is responsible for what happens is confused, and therefore, the accountability of the most powerful members of the Congress is reduced. This also tends to make effective reform more impossible of achievement.

If a person is to really understand and appreciate the inner workings of the Congress, he must take into consideration the import of the personal element. It is this element, as it expresses itself in the leadership, the internal power distribution, the seniority system, the relationships among the members, the ability to speak effectively at just the right moment, and the ability to sense the mood of one's colleagues, that makes the legislative machine function in the uncertain way it does.

Notes

1. Augustus Foster as quoted by Larry King, "Inside Capitol Hill: How the House Really Works," p. 69.
2. Clapp, *The Congressman*, p. 26.
3. *Congressional Record*, 78th Congress, 2nd Session, p. 5471.
4. John Kennedy, *Profiles in Courage* (New York: Pocket Books, Inc., 1957), p. 15.
5. As quoted in Clapp, *The Congressman*, p. 16.
6. Bella Abzug as quoted by Mike Waldman, "Rebel in the House," *Newsday* (1971).
7. Don Riegle, *O Congress*, p. 122.
8. As quoted by Robert Healy, "Committees and the Politics of Assignments," in Groenings and Hawley, *To Be A Congressman*, p. 112.
9. Riegle, *O Congress*, p. 112.
10. Everett Burkhalter, "Why I'm Quitting Congress," *Family Weekly* (December 27, 1964).
11. As quoted by Larry King, "Inside Capitol Hill," p. 60.
12. As quoted by Charles Clapp, *The Congressman*, p. 19.

Chapter VI

Political Parties in Congress

WHILE THE CONSTITUTION provides adequately for the structure of the Congress, it does not, beyond providing for periodic elections, address itself to the matter of recruiting and staffing, and it does not even mention political parties, which have come to play a key role in the process of staffing. Though overlooked by the founding fathers, it has been the political parties that have organized the Congress for action and have provided the motive power to make the machinery go. In the first Congress like-minded members began to form groups within the body and it is here that formal parties had their beginnings. As these groups became more formalized, they played larger and larger roles in the legislative proceedings. By 1809, only a decade after the adoption of the Constitution, a member complained, "all great political questions are settled somewhere else than on this floor."

Party politics in the United States Congress is frequently a complex puzzle, and some members find the goings on not totally to their liking. Don Riegle says, "For the most part, party politics is awful. The constant jockeying for position, the jealousies and backbiting leave me very cold."[1] One factor contributing to the confusion is the decentralized nature of American parties, both inside and outside the Congress. Because elections to Congress are primarily state and local affairs, representatives and senators are largely independent of the national party organization and even of the party leadership within the legislature. Because of the individual autonomy of members resulting from the decentralized and loosely disciplined party structure, what frequently occurs in the legislature are scuffles and skirmishes among various raiding troops rather than a confrontation between the well-disciplined ranks of the two major parties. Nowhere is the decentralized and undisciplined nature of American parties better evidenced than in Congress, where the leadership is fragmented and individual members act with a high degree of independence without fear of party retaliation. Thus, while the parties play a key role in the staffing and organization of the Congress, party regularity has not been a keystone of congressional operations.

Party Organization in Congress

In undertaking their functions in Congress, the parties have established elaborate machinery to provide leadership and direction for their members, including party conferences or caucuses, floor leaders, whips, steering and policy committees. The party conference or caucus was developed early as an instrument of party leadership and organization, tracing its origin back to the Jeffersonian era. Rather informal at first, the caucus gradually developed into a more formal structure for dealing with party organization and legislative programs. During his tenure as Speaker, Henry Clay used the caucus as an effective tool of party leadership in the House. With Clay's departure the caucus faded somewhat and did not reappear as an effective party instrument until the overthrow of Speaker Joe Cannon in 1911. Following the revolt, during the administration of Woodrow Wilson, committee chairmen, for a period, were responsible to the caucus. In the Senate the caucus was an effective instrument prior to the adoption of the seventeenth amendment. Popular election of senators made the caucus less effective.

From the 1920's until recent Congresses, the caucus has had a rather spotty record as an instrument of party leadership. The Republicans as a general rule have used their caucus more than the Democrats. The Democratic leadership allowed the caucus to atrophy from disuse because they feared that discussing controversial issues in the caucus would irreparably strain the tenuous bonds between the divergent elements within the party. The leaders also were inclined to view the caucus as a forum in which they might be openly challenged.

In recent Congresses there have been some indications of a revival of the caucus as an instrument of party leadership. Both Sam Rayburn and Lyndon Johnson preferred to run their respective houses largely without caucus sessions; their successors have been much more inclined to use the caucus as a sounding board of party opinion. In the House, John McCormack agreed to monthly caucuses of the Democratic party, and caucus power and influence have increased. At the opening of the 94th Congress, the Democratic caucus in the House, showing more muscle than had been apparent for years, created some real ripples in Congress by challenging the seniority system and making several significant changes in the rules. Whether this new-found vigor in the caucus will continue after the large number of freshmen members have been around for a while is a major question at this point.

While the increased willingness of party leaders to use the caucus means more participation for other members in the decision-making, it still may fall short of the results desired by many reformers. In fact, the broader participation for rank-and-file members may actually blunt the drive for reform. The impact of caucus positions also may be reduced by the lack of participation. Since House Democrats have established monthly meetings, the sessions have not always been well attended. In fact, attendance became so poor, shortly after adopting the monthly meetings, that caucus chairman Olin Teague called a "caucus on the caucus" to discuss the proper role for the party sessions.

Along with the caucus or conference, the parties also use a number of committees to carry out their internal functions. Among the most important of these are the policy or steering committees, the campaign committees and the committees on committees of each party. The Congressional Reorganization Act of 1946 provided for the formal establishment of party policy committees in both houses of Congress. However, both Sam Rayburn and the House Rules Committee were opposed to the idea of another power center in the House, and consequently the provision was stricken in the House. The Senate still liked the idea and policy committees were provided for in a rider tacked on to an appropriation bill; both parties established such committees. In the House, the Republicans converted their steering committee to a policy committee. In 1972, House Democrats also created a steering and policy committee to function as an arm of the party leadership.

The policy committees were an outgrowth of a desire for more responsible party action in the Congress. In theory, the policy committees were to establish the party's position on issues and party members would then join ranks to support the party's established position. In actual practice, the committees have never come close to fulfilling the role envisioned by those seeking a more responsible party organization in Congress. The committees have served more as a forum where party members and party leaders can come together and discuss party positions and develop party strategy, than as instruments of party leadership and control. Party leaders lack the control and discipline over individual members to effectively enforce policy positions as established by their policy committees. The primary function of the Democratic Policy Committee in the Senate has been to advise the floor leader on the scheduling of measures for floor consideration and the House Committee is still youthful and finding a role for itself. Though the Republicans have generally had more internal unity than the Democrats, their policy committees have not been a binding influence on party members either.

The steering committees have to a degree been supplanted by the policy committees; in fact, in the House the Democrats have combined the two. The Democratic Steering Committee in the Senate has taken on another role, functioning as a committee on committees. Recently, at the start of the 94th Congress, reform elements in the House were successful in transferring the same function from Democrats on Ways and Means to the Democratic Steering and Policy Committee in the House. The Republicans have used separate committees on committees in both houses for making committee appointments.

When the radical Republicans in the House were having problems with President Andrew Johnson, they were fearful the Republican National Committee would be used against them, so they set up their own campaign committee to help them in their re-election efforts. The House Democrats decided this was a good idea and set up a similar unit. With the adoption of the seventeenth amendment, the senators decided campaign committees could help them with their popular election efforts, so both parties created Senatorial Campaign Committees. The primary function of these committees is to assist their respective party members in their bids for re-election or election to Congress. The committees raise funds, do research, provide speech material and speakers and other services aimed at helping party members in their campaign efforts. The Republican congressional campaign units have, primarily because of access to greater financial resources, been able to employ larger staffs, provide more services and distribute more funds to party candidates than the Democratic units. These units do sometimes pose somewhat of a problem for the national party organization as they compete with the national committees for available money, speakers and other campaign resources.

Party Leadership in Congress

Other important cogs in the party machinery in Congress are the various leadership positions. In the House, the key figure in the majority party is the Speaker, and his chief assistants are the majority floor leader and the majority whip with his regional assistants. In the Senate, the principal party leader is the majority floor leader, aided by the party whip. In both houses the minority party's caucus also selects floor leaders and whips.

In earlier Congresses the party leadership was much more effective than today. During Washington's administration, Alexander Hamilton functioned as a sort of shadow floor leader in the House and his Federalist party was in complete control. With the 1911 revolt against the Speaker in the House, and the rise of the seniority custom for selecting chairmen, the role of the leadership became more difficult. Separating the party and committee leadership hierarchies created competing centers of power which frequently made the party leaders' roles more difficult. One of the major criticisms of the seniority system in Congress is its undercutting of party leadership and party responsibility. The chairmen of the powerful committees owe their positions of power, not to the party but to their abilities to be re-elected and pile up tenure on their committees. The elected party leaders often find themselves confronted with an entrenched group of men who do not share the party's objectives. The powerful and largely autonomous chairmen frequently become rallying points for party colleagues and may challenge the power and influence of the party leadership.

Problems in congressional leadership may also arise as a result of an innate conflict growing out of the traditional methods for selecting legislative leaders and the nature of American political parties. In his book, *Deadlock of Democracy,* James McGregor Burns notes that what we have in tht United States is really not a two-party system but a four-party system, with each of the major parties having both a presidential and a congressional wing. This is probably an oversimplification, especially for the highly heterogeneous Democratic party, but it does point up a situation that frequently makes effective party leadership in the Congress difficult to achieve. The customs and traditions which play such a paramount role in leadership selection generally favor those members who belong to the more conservative congressional wing of the parties. Thus we have a built-in conflict between the leadership and the members belonging to the more liberal presidential wing of the party. In the 91st Congress, nine of eighteen Democrats in "leadership" positions were from states carried by George Wallace and five from states carried by Richard Nixon; only four came from states carried by Hubert Humphrey. Consequently it is often the Democratic leadership that drags its feet on liberal legislation and becomes a thorn in the side of the more moderate element of the party. Seniority has posed a particular stumbling block for the Democratic leadership since the start of the New Deal. For thirty-six of the last forty years, the Democrats have had a majority in Congress, but have had difficulty getting their programs enacted. While the Northern, usually more liberal, element in the party has been growing and has become a sizable majority in the party, conservative Southerners have, because of their seniority, held a disproportionately large number of leadership positions. In the 92nd Congress, for example, Southern Democrats accounted for only sixteen of the fifty-five Democratic members in the Senate, but they held eight of fourteen chairmanships of major standing committees.

Another factor which may complicate legislative leadership is the relationship between party leaders inside and outside the Congress. When the same party controls the White House and the Congress, the President is the spokesman for his party, but this does not necessarily mean he will dictate the party's legislative program, or even that the congressional leaders of his own party will always agree with him. The President may find that his legislative proposals depend on the votes of individual members over whom he has little control, and on occasion even the leaders of his own party may oppose his program in Congress. As a general rule, however, it does make the role of the congressional leaders easier if their party occupies the Presidency. Party leaders can suggest to the White House how to apply such things as social invitations, personal phone calls, minor patronage positions, private audiences, etc. in a manner to most benefit party programs. When the party does not control the White House, its policy initiatives are left largely to the congressional wing of the party, and there are frequently many competing spokesmen for the party.

Effective party leadership may on occasion be hampered by an innate antagonism between the executive and legislative branches—an antagonism that is built into the system. Because the internal customs and procedures of the Congress have a tendency to bring to positions of power members representing rather narrow local constituencies quite different from the national constituency of the President, inevitable frictions result. Many members of Congress may have a good feel for their local constituency but may be almost totally out of touch with national sentiment. A good example of this is the attitude of many Democratic leaders in Congress toward their party's nomination of Franklin Roosevelt in 1932. They felt their party had selected the weakest candidate seeking the nomination. They didn't think he had mass voter appeal. Politically he proved much more astute than his party's congressional leaders, and subsequently his great personal charm often caught his congressional opponents off-guard. Because much of the leadership on legislative matters is personal, rather than institutional, the personality of the man in the White House can be a big factor in party leadership in Congress. Whereas Roosevelt was able to overwhelm many opponents with an outpouring of personality, Richard Nixon turned off many congressional leaders and members of his own party with his method of operation. Though he was one of the most political men ever to occupy the Presidency, even more political than Lyndon Johnson, he displayed incomprehensible political ineptitude in his dealings with Congress. He tried to run an almost completely "in house" operation, and the high-handed and arrogant attitude of men like Bob Haldeman and John Ehrlichman upset many members of Congress. Key members of the President's own party, such as Hugh Scott, minority leader in the Senate, were ignored or seldom asked for advice. For a President to operate in such a manner is to ask for trouble with members of Congress who are inclined to be suspicious of the executive anyway and highly jealous of their prerogatives.

Because frictions do develop between the executive and legislative wings of the party, it may be tempting for a President to use his position and influence to try to secure the election of members to Congress who are more in line with his own thinking. If he is successful, he may improve the chances of getting his programs through the legislature; on the other hand, if unsuccessful, he may be faced with a Congress even more resentful of efforts by anyone outside the body to influence them. Presidents have engaged in this political game with varying degrees of success. In 1938, FDR designated for purging a dozen Democrats who had been dragging their feet on New Deal programs. He used the WPA and other federal programs in an effort to secure the election of Democrats more to his liking. His campaign was not successful. In the 1960's, the neutrality of the White House and the National Committee was breached several times in congressional races. In 1962, Kennedy's staff and the National Committee assisted Charles Weltner of Georgia in his race, and they helped James B. Frazier defeat incumbent Wilkes Thrasher in Tennessee's third district.

Such efforts on the part of the White House and the National Committee are a risky business and may do little more than increase the tensions between the President and the party leadership in Congress. Of Roosevelt's efforts, his national chairman, Jim Farley, observed that he knew from the beginning that the purge could lead to nothing but misfortune, because in pursuing his course of vengeance, the President was violating a cardinal political maxim which demanded that he keep out of local elections. Of the 1962 effort to get the "right" Democrats elected, House Democratic Campaign Committee Chairman Mike Kirwan (D. Ohio) said:

> They ought not to be doing it. I'm for uniting everybody, not destroying one another. The National Congressional Campaign Committee never interfered in the primaries and certainly won't as long as I'm chairman.[2]

Other members also expressed resentment at the involvement of the National Committee in congressional elections, expressing the feeling that such action could lead to the election of Republicans.

In Tennessee, where liberal Democrats helped Frazier unseat conservative incumbent Thrasher, Frazier lost in the general election to Republican Bill Brock. Commenting on this turn of events, a Kennedy aide said,

> What did we lose? We got Thrasher off the Ways and Means Committee, where he was voting against us on "medicare." All it cost us was one more Republican in the House, a man whose legislative influence in the next ten years will be zero.[3]

Returns from such efforts by the President and the National Committee may prove rather meager. In the first place, the President's troops are at a disadvantage in that "they don't know the territory." They are challenging the incumbent on his own turf where he is often well-entrenched. Joe Martin, speaking of efforts to unseat him, noted, "I knew my district too thoroughly to be pushed around by the WPA. I was well acquainted with the deep feelings of the people in those hard times."[4] Also, such efforts may affect few election outcomes, but may create substantial disharmony among party members in Congress. In FDR's 1938 effort, only John O'Connor among those marked for defeat actually lost. After the election, disharmony among the Democrats grew considerably. The effects of such efforts on the party and their potential for producing the desired results should be carefully weighed before being undertaken.

Because of the highly personal nature of much leadership, the tradition and informality of internal relationships, the absence of centralized party control and the lack of effective disciplinary measures, the leaders in the Congress actually may weaken party influence in the legislative process rather than enhance it. The leaders are chosen not necessarily on the basis of party regularity, but on the basis of various other considerations—considerations which in many instances, as in the case of seniority, tend to undermine rather than strengthen party control. Because of the quirks of the system, those who rise to positions of leadership in the Congress may or may not reflect the general tenor of their parties.

Party Unity and Discipline in Congress

As noted earlier, party is only one of several factors influencing how members vote. Party unity and party discipline in the United States Congress are very different from that found in many

European legislatures. Consequences of a member's refusal to vote with his party are not nearly so great as in some other countries. Defeat of the majority party does not bring a new election and a reorganization of the government. Many members of the U.S. Congress, though they run under the label of a major party, largely discount the role of the party in their elections. Unlike candidates for Parliament in Great Britain, who are heavily dependent on their parties, candidates for Congress usually raise their own funds and run their own campaigns. Many members represent "safe" districts in which politics is based largely on personalities, a friends-and-neighbors pattern.

In the American system of representation, party loyalty is often outweighed by members' stronger commitments to district or constituent interests, philosophies or prejudices. As a consequence, many members operate frequently outside the influence of their party and its leaders, their votes not being bound by the party caucus. The leadership accepts this as a fact of life in Congress, and when a member pleads he must vote his constituency on a particular issue, they understand. The leaders also feel that when members are permitted to "vote their districts" on those matters of vital interest to their constituents, they may be more receptive to suggestions that they owe the party a vote on some other, less sensitive, issue.

As a consequence of these attitudes, discipline in the parties in the Congress is extremely lax. Though many feel a member has some obligation to support the party under whose label he runs, any efforts to impose effective sanctions or enforce strict party discipline are vigorously opposed. Nowhere in the world are a party's legislators as undisciplined by their leadership as in the U.S. Congress. Members win election to Congress running under a party label, but, once elected, vote against the party whenever they feel like it.

On rare occasions the leadership decides that members should be chastised for actions not in the best interest of the party. The Democrats, in particular, have had a problem with Southern members who refuse to support the candidates and platform of the national party. In 1964, two Democratic House members, Albert Watson of South Carolina and John Bell Williams of Mississippi, supported the candidacy of Barry Goldwater. This was too much for many of their liberal colleagues in the party, and a move was launched to discipline them when the new Congress was convened. It was proposed to strip them of their seniority and place them at the bottom of their committees.

The move against Watson and Williams touched off a great deal of rhetoric and theorizing about the role of the caucus and responsible party government. In a Joint Statement on Democratic Party Unity—1964 Election, Representative John Blatnik, speaking on behalf of those urging disciplinary action, stated that Democratic programs "must not be thwarted by a repudiated minority holding legislative positions of power which permit them to frustrate the mandate for programs." He went on to add that:

> Members who bolted the party should not be welcomed back with the same privileges of those who supported the National party candidates and platforms.[5]

He concluded:

> Party responsibility of elected officials cannot be built on the shifting sands of political expediency by those who carry the party label lightly and without regard to principles and policies on which the party is based.[6]

In the Democratic caucus of January 2, 1965, those favoring the disciplining of Watson and Williams charged:

> They have arrogantly challenged the historic right of responsible party government in the House of Representatives by demanding that they be given the same privileges, committee assignments, seniority, and other prerogatives reserved for loyal members of the Democratic Party.

They urged that caucus action against the two

> . . . will also serve notice that membership in the Democratic Party Caucus of the House is a privilege reserved for loyal Democrats, not an automatic right to be conferred without corresponding responsibilities. It also acknowledges the sound and historic role of the caucus in the achievement of party responsibility, the foundation on which responsible government is built.[7]

In this instance, Watson and Williams were stripped of their seniority. Subsequently, Watson resigned, returned to his home state, ran as a Republican and was re-elected to his seat. Williams accepted his demotion and shortly returned home to Mississippi where he was easily elected governor.

Following the punishment of Watson and Williams the Democratic leadership backed away from taking similarly tough stands in subsequent cases. A 1968 effort to chastise John Rarick (D. La.) for supporting George Wallace for President by taking his seniority failed in caucus, 87 to 85. Two years later, Harry Byrd, Jr., decided to run for the Senate in Virginia as an independent, rather than as a Democrat; he won re-election and was welcomed back into the Democratic caucus, no questions asked. In 1970 Representative John Conyers (D. Mich.) protested that five Mississippi representatives had run as candidates of a state party that had been refused recognition at the 1968 Democratic National Convention. He moved that the five be stripped of seniority and placed at the bottom of their committees; his motion was rejected in the caucus by a 111 to 55 vote.

The cases of Watson and Williams illustrate what the party leaders consider to be the futility of disciplinary actions against such members. Watson was re-elected as a Republican and Williams' career was not severely hampered. Congressmen such as Williams, Watson or Rarick are not greatly disturbed by the prospects of party sanctions against them. Such action on the part of the national party may reflect to the advantage of the member with his local constituency.

While the Republicans operate with somewhat more unity and discipline, the consequences of the party leadership's failure to punish party disloyalty is apparent in congressional voting records. In 1968, the average Democrat voted with the majority of his party 57 percent of the time, Republicans, 63 percent. In the House, Southern Democrats voted with a majority of their party only 39 percent of the time. A number of conservative Southern Democrats rather consistently vote more with the Republican party than with their own.

As has been demonstrated Democrats, in particular, have had an extremely difficult time maintaining any degree of party unity in their legislative party. A major element in the Democratic disunity is that the legislative party includes at least three rather distinct groups of Democrats: Southern conservatives, members elected by big-city party machines, and a growing number of ideal-

istic young liberals. The Southern conservative wing of the party
has frequently been an embarrassment to Democratic Presidents
and the party leadership in Congress. Some members have described them as "Republicans with Southern accents." They run
under the Democratic label, but are much closer to the Republicans on most social and economic issues. The pattern has been for
these Southern Democrats to vote for Democratic leaders, receive
their committee assignments as Democrats, then proceed to vote
against their party on many major issues.

The Southern wing of the party has for years maintained a
distinct identity within the party, developing its own whip system
for getting out the votes on certain issues. This wing was frequently
joined with Republicans in Congress to form the so-called Conservative Coalition and block numerous pieces of liberal social and
economic legislation. Because of the alliance, Democratic majorities in the Congress have often been more apparent than real. Joe
Martin recounts how, as Republican minority leader in the 1950's,
he would go to Howard Smith (D. Va.) or Eugene Cox (D. Ga.)
and say, "Why don't you see if you can't get me a few Democratic
votes on this issue?"[8] In many instances they were willing to
cooperate.

Frequently the Southern Democrats have been more than willing to join with Republicans in voting down programs of their
party. In the late stages of the 85th Congress, for example, Southern Democrats refused to support their party on more than eighty
crucial votes in the House. While these members run as Democrats
in their home states because the Republican party is decidedly a
minority party, they feel no strong obligation to support the candidates and programs of the national Democratic party. John Bell
Williams (D. Miss.), against whom the party finally took disciplinary action in 1965, said in his first speech in the House:

> I did not come here as a Democrat necessarily, because we
> have only an insignificant number of Republicans in my dis-
> trict, so I do not have to vote along partisan lines. . . .[9]

He went on to add that his political party loyalty was to the
Mississippi Democrats who had nominated and elected him to
Congress. Years later, in opposing John Conyers' motion to strip
the Mississippi delegation of their seniority because they were can-

didates of a party not recognized by the Democratic National Convention, Representative Jamie L. Whitten (D. Miss.) argued that the delegation had been duly elected by the voters of Mississippi and therefore the party caucus had no authority to intervene in the people's decision. This concept of the relationship between state and national party organizations enables the Southerners to vote against their national party leadership with impunity. As an eight-term congressman, John Bell Williams never once supported a national Democratic candidate for President, and in the 87th and 88th Congresses he voted with his party less than twenty percent of the time.

The present system of party leadership and discipline through its failure to condemn such party disloyalty makes it extremely difficult for the party leadership to put through any organized program of legislation. Because members are allowed to wear the party label so lightly and to cast their votes without regard to the principles and policies on which their parties are based, the leadership is frequently defeated by a coalition of party dissidents. Still, as indicated earlier, the leadership is extremely reluctant to impose sanctions and discipline those who take their loyalty to the national party and its programs lightly. This has long been a pattern in the Democratic party. Many of the Southerners who stalked out of the 1948 Democratic Convention in Chicago and supported Strom Thurmond rather than Harry Truman for President appeared to take their seats at the start of the 81st Congress and were allowed to participate without protest. Current trends seem to indicate that time may eventually do what the party leadership has not been inclined to do, i.e., bring more unity to the parties in Congress. Both Strom Thurmond and Albert Watson have left the Democratic party and joined the Republicans, and there has been a gradual trend toward the election of more Republicans in the place of conservative Democrats. In 1951 among the Southern members in the 82nd Congress, there were 116 Democrats and six Republicans in the House and twenty-six Democrats and no Republicans in the Senate. By 1973, the Southern delegation in Congress was made up of eighty-four Democrats and thirty-seven Republicans in the House, sixteen Democrats and ten Republicans in the Senate. Furthermore, more of the Southern Democrats being elected were more moderate than their predecessors. At the same time, the number of Democrats controlled by the big-city machines who frequently had ties with the Southern wing of the party is also declining. The upshot of all this is that gradually the moderate wing of the Democratic party is growing, a development that should bring more unity in the party's legislative wing and make it more receptive to national leadership.

Parties and Policies

American political parties, and more particularly the party leadership in the legislatures, do not to any great extent serve as a source of creativity and initiative for public policies. Their primary objective is not the formulation of policies, but rather the devising of the strategy necessary for getting the legislation they desire enacted and for preventing the enactment of that which they oppose. The principal role of the party in the legislative process then has been in the organization and selection of leaders in the Congress. Most policy initiatives today come from outside the Congress, from the executive, special interest and citizens groups. Within the Congress, most legislative initiatives come from individual members or groups of members rather than from the parties. The policy committees, as noted earlier, are not effective instruments for molding party positions on policy questions and bringing party members in line to vote the party position. The parties generally are much more effective on organizational and procedural issues than on policy issues. Because of the absence of any marked degree of party responsibility or effective disciplinary action, the legislative parties are not highly effective instruments for the development and enactment of specific policies. The major contribution of the parties to legislative policy-making is through their organization of the Congress and their contributions as interest aggregators and instruments of compromise. While they do not formulate and enact many policies themselves, the parties do facilitate legislative action.

Summary

There are various reasons why parties do not provide more vigorous leadership in our legislatures—our federal system, the structural arrangement of governmental machinery, the fragmentation and decentralization of power within the legislatures and the absence of any effective disciplinary tools at the disposal of the party leaders, plus their reluctance to use those tools which are available. Probably the most important factor, however, is the strong independence of the individual legislator born of the fact that he is not dependent upon the party for election. Election to Congress or the state legislature is primarily a state and local matter, thus making each candidate's election or re-election dependent almost entirely upon his ability to satisfy the unique demands of his constituents. Many legislators share the sentiments expressed by Senator John Sherman Cooper when he stated, "Today it is my duty and my desire to support the people of Kentucky, the people whom I represent." Since the legislator feels his first obligation is to his individual constituency, this tends to reduce the party's influence and control over him. If party demands and constituent demands are compatible, then all is well; but if it is a choice of satisfying the party or his constituency, the legislator usually feels it is safer to disappoint the party. This is not to say that the legislator's identification with the party is without any significance whatsoever. In fact, the party is very important to him, but not necessarily crucial. Individual congressmen, such as Strom Thurmond, Albert Watson and Wayne Morse, could win elections running under the label of either party. In the U.S. Congress, a member can be either a Democrat or a Republican simply by calling himself one or the other. The party really doesn't determine who belongs; this makes control and discipline most difficult. In a report on American political parties in 1952, the American Political Science Association called for more responsible parties and implied that the elected representative should follow his party on key issues. However, it would appear that those demanding more "responsibile party government" in American legislatures, after the British model, may be destined to disappointment. Most of their suggestions for legislative change fail to fit the character of the American party and legislative systems, especially the latter with its direct responsibility of representatives to their constituencies and the specialized and powerful committees presided over by the senior citizens of the legislative ranks. Party leadership and voting unity cannot be imposed through organizational devices, but must be based upon some basic changes in the underlying system.

Notes

1. Riegle, *O Congress*, p. 128.
2. Mike Kirwan as quoted in "Democrats Debate 1964 'Purge' of Dissidents," *Congressional Quarterly* (April 26, 1963).
3. Kennedy aide as quoted in *Congressional Quarterly* (April 26, 1963).
4. Joe Martin, *My First Fifty Years in Politics*, p. 80.
5. Statement to the Democratic Caucus, January 2, 1965, on the purge of John Bell Williams and Albert Watson.
6. *Ibid.*
7. *Ibid.*
8. Joe Martin, *My First Fifty Years in Politics,* p. 80.
9. John Bell Williams, *Congressional Record,* 80th Congress, 1st Session.

Chapter VII

Organized Interests and Congress

IN OUR HIGHLY pluralistic society, political parties and elections are not the only legitimate vehicles for political action. Though interest groups, like political parties, are not mentioned in the Constitution, their activity is recognized as a legitimate part of democratic government through the guarantee of the "right to petition." Since a pluralistic democratic system such as ours does not have autocratic decision-makers, decision-making must inevitably become a group process. And though interest groups and their role are not specifically mentioned in our Constitution, they have become such an integral part of our policy-making process that it is hard to imagine Congress functioning without them.

But, while they have become an essential element in the legislative process, interest groups, because their ends are always "special," are sometimes assumed to be contrary to the general public interest and thus antidemocratic. In this vein, Speaker Thomas Reed once said that veterans' groups got together and resolved three things: "We saved the country; the country wouldn't have been saved if it hadn't been for us; we want it." Consequently, lobbying has a rather bad connotation for many Americans, who see the groups as being out to subvert the public interest to the benefit of their own narrow interests. For many, the term "lobbying " and "lobbyist" call up sinister meanings with visions of shady characters with bags of money skulking through the corridors, buttonholing senators and representatives and hosting parties where the liquor flows freely and glamorous women fascinate legislators into doing their will. Because the news media traditionally have focused on the unsavory aspects, the term "lobbying" calls up visions of Dita Beards, ITT, laundered money, milk association funds and big-oil money. Says one professional, "When I say I'm a lobbyist, it's about the same as saying I'm a pimp." Consequently most lobbyists refer to themselves as "legislative counsels," "legislative liaison men," etc. The term "lobbying" is an imprecise one, and as Frank Daniel, chief lobbyist for the National Rifle Association, points out, a lot depends on one's definition of the term. In any legislative battle, he says, the losing side calls the other side a lobby.

In spite of some misgivings about lobbying and lobbyists and their roles, the struggle among competing groups generally has been accepted as an essential element in the democratic process. Today the lobby is probably the most effective means for approaching the Congress, and in many instances group pressure politics are even more important in the legislative process than party politics. In our nation of "joiners" nearly every citizen belongs to at least one group, and groups of all types and sizes have come to be active participants in the legislative process. Ranging from trade associations to ad hoc citizens groups, interest group spokesmen constantly press their causes before the Congress. Each year about 500–600 lobbyists register with the clerk of the House and the secretary of the Senate, and because many groups do not consider their principal function as lobbying, the registered lobbyists represent only the tip of the iceberg. In the relatively new interest area of environment-conservation alone, the following groups have been active: the Izaak Walton League, the Sierra Club, the National Audubon Society, the National Wildlife Federation, the Citizens Committee on Natural Resources, the League of Conservation Voters, Environmental Action, Friends of the Earth, Zero Population Growth and the Wilderness Society. Consideration of a particular measure can bring lobbyists flocking to Capitol Hill to make their cases. In 1962 Senator William Fulbright observed that "lobbyists on Capitol Hill working on the sugar bill are as thick as flies." Around Washington normally there are about eight to ten lobbyists for each member of Congress. At certain times the odds are even higher.

Roles of Interest Groups

Today, the relationships between the legislators and the lobbyists have become so interwoven, it is hard to understand the workings of one without the other. And, while many people still harbor strong suspicions of the workings of "special interests" in democratic government, most feel as a state legislator friend said, "They are a necessary evil." In the final analysis, interest groups perform a number of roles that contribute substantially to the more effective functioning of our democratic processes.

With the volume of legislative proposals considered and the limited staffs available, legislators are hard pressed to be knowledgeable and informed about the measures on which they must vote. Interest groups perform a most valuable function by helping to educate and inform both legislators and the public. Many congressmen say their effectiveness would be reduced without the information and help provided by the lobbyists. Many groups work hard to build reputations as reliable sources of information and provide members of Congress with expert information and insights on complex legislative issues. Such groups also help members determine constituent attitudes on particular measures, and most members feel the lobbyists perform a real service in helping them to anticipate the various consequences of a particular proposal. One member says:

> Any member of Congress who doesn't have his door open to the lobbyist just isn't a good member. I learn a hell of a lot from them.[1]

As a general rule, the overworked office and committee staffs welcome the free services of the lobby groups, and these groups in turn are eager to be of service. After a while members and their staffs learn who is reliable and who is not, and they come to depend heavily on those who have knowledge and skills in particular areas. In this way a member may have access to specialists he cannot afford on his personal staff. Information on issues on which the member and his staff are not well informed is particularly welcome. These groups, many with narrow, specialized interests, are frequently in a position to be much better informed in a particular legislative area than are the members themselves. They often have resources and information in terms of statistics, field interviews and the impact of existing legislation, not readily available to members. They may be in a superior position to assess whether a particular piece of legislation is having the desired impact and merits continuation or whether Congress is just spinning its wheels. Access to such information is invaluable in effective policy-making.

In availing themselves of the services and information of such groups, however, the legislators must always keep in mind that they are the spokesmen for specialized interests and they do have their own axes to grind. In the words of Wright Patman (D. Texas), "Too frequently we take the presentation of lobbyists as facts when such information is really a lopsided plea from selfish interests."[2] Keeping this fact in mind, however, the member can gain valuable information from these groups, and by balancing the views expressed by various competing groups, he can arrive at an informed decision on what is in the public interest. An important element in the democratic policy-making process is the widest possible dissemination of information and viewpoints from diverse and antagonistic sources within the society. Thus, it can be most informative and helpful to members of Congress and their committees to hear the differing views of the various advocates testifying on the opposite sides of a legislative issue. By weighing these views along with those expressed through elections, letters, telegrams and other channels, the elected representative can arrive at a more informed judgment than would otherwise be the case.

As noted previously, the primary purpose of the interest group's existence is the promotion of a particular interest or position. In carrying forward this objective, however, groups may perform a variety of other functions which are beneficial from the standpoint of more representative governmental policy. The framers of the American Constitution chose a system of territorial representation rather than a functional system. Representatives elected from single-member, geographical districts do not represent all the myriad interests composing our extremely heterogeneous society. Therefore interest groups perform a significant representative function by supplementing our rather imperfect system of territorial representation. This, in turn, serves a system maintenance function by providing an escape valve through which interests may release their tensions and frustrations. Many interests are not directly represented through the elected members of Congress, but they have an opportunity to express themselves and make their weight felt in the legislative process through groups to which they belong. This prevents feelings of alienation and desperation which might otherwise develop and undermine the stability of the system itself. In this respect the interest groups perform a stabilizing function in our democratic system.

Along somewhat the same lines, interest groups are a stabilizing factor in the system and help to make the legislator's job easier through their interest aggregation function. In our system, with all its various competing interests, effective government is possible only through compromise. Interest groups often facilitate compromise by forming coalitions and alliances and by carrying on extensive campaigns to create widespread support for their positions. Frequently, by the time a highly volatile issue reaches the voting stage in Congress, most of the really controversial issues already have been fully debated and mutually satisfactory arrangements made among the various competing interests. Interest groups often play a key role in this process.

Yet another way in which interest groups make a contribution to the legislative process is in their initiation of legislative proposals. The pressures behind most legislation builds for years and years, but in many cases interest groups play a key role in keeping such pressures alive and growing. Each group has its particular interests and problems which it feels merit governmental action, inaction or retreat from action. In this respect, lobbyists get involved in the legislative process in numerous ways. Many measures have their origin with interest groups, but since they cannot introduce measures directly, one of their first tasks is to find a congressman willing to drop the bill into the hopper. For most groups this is a relatively simple matter. Once the measure is in the mill, they must turn their efforts to getting enough votes to get the bill out of committee, stirring up public interest in the measure, lining up votes for floor action, and making sure that the promised votes are actually cast. A key point of involvement is in the drafting of the bill and helping to fix the language to achieve the desired effect. It is standard procedure for committee staffs to consult lobbyists on both sides of an issue when drawing up a bill. For example, when the Auto Safety bill was being drawn up in the Senate committee,

Ralph Nader was in one anteroom and Lloyd Cutler, lobbyist for the auto industry, was in another. Senate aides hurried back and forth between the two as the final version was hammered out. As long as the staffs and the committee members do not abdicate their responsibilities to the lobbyists, this arrangement probably results in sound legislative proposals, although the groups do have ways of getting preferential provisions written into bills. One senator estimates that the initial drafts of about half the laws passed have their origin in lobby offices. This is probably an exaggeration, but groups have considerable input into the legislative process.

Closely related to the initiating function is another function which we might call the "watchdog role." Since these groups tend to concentrate on those measures that affect them directly, they usually go over such measures with a fine-tooth comb and anticipate all implications for their activities. Frequently they will discover mistakes or flaws in the wording of a bill, or will point up implications not anticipated by the framers. This enables the legislature to correct these defects and improves the final legislative product. Thus, while the interest groups and their hired lobbyists are concerned primarily with promoting their own particular legislative interests, their actions have a number of spin-off effects which are a positive contribution to the legislative process. Most members of Congress are aware of this and frequently make use of the services available from these groups. While there are inherent dangers to such an arrangement, the end result probably is sounder and more representative legislation.

Lobbying Techniques

In striving to achieve their legislative objectives, interest groups employ a variety of techniques with varying degrees of success. One of the most common and widely used lobbying techniques is the direct contact. Group representatives, either professional lobbyists or interested citizens, visit individual members and present their cases directly. For the direct contact to be effective, the lobbyists must be well-informed and present their cases succinctly and convincingly. The good lobbyist is one who knows his legislative objectives, has his facts clearly and firmly in hand, can present his case with conviction, and proceeds with directness. Because they operate on such tight schedules, congressmen are more appreciative than is generally known of those who respect their crowded schedules. Therefore, the lobbyist will generally have only a few minutes in which to make his case and will make a more favorable impression if his presentation is thorough and to the point, but brief.

Groups must be very careful in their selecton of lobbyists to handle their direct contacts with members of Congress. An individual who gives members the impression of talking down to them, who is overly pushy, or who displays other traits that rub them the wrong way can do more harm than good. Many groups try to hire former legislators or others with considerable governmental experience who have large numbers of friends in Congress and ready access to the legislative process. A 1966 survey by *Congressional Quarterly* turned up twenty-five ex-congressmen or other former federal employees as registered lobbyists. Among them were Earle Clements, former senator from Kentucky, as lobbyist for the American Tobacco Institute; George M. Grant, one-time chairman of the Forests subcommittee of the House Agriculture Committee, as lobbyist for the National Forest Products Association; and John Harvey, former deputy commissioner of the FDA, lobbying for the Drug and Allied Products Guild, Inc. One major advantage to having a former member as a lobbyist is the built-in access he has to the process. As former Illinois Senator Scott Lucas observed of his own lobbying efforts:

> The Senate is a club and you're a member until you die—
> even if you get defeated for re-election. I can see anybody in
> the Senate almost any time.[3]

Some lobbyists, such as Clarence M. Mitchell, Jr., of the NAACP, know most members personally and develop such relationships that they have ready access to most offices. Mitchell makes appointments only with those members he doesn't know well. Lobbyists able to build this type of working relationships can be most effective in making direct contacts with members.

Another technique used by many groups is that of providing a variety of services and assistance to members of the Congress. Much of this is very legitimate assistance and contributes to the effectiveness of the legislators, while other aspects are quite questionable and may verge on bribery. It was previously noted that many groups provide the Congress with invaluable information, statistics, expertise and similar assistance in drafting and passing sound legislation. Many members frequently contact lobbyists for such services as speech-writing, preparation of reports, answering certain correspondence, writing bills, entertaining out-of-town visitors, and a variety of other tasks. By aiding congressmen in this way, the lobbyists build up political credits that can be cashed in later.

Lobbying today also involves groups extending to members of Congress various amenities and courtesies which many view as a sort of "social seduction." In this respect, groups may provide free a variety of products and services to members, or provide them at less than cost. A member may be able to lease a new car from a dealer in his district each year for one or two hundred dollars; a pharmaceutical firm may keep a drawer in the congressman's file cabinet stocked regularly with their products; businesses in his state or district may provide free plane rides back home; or he may be invited to speak before certain groups for a lucrative honorarium. The ultimate objective, of course, is to insure easier access to the members to present the group's special cases.

For three years now the Pharmaceutical Manufacturer's Association has sponsored the nightly "Meet the Member" radio show. The show presents a biographical sketch of a member of Congress and PMA provides the member 2,000 free copies of the program transcript for his own distribution. PMA says this free publicity is just its effort to try "to even the odds a little." In another type of service, the Maritime Union loaned $25,000 to Senator Mike Gravel (D. Alaska), who needed ready cash for his re-election campaign. Gravel was a strong supporter of a measure requiring the use of American vessels to transport at least 30 percent of all imported oil, a measure the union also favored. Acceptance of these types of services from groups having special interests raises some serious questions as to the member's independence and objectivity in arriving at decisions affecting these donors.

Probably the most effective means interest groups have of influencing the legislature is through their political activities. With the exception of nominating candidates for public office, interest groups engage in about the same political activities as political parties. This involvement places them in a position to exert considerable influence on the elective members of Congress. Many groups have extensive resources, in terms of both manpower and finances, that they can bring to bear on congressional elections. Few candidates relish the prospect of being opposed for election or re-election by well-financed and well-organized interest groups.

Since votes at election time are really the lobbyists' best currency in dealing with members of Congress, many groups are quite active politically. One of the most active and successful groups politically is COPE (Committee on Political Education), the political arm of the powerful AFL-CIO. COPE can be a powerful ally to those it supports and a potent threat to those it singles out for opposition. COPE has both the money and the manpower to engage in extensive political activity and this is evidenced by the range of its involvement. *How to Win: A Handbook for Political Education* is a manual published by COPE telling its local union affiliates how to recruit workers, raise funds, generate publicity, get out the voters, and engage effectively in other political efforts. Using sophisticated methods, including computerized voter identification lists and professional pollsters, COPE has put together a vast store of "political intelligence" for use in its campaign activities. COPE maintains individual files on each member of Congress and publishes a score sheet near the end of each Congress ranking each representative and senator on votes of direct interest to organized labor. COPE has voting records on members going back to the turn of the century and maintains voluminous files on those candidates it will likely oppose. Information is provided from these files to the opponents of those the unions seek to defeat. In addition, COPE collects data on registration laws and voting patterns, and union members are inundated with its leaflets, pamphlets, posters and handbills on political issues. Candidates endorsed by COPE also benefit from its political war chest. Normally each senatorial candidate endorsed will receive about $10,000 and each House candidate about $2,500. But while COPE makes substantial campaign contributions, the voter registration and voter turn-out drives are probably the key elements of its political activity. Though efforts don't always meet with success, COPE maintains a good political batting average. In a 1968 congressional contest between Frank Kemp (R. Colo.) and Byron G. Rogers (D. Colo.), Kemp said COPE's support of his opponent was a key factor in Roger's victory. He said the key element was COPE's get-out-the-vote effort. In the 1968 elections, 185 representatives and fifteen senators endorsed by COPE were elected. In 1970, however, Senators Ralph Yarborough (D. Tex.) and Albert Gore (D. Tenn.), both of whom COPE supported, were defeated. COPE *was* able to help Senator Harrison A. Williams, Jr. (D. N.J.), withstand a strong challenge in his state.

The success of labor's political activities and its influence are attested to by the number of groups who are now emulating their example. The American Medical Association has now established a political arm (AMPAC); business and industry now have BIPAC, formed primarily to counter COPE; and the bankers have Bank Pac. More and more interest groups, again following labor's lead, have started evaluating the performance of members of Congress. The significance and impact of such ratings depend on a number of factors—the size and influence of the group, the nature of the issues involved, and the nature of the member's state and district. A poor rating from the American Farm Bureau Federation or the Farmers' Union is not of great concern to the representative of a Michigan district heavily populated by General Motors employees. On the other hand, being named to Environmental Action's "Dirty Dozen" in an environmentally conscious district could be quite detrimental. Several Republican members in particular have objected to such group ratings, contending that most rating groups lean toward the Democrats and tend to make Republican members look bad. They had never objected, however, to ratings by such conservative-leaning groups as the American Constitutional Union or Americans for Constitutional Action. The real significance of such ratings of members is the actual support or opposition that goes along with the ratings in the form of campaign contributions, volunteer workers, campaign publicity, etc. Endorsement or opposition by some groups is cause for deep concern while others are virtually ignored.

Spurred by labor's political success, many business groups have encouraged their members to become much more active politically. The Chambers of Commerce across the country now sponsor "Meet Your Congressman" gatherings and encourage their members to contact their congressmen. The AMA has encouraged doctors to be more politically involved and has levied extra assessments to oppose national health insurance programs. The GMA (Grocery Manufactures of America, Inc.) sends out detailed instructions to its members on how to organize company task forces, how to contact members of Congress, and what to say when they do.

In the final analysis, however, it is through their campaign contributions that the organized interests make their biggest impact on the legislative process. Most members are not quite so bold as the representative who reacted to a fifty-dollar contribution from a merchant marine company by telling the firm if that was all it could afford he didn't want anything to do with it. The company responded with $200. However, lobby money buys a lot of fund-raising tickets and finds numerous other ways to get into the campaign coffers of those running for Congress. For years the petroleum industry has been one of the most effective lobbies in Washington and contributions of the oil tycoons over the years have been on the spectacular side. This list of contributions from oil company executives runs for several pages in the campaign finance records of the Citizens' Research Foundation in Princeton, New Jersey.

While a substantial campaign contribution doesn't necessarily buy a vote, it does help insure a sympathetic audience—a chance for the special interest to be heard. The appearance of such citizen-oriented lobby groups as Nader's Raiders and Common Cause, and the concern over campaign finances developed as an aftermath of Watergate, will make many groups and candidates much more cautious about offering and accepting contributions. As long as the present system of private financing of campaigns is continued, however, the campaign contribution will remain a substantial tool in the hands of the special interests.

Rather than direct their efforts toward 535 individual members, many groups feel they can have much more impact by working through the much smaller committees of Congress. Besides, many lobbyists feel that from 70 to 90 percent of the members don't have enough power and influence in the legislative process to warrant buying them lunch anyway. Working at the committee stage, group representatives often are able to bring about desirable changes or to sidetrack a measure. In its final opposition to Medicare, the AMA concentrated its efforts on getting Eldercare substituted at the committee stage. Groups often have their own alternative measures or amendments proposed at the committee stage. Because the committees specialize in certain areas of legislation, this sometimes enhances the influence of particular groups in these smaller units of Congress. Certain committees may become the strongholds of particular interests—the postal workers, the Indians, the conservationists, etc.

Also at the committee stage, group spokesmen have an opportunity to present their testimony. Many feel, however, that committee testimony is of dubious value as a lobbying technique. Nevertheless, the committees feel obliged to schedule hearings and the lobbyists feel compelled to appear and testify. Such testimony is frequently a defensive action, but the groups consider it necessary to counter the claims of the opposition. Such testimony is used primarily as a supplement to other lobbying techniques.

Much of the lobbying effort of many interests is not directed at the member of Congress personally at all, but rather at his constituents. Because many members tend to "vote their constituencies," the groups feel the most effective lobbying they can do is among those who elected the member. As one Michigan member observed, "A call from the district from someone you know who will be affected by a bill is far more effective" than a contact by a professional lobbyist. Therefore much lobbying effort is directed toward generating support among constituents which will result in their writing, phoning or visiting their representative or senator. Some groups are capable of generating massive letter-writing campaigns and others can have hundreds of members on Capitol Hill in no time. They feel this is much more impressive in many instances than trying to make their own case.

Over the years the style of lobbying has changed considerably as groups have come to rely more and more on advertising, media, letter-writing and telephone campaigns and other indirect methods. Many groups, such as the 700,000-member National Rifle Association, can generate letter-writing campaigns which flood congressional offices almost overnight. On the Landrum-Griffin Bill passed in 1959, the Chamber of Commerce generated almost a million messages to Congress. The 1961 aid-to-education bill prompted a massive letter-writing campaign by education interests. In 1962 the U.S. Savings and Loan League staged a campaign against a proposal in Kennedy's tax bill to withhold taxes on dividends and interest. In one month the campaign flooded Capitol Hill offices with thousands of letters. Such overwhelming onslaughts of mail, of course, do not appear as spontaneous reactions of constituents, but they do indicate large numbers of voters who are capable of being mobilized on certain issues, and for a member looking for a way out on a particular issue, they may provide a ready explanation for his vote. Usually, however, the more spontaneous such efforts appear, the more effective they are.

The increased emphasis on working through constituents using indirect methods has made lobbying quite expensive. Tremendous amounts of money are spent by interest groups through radio and television programs, newspaper advertising and pamphleteering. Many organizations spend small fortunes on elaborate slick, full-color brochures and public relations campaigns. Others feel such efforts are largely wasted, or they cannot afford the expense of such productions. In its champaign against Medicare, the AMA in one year printed and distributed fourteen million pamphlets, ran ads in major newspapers, in eleven national magazines, thirteen farm publications, aired radio and TV spots, and showed a film on television. The campaign cost millions of dollars. Public relations has come a long way in politics and today no major group or organization would be comfortable without a broad-based appeal for public support. Along with all the commercials selling toothpaste, detergents and soft drinks, the public gets the soft-sell from the pharmaceutical manufacturers, the petroleum industry and many, many others. Currently the petroleum industry is spending millions to improve its public image, which was tarnished by the "energy crisis." In 1967 the Pharmaceutical Manufacturers Association launched a massive advertising campaign involving expenditures in excess of one million dollars per year. From 1967 to 1969 the association ran eight advertising inserts of eight pages each in *Reader's Digest*. It also distributed short articles promoting the drug industry point of view and ran extensive "educational ads." In mid–1969 the drug association switched to a more low-key approach, producing a consumer information program involving the distribution of hundreds of thousands of pamphlets and furnishing free speakers for local audiences. It also produced and distributed to TV stations a twenty-eight-minute, $150,000 color film on the drug industry. All of this, of course, is aimed at creating a favorable public attitude toward the industry which will eventually pay dividends in terms of favorable public policy. PMA does not place all its eggs in the indirect lobby basket, however; as one executive notes, ". . . we encourage our companies, particularly during recess periods, to get congressmen over to their plants." Most groups, even those with huge PR budgets, appreciate the value of some direct contacts with those who make the laws.

Growing out of the concept that organized action produces more impact politically than individual effort, interest groups would be expected to appreciate the advantages of political alliances and coalitions. On many issues, groups will seek to line up support among other groups, among agencies of the government, and among the members of Congress. Such working coalitions can be most effective on particular pieces of legislation. During the Nixon administration a coalition of more than eighty different organizations was formed under the title of the Emergency Committee for Full Funding of Education Programs. Organizing into teams, group representatives contacted each congressman at least once. On one occasion the group helped to get $1 billion more appropriated than Nixon had requested in the budget. Another type of alliance that is frequently very effective is that of interest groups working jointly with certain members of Congress. Such alliances are quite common among large government contractors and the delegations from states where these firms are located. In 1973, at the urging of the influential Texas delegation, Congress voted $300 million for the F–111 and A–7 airplanes for which the Pentagon had asked no funds. Both planes are built by contractors home-based in Texas. Currently the Rockwell Corporation is lobbying for appropriations for the B–1 bomber which will cost at least $76 million each. Already Rockwell has shown members how many jobs the B–1 production will mean in their home states and districts, and Rockwell has the California delegation on its side. Many groups, such as Common Cause, try to work in tandem with other groups when possible as they feel this enhances their influence. And proving the adage that politics makes strange bedfellows, the Kansas WCTU (Women's Christian Temperance Union) had as a major source of its funds for years the bootlegging interests of the state. The alliances and coalitions may appear incongruous at times but they can be effective.

Many people mistakenly assume that professional lobbyists lurk in the hallways of the Capitol looking for members whose votes they can buy. Today lobbying has become much more subtle and sophisticated than the outright bribe. Some members may play poker with lobbyists who contact them and appear before their committees *and the members win consistently.* But, on the whole, bribery is a little-used tool of the modern-day professional lobbyist. In the first place, the risk is too great, and in the second place, it is too expensive to buy all the votes needed to insure victory on most issues. In a well-publicized case in 1956, a bribery attempt by a representative of the petroleum industry on a pending natural gas bill backfired, causing Senator Francis Case (R. S.D.) to vote against the bill which he had originally supported and creating such a public furor that President Eisenhower felt compelled to veto the measure which he also had supported. The consequences of a misdirected effort to bribe a member can be calamitous, as indicated, and most lobbyists feel there are much less risky and more effective means of promoting their legislative objectives.

Group Influence

Largely unnoticed by the general public and virtually ignored by the news media, interest group influence is pervasive in the legislative process. In fact, some sources, including Ralph Nader and his group studying Congress, feel that lobbyists and the special interests they represent have captured control of the House and Senate. There can be no doubt but that organized interests and their representatives have tremendous influence in the Congress and on its decisions. Many examples attest to this substantial influence. As Speaker, John McCormack acknowledged that he checked all appointments to the House Education and Labor Committee with former two-term representative from Wisconsin and head lobbyist for the AFL-CIO, Andrew Biemiller. The Pharmaceutical Manufacturers Association was able to get two of its attorneys on an informal Senate committee drafting drug legislation. The 1962 legislation making lobbying expenditures a tax-deductible business expense, a measure supported by virtually every major lobby group in the nation, breezed through Congress. Not a single opposing vote was cast in the House and the vote in the Senate was 51 to 13 in favor of passage.

While such groups as those pushing for civil rights and environmental legislation attract the most attention, equally impressive but less spectacular in their actions are the hundreds of business and professional groups. Quietly, but effectively, these groups go about making their weight felt in the legislative process in a great variety of ways.

Many choose to concentrate their efforts, zeroing in on a few key members or a key committee. For years the legislation regulating import quotas on sugar was quietly drawn up in the House by the lobbyists representing the sugar interests and Representative Harold Cooley (D. S.C.), chairman of the House Agriculture Committee. Asked whom he contacted, one sugar lobbyist said he talked to one member—Harold Cooley. He added, "There aren't five men in Congress that understand it [the sugar bill], but I do."[4] In the same vein, Cooley once told his House colleagues that sugar quota legislation was so complicated that they should take his quota recommendations "on faith." The lobbying of foreign agents on sugar legislation finally reached such proportions in 1962 that it touched off an investigation. The committee has since reasserted its prerogative to draft sugar import quotas.

Frequently groups are in a good position to exert influence on a key committee, and if they hope to succeed, the committee may be the only place to exert influence. In a letter to its members in 1962 on the "Truth in lending bill" sponsored by Senator Paul Douglas (D. Ill.), the U.S. Chamber of Commerce noted that its best chance to block the bill was while it was still in subcommittee, where five to ten members still favored the chamber's position. If the bill cleared committee, it would no doubt breeze through the full Senate. In 1966, the auto lobby ignored the Senate committee handling auto safety legislation, headed by Senator Warren Magnuson (D. Wash.) to concentrate its efforts on the House committee headed by Representative Harley O. Staggers. The industry was successful in getting a watered-down version of the auto safety measure, and a similar bill on tire safety wasn't even reported out by the committee.

Another place where groups may sometimes concentrate their efforts with success is in the House Rules Committee. An example was the federal land use bill proposed in the 93rd Congress. The bill breezed through the House Interior Committee, 26 to 11, and went on to the Rules Committee where it was bottled up by a 9 to 4 vote. The principal reason was the last-ditch lobbying efforts of such groups as the U.S. Chamber of Commerce and the Liberty Lobby, which contended the measure would hurt property values, retard growth, and involve the federal government in local zoning matters. Representatives of these groups were able to prevail upon

Nixon to withdraw his support and the Rules Committee obligingly prevented the full House from considering the measure.

The committee system facilitates the lobbying activities of the interest groups. They can concentrate their efforts on smaller groups of members and upon those committees and committee members most likely to be favorable and in the house where the chances of success are greatest. As noted, certain committees may become the spokesmen in the Congress for certain special interests, and these interests may have undue influence on legislation affecting them. Interest group influence in committees also may be enhanced by the fact that members operate with a considerable degree of anonymity in committee and may be much more receptive to helping to kill a measure in committee than to voting against it on the floor. Consequently, the committees and subcommittees of Congress are the targets of some of the most intensive lobbying efforts carried on by the special interests.

The power wielded by the various interest groups in the legislative process is difficult to assess. As with so many other questions involving power and influence, many factors come into play. On some issues interest group lobbying may have a determining impact, while on other issues, it may be of little consequence. Some lobbyists and some groups are much more effective than others. What makes the difference? Why are some groups highly effective, while others that appear to have all the ingredients for power, have only slight influence?

For decades the petroleum lobby has been regarded as one of the most influential in Washington. In fact, operations of the oil lobby have become such a fine art that the oil companies and their allies in Congress and in the executive agencies operate almost as a subgovernment in the Capitol. Only recently has their influence shown any decline. In 1969 the oil depletion allowance was reduced for the first time in forty-five years. What are the ingredients of such influence in the legislative process? The oil industry has more than 200 "Washington representatives" to speak for more than a dozen associations. Best known of these is the American Petroleum Institute, which alone has more than 400 employees and an annual budget of $19 million. Principal Washington spokesman for API is Frank N. Ikard, former U.S. representative from Texas and a close friend of Wilbur Mills and other members on the House

Ways and Means Committee. One hundred eighty-one "little" producers make up another of these groups, the Independent Petroleum Association of America. This group has grass-roots support in Congress. In addition to its own associations, the petroleum industry also is a major voice in groups such as the National Association of Manufacturers and the U.S. Chamber of Commerce. And it has close connections with many of the country's most prominent families—the Mellons, the Pews, and the Rockefellers.

Probably the principal source of its influence, however, is the number of very close friends the industry has had in government positions of power. The industry works hard and spends heavily to insure that those elected to Congress from oil-producing states look favorably upon the industry. With twenty states as primary producers of oil and with the industry working to see that its friends are elected, there are usually a substantial number of hard-core oil senators and representatives. The Bob Kerrs, Lyndon Johnsons and Sam Rayburns are gone from Congress, but the industry still can count on members such as Dewey Bartlett, a former oil man; Russell Long, whose family has become rich on oil; John Tower, Lloyd Bentsen, and Henry Bellmon, among others. Also there are more than one hundred energy company employees now working for the Federal Energy Administration. So, while the oil lobby has slipped a bit, its current influence on legislation is not to be discounted.

While the petroleum industry lobbies with a high degree of success, another giant of American industry gets very little mileage from a low-key lobby effort. General Motors, which has 123 plants in 95 congressional districts employing over 800,000 people, with dealerships in probably every congressional district in the country, and with an income of $25 billion, demonstrates little legislative political clout. An excise tax on automobiles which GM would like repealed has been on the books for thirty-eight years. One of the big problems is that GM lacks credibility in the Congress. This reduces substantially the impact of any lobbying efforts it engages in.

An extremely important element for the success of any lobby effort is that the group and its lobbyists have the confidence of the members they are seeking to influence. They face an extremely difficult, if not impossible, task in selling their case to those who do not trust them. The interdependence of the member of Congress and the lobbyist demands that their relationship be based on integrity and mutual trust. Dale Miller, one of the most successful professional lobbyists in Washington, says, "I think a person acquires influence in Washington through integrity and effort—not through contacts."⁵ Political science professor Lester Milbrath writes:

> It is extremely important that a congressman think of a lobbyist as a kind of doctor that he can depend on. Unless a congressman has real confidence in a lobbyist, that lobbyist simply does not have much influence. The greatest compliment one can get is for a member of Congress to say, "Whatever that fellow tells you, you can depend on it."⁶

The lobbyist who misrepresents something or deceives a member is through, his credibility is destroyed and the word spreads quickly. The effective lobbyist does his homework carefully, is well-informed, knows what his objectives are and the best way to achieve them. Those who don't know much are soon discredited. Lobbyists operating on Capitol Hill range from the inept and uninfluential to the extremely powerful.

Regulation of Lobbying

Because lobbyists speak for and try to influence legislation on behalf of specialized interests, most citizens and legislators feel they must be regulated by law. However, because lobbying involves the constitutional right to petition, effective regulation, without infringing upon this constitutionally guaranteed right, becomes a delicate matter. For this and other reasons, the few feeble efforts that have been made to regulate the activities of the groups lobbying Congress have been quite ineffective.

Only about twenty members of Congress have been formally accused of corrupt practices since 1900 and fewer than half of these cases involved lobbying. The first investigation of lobbying came in 1913, and legislation directly regulating lobbying was not passed until 1946. The so-called Federal Regulation of Lobbying Act was passed as Title III of the Congressional Reorganization Act of 1946, and actually is not a regulatory measure but a reporting and disclosure requirement. The law deals only with direct efforts to influence Congress, and simply requires quarterly reports from lobbyists giving their names and addresses, those from whom they receive money, those with whom they spend money, the bills in which they are interested and publications carrying their propaganda. These reports are filed with the Clerk of the House and Secretary of the Senate and are buried in the *Congressional Record*.

As a measure for regulating lobbying, the law is so full of loopholes that it is unenforceable. The Supreme Court has widened these loopholes even further by holding in the *Rumely* and *Harriss* cases[7] that the law applies only to direct efforts to influence Congress and only to groups that have as their primary objective the influencing of Congress. Under this interpretation, groups engaged in substantial lobbying efforts have declined to register, saying their primary function is not lobbying. Regarding themselves as exempt, such groups as the NAM, ADA, Chamber of Commerce, Americans for Constitutional Action, American Public Power Association, American Bankers Association, National Rifle Association, among others, have not filed for years. Even the committee for Government of the People, which opposed the Supreme Court's one-man, one-vote decision and lobbied for an amendment to change it, refused to file. The committee was chaired by Senator Everett Dirksen and had Senator Frank Church as cochairman. In 1973 one of the most intensely lobbied issues in Congress was the Alaska pipeline bill. Two major groups were the Alaska Public Interest Coalition, a combination of more than two dozen environmental and public interest groups, and the Alyeska Pipeline Service Company, a consortium of Exxon, Mobile, Atlantic-Richfield, Standard Oil of Ohio, Phillips and Union oil companies. Neither of these groups reported lobbying expenditures because they contended they only "gave advice" on this issue.

Furthermore the law is virtually toothless as far as enforcement. The bill fails to designate anyone to enforce the reporting provisions or to investigate the validity of the reports. Consequently, with no one designated to report violations, no one does. The already overtaxed Department of Justice has little time for investigations of lobbying violations, and there have been only four prosecutions and one conviction for violations since 1946. What we have is a disclosure law with no effective enforcement agency.

The existing law has a number of other loopholes as well. It requires no information on the lobbying organization itself, such as size, organizational structure, affiliations and other pertinent data which could be useful to the legislator in identifying the group. Current provisions also enable many groups to evade the intent of the law, in fact, probably encourage false and devious reporting. Most groups seldom report as lobbying expenses the costs of research, mailing, office staff, advertising, and many other aspects of indirect lobbying campaigns. Consequently the expenditures reported are only the tip of the iceberg. In 1950, 312 organizations reported spending $10.3 million on lobbying. Since then the amounts reported have declined, though lobbying activity has certainly intensified. In 1965, 304 organizations reported expenditures of $5,484,413, while in 1966 only 296 organizations reported spending $4,656,872.

Bills to strengthen the current lobbying regulations have been introduced for nineteen consecutive years, but have quietly withered on the legislative vine. "Nobody," explains Representative Morris Udall (D. Ariz.), "is lobbying for them." However, more stringent enforcement of the regulations already on the books would help to improve the congressional image in this area. Some abuses are clear-cut and flagrant. In 1974, when federal strip mine legislation was under consideration in the House, Wayne Aspinall, a $1750-a-month lobbyist for the coal mine interests and former chairman of the House Interior Affairs Committee, moved about freely on the floor genially twisting the arms of his former colleagues. The voters of his district had voted him out, largely on the issue of conservation, and now they sat rather helplessly in the galleries and watched him lobbying vigorously among his former associates who declined to enforce the House rules against him. It is this type of open abuse that raises questions of undue influence from special interests in Congress. Stricter enforcement of the existing rules would improve the ethical climate.

Conclusion

Interest groups and lobbyists have become an integral part of our legislative process, an important representative element in our highly pluralistic society. Former New York Congressman Emanuel Celler has written, "Legislation will be improved when more and more people learn to intervene directly in the conduct of our national affairs."[8] One of the most effective ways for the rank-and-file citizen to get involved is through interest groups. As our society becomes more fragmented and impersonal, good representative lobbies take on an even more important role. Also, as the issues faced by the Congress multiply and become even more complex, members must depend increasingly upon pressure group spokesmen with special expertise to help them understand and act on vital issues.

As a general rule, lobbyists are neither sinister nor malicious. The modern-day lobbyist is much more sophisticated in his techniques than the women-and-liquor plying version of much popular writing. Members are likely to be resentful of anyone who acts as though he owns them or tries to dictate to them. Most lobbyists seek not so much to apply pressure as simply to be allowed to make their case. Their approach is one of soft-sell rather than demanding or threatening. They don't waste a lot of time trying to win over die-hard opponents but concentrate on those already inclined in their direction.

While the interest groups play a vital role in our democratic system, their activities also harbor a vast potential for corruption and wrongdoing in the legislative process. Interest group contributions to the political campaigns of members of Congress pose some difficult questions that the Congress cannot continue to sweep under the rug. In 1972–73, one out of every seven members of the House and Senate received contributions from the milk co-ops. David R. Bowen (D. Miss.), newly assigned to the dairy subcommittee of the House Agriculture Committee, received $32,000 in co-op money over a sixteen-month period. Ed Jones (D. Tenn.), chairman of the dairy subcommittee, got $12,000, and Frank A. Stubblefield (D. Ky.) received $5,000. Over the sixteen-month period the co-ops distributed a total of $213,000, some of which was returned. This episode is repeated many times over as interest groups seek to insure that they have access to those committees and those members who deal with legislative matters of prime interest to them.

Some years back Emanuel Celler, former chairman of the House Judiciary Committee, wrote:

> I sometimes think that the political maturity of a people is best indicated by the extent to which they insist upon high moral standards in the conduct of their public affairs.[9]

Watergate has caused Americans to become quite politically mature and they are now going to insist that public officials, including members of Congress, face up to a number of moral issues they have avoided for many years. Campaign finance is one such area.

The voters are going to demand that elected officials demonstrate their resolve to place public interest above private gain. And, as long as Congress continues to operate as it has in the past, it is not likely that it will rise much in public esteem.

Notes

1. As quoted by Lester Milbrath in *The Washington Lobbyists* (Chicago: Rand McNally & Co., 1963), p. 222.
2. Wright Patman as quoted by Larry King in "Washington's Money Birds," *Harper's* (August, 1965), p. 53.
3. Scott Lucas, *Ibid.*, p. 50.
4. As quoted in ". . . All Those Sugar Lobbyists Go Tweet Tweet Tweet," *Newsweek* (July 30, 1962).
5. Dale Miller as quoted by Larry King in "Washington's Money Birds," p. 51.
6. Lester Milbrath, *The Washington Lobbyists,* p. 211.
7. *U.S.* v. *Rumely,* 345 U.S. 41 (1953) and *U.S.* v. *Harriss,* 347 U.S. 612 (1954).
8. Emanuel Celler, *"Pressure Groups,"* p. 1.
9. *Ibid.* p. 3–4.

Chapter VIII

Congress and
the Judiciary

IN THE AMERICAN system of government, the judicial branch enjoys a certain mystique that neither the executive nor the legislative branch has. Somehow, in the minds of many, the judges, once they don judicial robes, cease to be involved in politics, unlike presidents, governors, and legislators. French nobleman Alexis de Tocqueville noted that if there was an aristocracy in America it occupied the judicial bench. The courts occupy a special niche in the American political system. Over the years their impact on the political process has been substantial.

Under the concept of separation of powers and checks and balances, the role of the judicial branch relative to those of the legislative and executive branches is really rather passive. In fact, Montesquieu, often regarded as the father of the idea of separation of powers, wrote in *The Spirit of the Laws*:

> Of the three powers above-mentioned, the judiciary is in some measure next to nothing: there remain therefore only two; and as these have need of a regulating power to moderate them, the part of the legislative body composed of the nobility, is extremely proper for this purpose.[1]

Montesquieu didn't see the judiciary as being an effective check in the system of separation of powers. Likewise, Alexander Hamilton in *The Federalist* No. 78 wrote:

> The judiciary, on the contrary, has no influence over either the sword or the purse; no direction either of the strength or of the wealth of the society; and can take no active resolu-

tion whatever. It may truly be said to have neither FORCE nor WILL, but merely judgment; and must ultimately depend upon the aid of the executive arm even for the efficacy of its judgments.[2]

By 1787, the time of the framing of the American Constitution, the doctrine of separation of powers had become an axiom of free government, and though Hamilton and others of the framers may not have viewed the judiciary as a co-equal branch of government, they felt it was an essential part of the system. In actual practice the balance of powers among the three branches has proved quite delicate, and through history first one branch, then another has asserted itself to play a dominant role in the governmental process.

Under the leadership of the forceful Chief Justice John Marshall, the Supreme Court became probably *the* major force in laying the groundwork for a strong federal government. Seizing the initiative and exercising the power of judicial review* propounded so effectively by Marshall in the landmark case of *Marbury* v. *Madison,* the Supreme Court played a key role in forwarding Hamiltonian concepts of a strong federal government. From the time of Marshall to the end of World War II, the court was again rather passive, acting primarily as a restrainer on the other branches of government. However, throughout the 1950's and '60's the court once again seized the initiative. With neither the Congress nor the President taking action in such areas as civil rights, segregation, and legislative reapportionment, the courts stepped in to take the lead in finding solutions to these difficult issues and attempting to correct glaring inequities. Consequently, throughout the '50's and '60's the most substantial impact in domestic affairs was a result of judicial action rather than congressional or executive action. Because many of these issues were highly controversial, the courts did not take action in such areas without encountering volatile criticism and opposition.

As originally conceived by the framers of the Constitution, the Supreme Court was to be insulated from direct popular will.

---

*Judicial review is the power assumed by the courts of reviewing the acts of the legislative and executive branches and determining their constitutionality.

However, social and demographic changes, coupled with developments in mass communications techniques, have altered substantially the role of the President and the Senate and also have helped to transform the federal courts from distant and passive arbiters into representative and active instruments of social change. No longer are the courts insulated from the groundswells of public sentiment, and their responses to such sentiments may lead to conflicts with the other branches of government.

When the courts respond to popular sentiment and when they initiate action in certain areas, oftentimes rather controversial areas where neither the President nor Congress has found it expedient to act, they risk generating criticism and opposition, especially in the legislative branch. Frequently, the interests served through such court action are opposed to the interests of those served by members of Congress. In such instances the courts usually come under intense fire from those members in Congress who charge that such actions are an abuse of judicial power and that the proper role of the courts is to "interpret," not to "make law."

Under such circumstances the courts must maintain a good defense because they are to a great extent at the mercy of the legislature and in constant jeopardy of legislative ire. The extent of congressional authority over the courts is substantial.

Legislative Powers

The United States Constitution establishes only one court—the Supreme Court. All other courts in the federal system are creations of the legislature and as such can be abolished by the Congress. Following the elections in 1801 when the Federalists were swept out of office by a Democratic landslide, John Adams stayed up most of the night preceding Jefferson's inauguration signing judicial appointments—the "midnight judges"—to keep that branch under Federalist control. Once in office, the Democrats in Congress abolished the circuit courts because they had been staffed by Adams with Federalists.

While the Supreme Court could be abolished only through a constitutional amendment, its size is left to the discretion of Congress. As a consequence, its size has been altered from time to time, usually with a particular objective in mind. In an 1869 decision, a majority on the Supreme Court struck down the Legal

Tender Acts. Subsequently two new justices were added to the court, and they helped reverse the earlier decision when a similar case came before them.

Periodically, as a result of clashes between the two branches, Congress will try through various means to curtail the powers of the courts. Such actions led Woodrow Wilson to note:

> The power of the courts is safe only during seasons of political peace, when parties are not aroused to passion or tempted by the command of irresistible majorities.[3]

Actually only a relatively small part of the Supreme Court's jurisdiction is controlled by the Constitution, and while constitutional theorist Raoul Berger contends in *Congress* v *The Supreme Court* that the framers did not intend for Congress to have the authority to change the court's appellate jurisdiction, Congress has assumed that it has this prerogative. Over the years numerous bills have been proposed which would have limited the jurisdiction of the federal courts in various ways. The first amendment adopted after the Bill of Rights dealt with the jurisdiction of the Supreme Court. In 1964 the House passed a measure which would have removed legislative apportionment cases from the jurisdiction of the courts. The so-called Dirksen-Tuck Bill would have allowed at least one house of state legislatures to be based on something other than population and would thus have modified the jurisdiction of the federal courts. In 1968 the Senate Judiciary Committee reported a bill that would have limited the federal courts' authority to review certain state court decisions on criminal confessions. Such legislation is proposed regularly in the Congress as major decisions of the courts affect someone's constituents adversely. However, unless the Congress is really upset with the courts, the likelihood of such measures passing is quite slim.

Nonetheless, the fact remains that the courts are for the most part within the power of the Congress, which can alter their operations drastically upon its whim. For example, Congress controls the salaries and the budget of the federal courts. In 1964, while voting themselves a 33.3 percent raise, the Congress pettily declined to vote Supreme Court Justices a raise. Many members were unhappy at the time with the court's apportionment decisions. When it comes to budgets, Congress may deny even the most meager requests from the judiciary. By comparison, the annual budget of the

FBI is usually larger than the budget for the whole federal court system. Former Chief Justice Earl Warren once observed, "It is next to impossible for the courts to get something from Congress." This is particularly true if the courts have rendered decisions recently with which Congress is in disagreement.

Another way in which the Congress has influence over the courts is through its impeachment and confirmation roles. Most federal judges serve for life with good behavior, but they are subject to impeachment by the Congress. Though impeachment is not a tool Congress has turned to often, it is a sort of "gun behind the door" which may be used to bring the courts more in line with congressional thinking. In our entire history only one Supreme Court Justice, Samuel Chase, has been impeached. John Randolph, a caustic and rabid partisan, handled the prosecution for the House but the Senate failed to convict Chase. Chase was one of a number of Federalist judges appointed by John Adams whom Jefferson and his Democratic allies in Congress set out to remove through impeachment. A key question raised in the proceedings was whether a judge could be impeached who had committed no "indictable offense." The Senate split on each vote with the Democrats failing to get the necessary two-thirds vote for conviction. Disgruntled at the failure of his efforts, Jefferson snorted that impeachment of federal court justices was "a farce never to be tried again."

However, threats of impeachment have been raised on various occasions whem members of the federal bench have performed in a fashion disapproved of by Congress. In April, 1970, then House Minority Leader Gerald Ford took the floor of the House and urged that Justice William O. Douglas be impeached. Ford accused Douglas of espousing "hippie-yippie style revolution," writing for pornographic magazines, and links to "left-wing organizations." In his attack, Ford said of impeachment:

> The only honest answer is that an impeachable offense is whatever a majority of the House of Representatives considers it to be at the given moment in history; conviction results from whatever offense or offenses two-thirds of the other body considers to be sufficiently serious to require removal of the accused from office.[4]

A few years later Ford did not appear nearly so eager to apply the same criteria to fellow Republican Richard Nixon as President. A subcommittee of the House Judiciary Committee investigated charges against Douglas and reported no grounds for impeachment. On the whole, Congress has resisted being stampeded impetuously toward impeachment. However, as the Nixon case demonstrated, impeachment is an ever-present check which may be used by the Congress against the executive or judicial branches.

Congress is also an important participant in the process of appointing members to the federal judiciary. The Constitution requires congressional confirmation of federal judges appointed by the President, and custom and tradition have given legislators even further influence in the actual selection of judges for the lower federal courts. It has become common practice for the President to observe "Senatorial Courtesy" and clear his appointments to federal judgeships with the senior senator of his party from the state where an appointment is to be made. A strong objection from a senior senator may be enough to cause the President to seek another nominee, or if the President persists, to block confirmation by the Senate.

As a general rule, Presidents do not have much difficulty in getting Senate confirmation of their appointments to the federal bench. On occasion, however, the Senate may have serious reservations about a nominee and may raise such strong objections as to bring about withdrawal of a nomination or else a rejection of the President's choice. When Lyndon Johnson nominated Francis X. Morrissey, a close friend of the Kennedy family, for a vacancy in a district judgeship in Massachusetts, serious questions of his qualifications to serve on the federal bench were raised in the Senate. Finally, as a result of the vigorous congressional criticism, the nomination was withdrawn. On some occasions more than others the senators take their confirmation function much more seriously. Many senators feel this is a task they must take seriously and give careful consideration. In reviewing one of President Nixon's nominations for the Supreme Court, Senator Harry Byrd observed:

> When the Senate fails to give adequate attention to a Supreme Court nomination, it fails in its constitutional duty to make certain the men on the bench have the requisite knowledge and integrity—and requisite concept of the judicial role.[5]

The last clause in Senator Byrd's remark is a key to the struggles that sometimes arise over confirmation of judicial nominees. Not only does the Senate concern itself with the qualifications of the nominees, but also with their judicial philosophy, and this may sometimes lead to some stirring battles over confirmation. When Woodrow Wilson nominated Louis Brandeis for a seat on the Supreme Court, there was no real doubt of his legal qualifications, but many senators had strong reservations about his economic and political philosophies. He won confirmation on a close, almost straight party vote. On the other hand, Richard Nixon's nominations of Harold Carswell and Clement Haynsworth raised serious questions, even in the minds of fellow Republicans, about the nominees' qualifications to serve on the nation's highest court. Nixon's experience illustrates that the President cannot assume that all he has to do is pick someone with a judicial background and experience and send the name to the Senate for its stamp of approval. In recent years in particular, the Senate has shown an inclination to review nominees for the federal bench with much closer scrutiny than at certain times in the past. Both Presidents Johnson and Nixon were somewhat embarrassed by not having screened court nominees more carefully.

Legislative-Judicial Friction

The constitutional system of separation of powers and checks and balances builds into our system a certain amount of inevitable friction between the different branches of the government. The courts are placed in a position wherein they either must play a totally passive role in the government process or else run the risk of incurring the wrath of the other two branches, especially that of the Congress. And, as Woodrow Wilson noted, unless the judiciary can check the legislature, the courts are of comparatively little worth as balance wheels in the system.[6] When the courts exercise the power of judicial review, they frequently substitute their concept of what is constitutionally correct for that of the Congress. This, rather inevitably, is not going to sit too well with some.

When the courts venture into areas of controversial economic, social and constitutional issues, there is no way they can avoid stepping on some legislative toes. There are those who feel that when the courts in their decisions espouse certain economic or social philosophies, they have usurped powers to which they are not entitled. Expressing such views of the judicial self-restrainers, Senator Harry Byrd observes:

> But I do say that it is unwise for the court to forge ahead in social movements outside of the confines of the case before it, and in areas which properly are legislative.[7]

It is, he adds, unwise to "legislate" from the judicial bench. Thus, when the courts, even though their actions may stem from the inaction of the legislative and executive branches as in the areas of civil rights and legislative apportionment, take action on one of these volatile issues, they will inevitably encounter rather strong criticism. There are almost always elements in the Congress ready to set out after the courts, and decisions in such touchy areas as civil rights and apportionment provide such elements a convient opportunity to vent their emotions toward the courts.

The courts also lay themselves open to legislative attacks when they render decisions in cases involving the internal affairs of the Congress. As a general rule, the courts leave it up to the two houses to resolve their own internal disputes; however, on rare occasions they may feel they have no choice but to become involved. A recent case was that of *Adam Clayton Powell, Jr., et al.* v. *John W. McCormack, et al.* involving the refusal of the House of Representatives to seat Powell as a duly elected representative from his Harlem district. In presenting their case, the House lawyers argued that this was not a "justiciable" issue, but was a matter to be resolved internally by the House. In the District of Columbia U.S. District Court, Judge Hart dismissed Powell's plea, saying that if the court rendered a decision in the case it would "crash through a political thicket into political quicksand."[8] Powell then appealed his case, and the Supreme Court in reviewing the case held that it could judge and even set aside an internal action of a house of Congress when an unconstitutional act was involved. The court held that Powell had been denied his seat unconstitutionally. However, recognizing the perilousness of their venture into such internal affairs of Congress, the justices stopped short, saying the court did not have the authority to order Powell's reinstatement. This decision is a lot like John Marshall's classic decision in *Marbury* v. *Madison*. In the Powell case, the court asserts its authority to decide the constitutionality of legislative actions, even those internal, but does not go so far as to order reinstatement which the House could simply refuse, leaving the court little or no recourse.

This was a tactically wise decision by the court, for it placed the House on notice that even their internal actions were subject to constitutional restraints and could be reviewed in this light by the courts; yet it did not go so far as to order any congressional action which could cause the Congress to rise up in retaliation against the court.

Summary

Historically the relationship between the courts and Congress has been one of watchful wariness. The Congress, jealous of its legislative prerogatives, has on occasion become quite agitated when it has felt that the courts have overstepped their constitutional role and have encroached upon the legislative function. Such instances have produced a rash of legislative proposals for limiting the powers and jurisdiction of the courts. Generally when the President and Congress have asserted themselves, the courts have been less inclined to take the initiative and innovate. Realizing that nothing produces dissatisfaction and criticism more rapidly than innovation and change which is sure to rattle certain elements in Congress, the courts have moved in these areas only when they saw no other recourse. Appreciating that they are largely at the mercy of the Congress, the courts have generally tried as much as possible to avoid open and direct confrontations with the legislative branch. And while the relationship at times becomes somewhat strained, the two branches have, considering the innate tensions of the system, been able to function rather well.

Notes

1. Charles-Louis Montesquieu, *The Spirit of the Laws* (1748: rev. ed., trans. Thomas Nugent, 1873).
2. *The Federalist*, p. 504.
3. Woodrow Wilson, *Congressional Government* (New York: Meridian, 1956), p. 40.
4. *U.S. News and World Reports*, 68 (April 27, 1970), p. 26.
5. Harry Byrd, *Congressional Record* (October 15, 1969), p. S12626.
6. Wilson, *Congressional Government*, p. 36.
7. Byrd, *Congressional Record*, p. S12627.
8. *Adam Clayton Powell, Jr., et. al.* v. *John W. McCormack, et. al.*, Civil Action No. 559–67, U.S. District Court of Columbia.

Chapter IX

Congress and the Executive

EVERY AMERICAN YOUNGSTER is informed in his first civics course that the United States system of government provides for a separation of powers wherein the legislative branch makes the laws, the judicial branch interprets the laws, and the executive branch administers or carries out the laws. While President, Dwight Eisenhower told a cheering audience in Rensselaer, Indiana, "Congress makes the laws; I execute them." This concept has become so much a part of the American governmental myth that few people stop to realize that in reality the system really doesn't function nearly so neatly and so simply. The constitutional framework and the formal powers vested in each branch are such that there is almost constantly a pulling and tugging between the Congress and the Presidency. Add to this the fact that the President is elected by a national constituency while congressmen are elected by state and local constituencies that are quite atypical nationally, and you have further tensions built into the system.

Traditionally there has been a struggle for supremacy between the legislative and executive branches. Our system of shared governmental powers and checks and balances makes such a contest inevitable. While the Constitution outlines the powers of each branch, there are numerous points of overlap, and much of the terminology used is broad and open to interpretation. Article II, outlining the powers and duties of the President, is the most loosely drawn chapter of the whole Constitution. In the words of Abel Upshur, Secretary of State under President Tyler and an able constitutional lawyer, ". . . the Convention appears to have studiously selected such loose and general expressions, as would enable the President, by implication and construction either to neglect his duties or to enlarge his powers."[1]

Under this arrangement, vigorous assertion by either branch of its powers and prerogatives will probably elicit some counter-action from the other. American political history has been marked by such challenges and counter-challenges on the part of Congress and the Presidents. While the formal powers and authority of the U.S. President are substantial, relations between Presidents and Congress have been influenced, to a marked degree, by the attitude and assertiveness of the occupant of the Presidential office.

Both George Washington and John Adams were careful to avoid even the slightest suggestion that they were encroaching upon the prerogatives of the Congress. Many of their successors have been much less inclined to remain aloof from congressional politics, and on numerous occasions Congress and the President have been locked in an unending battle for supremacy in the governmental process. In 1864, a group of irate congressional leaders in the Wade-Davis Manifesto told President Lincoln that he must understand "that the authority of Congress is paramount and must be respected." They then added, "If he wishes our support he must confine himself to his executive duties—to obey and execute, not to make the laws."[2] Little inclined to be dictated to by a group of reactionary radicals, Lincoln came to regard the Congress as a more or less necessary nuisance.

However, following the Civil War, the country experienced a period when the Presidency was largely overshadowed by a dominant Congress, a situation which persisted with only brief interludes of strong executive leadership until the New Deal and Franklin Roosevelt. In 1893 a Washington correspondent reported that the President had scarcely any influence at all on legislation or Congress. After brief periods of vigorous executive action under Teddy Roosevelt and Woodrow Wilson, the 1920's were a period when the White House provided relatively little leadership on policies and programs. The Great Depression of the 1930's and World War II touched off a period of executive dominance in American government, and the years since the end of the war have witnessed a tremendous growth in executive power in democracies through-out the world.

President as Legislator

Presidential involvement in the legislative process is not new, but in fact, quite obviously was intended by the Founding Fathers. It has, no doubt, reached proportions unimagined by them. Today the President is not just a participant, exercising a negative influence through the veto; he has become the chief legislator, the prime moving force in the whole policy-making process. The President's role as the principal figure in the legislative process is the outgrowth of a number of factors—his formal powers, his role as party leader, the absence of effective leadership in Congress, the growing complexity of issues and programs, and the unity of his office.

The Constitution grants to the President a number of powers which give him a key role in the legislative process. Probably the most direct of these powers is the veto. Given to the President ostensibly to protect his office from potential congressional aggression, the veto has been used by strong Presidents to make the Presidency virtually the third house of Congress. The use of the veto, or the mere threat of it, may give the President a strong bargaining tool with the Congress. Through its judicious use, a President can have considerable influence. Franklin Roosevelt sometimes told his Budget Director to give him a bill he could veto simply as a reminder to the Congress of this Presidential power.

The President also is authorized under the Constitution to call special sessions of the legislature and may use this power to influence action taken by the Congress. In accepting the Democratic nomination in 1948, President Truman announced he was calling a special session of the Congress. He said that his duty as President required that he use every means within his power to get the laws the people needed enacted. In taking this course, Truman placed the burden of action, or inaction, on the Republican-controlled legislature.

Another constitutional duty of the President is to deliver an annual State-of-the-Union address to the Congress. A good writer but poor speaker, Thomas Jefferson established the precedent for having his message read before the Congress. Woodrow Wilson revived the practice of delivering the message in person and used the addresses as a device to assume leadership over the legislature. Through his message on the State of the Union and other special messages to the Congress, the President can seize the initiative and set the agenda for legislative action. With the development of modern communications media, especially television, the President can use his messages to cultivate support for his legislative programs and bring pressure to bear on the Congress.

While his formal constitutional functions and powers provide him some leverage, it is through more informal methods that the President really makes his influence felt in the legislative process. As Lord Bryce noted in his classic study of American government, it is the political parties that provide the motive power that makes our legislature go.[3] Constitutional structure, however, places substantial obstacles in the way of effective party government. To a certain degree these obstacles are overcome by the merger of the popularly-elected leader and the mass political party in the President. While the nominating processes assure the separation of the Presidential and congressional parties, the initiatives of the President can go a long way toward the effective functioning of the American party.

The Congress is not organized to lead; power there is widely diffused and rests in many different centers. The White House, on the other hand, is a superb command post with substantial political resources. In exercising his leadership in the Congress, the President's party is both his burden and his support. The President must perform a dual role: he is both the leader of the whole country and the leader of his political party. Sometimes it may be difficult to reconcile these two roles; yet some of the most outstanding achievements of our government have been the result of the leadership of partisan, often highly partisan, Presidents. The President's party may provide him a base of power from which to exert effective leadership in the legislative branch. As President, Thomas Jefferson attended the caucuses of his party's members in Congress, and, according to rumor, even presided over some of them. While toady's Presidents do not preside at their parties' caucuses, the political parties remain one of the most effective channels through which the President exerts leadership in the legislature.

While the President may draw power from his position as party leader, this role may also pose problems for him. Recent Presidents have frequently found themselves faced with a majority of the opposing party in one or both houses of the Congress. Under these circumstances, the President's role as leader of his party may cost him more support than it gains. Even in those cases when the President has a majority of his own party in the Congress, there is no assurance the party members will fall readily in line behind his leadership. Because of the nature of our electoral system, the President and members of Congress who bear the same party label are divided by dependence upon and responsibility to different sets of voters. This party system brings into the Congress many members who will not support the President's legislative programs. Thus, the President frequently finds himself leading only part of his party. Like it or not, he may have to share leadership with other notables in the party, and frequently he must endure attacks on his integrity by members of his own party. He is faced with the difficult task of convincing often dubious congressmen that what the White House wants of them is in their own best interest.

What resources and tools can the chief executive bring to bear in this task? The executive office provides an elaborate apparatus to aid the President in his leadership efforts, and the President has sufficient weapons to make his leadership felt. The tools for achieving legislative discipline behind Presidential programs can, however, disrupt as well as unify. To be effective, they must be employed with tact and finesse. A young Kennedy aide reportedly told a veteran congressman that if he didn't vote the right way, every military base in his district would be closed. Such heavy-handed tactics may render Presidential powers ineffective in persuading members to support the President.

Used more tactfully and judiciously, the powers of the executive can be effective in lining up support in Congress. While patronage has become limited over the years, the White House still controls enough jobs and other favors to wield considerable influence. As Liaison Official in the Post Office, Mike Monroney kept a card file listing favors granted members of Congress. The list was then used in persuading members to support Presidential legislation. As chief budget planner and director of the vast federal bureaucracy, the President is in a position to bring pressures to

bear on Congress. For example, when Congress revealed some reluctance to appropriate the funds requested for the Post Office
Department in the 1950's, Postmaster General Arthur Summer-
field simply ordered a halt to mail deliveries on Saturday. Congress quickly saw the light and the Post Office Department got its
money.

The great prestige of the Presidential office is another advantage the chief executive may use on the Congress in a number
of ways. There is a certain hard-to-explain aura about the Presidential office that very subtly enhances the power of its occupant.
In Dallas, just before the assassination of John F. Kennedy, Senator Ralph Yarborough twice refused to ride in a limousine with
Vice-President Johnson. A month later he was swimming in the
White House pool with *President* Johnson. Many congressmen
find it is extremely difficult to tell the President "no" when seated
in the oval office or the second floor study. A well-timed call from
the President can also be a decisive factor in lining up key votes
in Congress. Early in 1964 the Senate Finance Committee passed
a proposed tax cut amendment. President Johnson felt the action
was premature and during their luncheon recess each member of
the committee got a personal call from the White House. When the
committee returned to session after lunch the amendment was re-
considered and voted down.

The prestige and popularity of the Presidential office can be
of value to a member of Congress in his bid for re-election. Thus,
the granting or withholding of Presidential blessings in the campaign becomes another tool in the arsenal of the chief executive.
A Kennedy aide, when asked about executive pressure on the Congress, responded, "I don't think you'll see any arms all out of
shape from Presidential twisting, but we know who votes against
us and we won't embarrass them by campaigning for them." Lawrence F. O'Brien, chief legislative liaison man for both Kennedy
and Johnson, observed, "The White House certainly remembers
who its friends are, and can be counted on to apply significant assistance in the campaign." Those who challenge the President may
find themselves placed in embarrassing political situations. A California congressman who persistently challenged Kennedy's foreign
aid program was conspicuously absent from the platform guests
when the President visited the representative's home district, a

rather considerable political affront. In a closely contested election, Presidential endorsement, or the absence thereof, can be a significant factor.

The aura and prestige of the Presidency coupled with the unity of the office place the President at an advantage over the Congress in a number of respects. The President is "Mr. President," but there is no "Mr. Congress." The President speaks for the whole nation and with one voice, whereas the Congress speaks for many constituencies and with many voices. Mike Mansfield, in spite of his quiet dignity and refreshing candor, is not in the same weight class with the President. The White House, in the words of Teddy Roosevelt, "is a bully pulpit," and using his opportunities wisely, the President can exert impressive public pressure on the Congress.

Andrew Jackson was the first President to go over the heads of the elected representatives directly to the people, but Jackson lacked the great power of publicity available to the modern-day President. The development of instantaneous nationwide commucations has greatly enhanced the powers of the Presidency vis-à-vis the other branches of government. By using the power and prestige of his office and current communications media, the modern-day President can take his case directly to an audience of millions. A popular President, using his ready access to the media effectively, can put the Congress at a severe disadvantage. With only the radio available, Franklin D. Roosevelt turned the Presidential "fireside chats" into a powerful instrument, and it was said that he had only to glance at the microphone to quiet a group of clamoring congressmen. Speaking of Roosevelt's "fireside chats" one Indiana farmer observed, "I listen to the President on the radio, and I know what he's sayin' ain't so, yet I find myself believin' him."[4] Television has further enhanced the power and influence of the President in this respect. Today a prime test of the political skill of the President as a leader is the effectiveness with which he employs the facilities of the mass media in molding and mobilizing public opinion behind his programs.

In spite of his substantial apparatus for bargaining and dealing with the Congress, the President quickly finds that he faces a formidable task in getting his legislative proposals enacted. Even with his own party controlling the two houses of Congress, as the

President seeks to lead, he frequently discovers that many of those members he counts on end up opposing him. Sectional interests, factionalism, congressional jealousy, even the mood of the country, may interfere with Presidential leadership. Though his party held overwhelming majorities in both houses, John Kennedy frequently was confronted by a hostile House. Furthermore, a President whose party has controlled Congress for some time faces an experienced and politically sophisticated leadership which may challenge his leadership. The President may well face a situation in which those challenging his leadership are more secure politically then he. John Kennedy, for example, faced chairmen in the House of whom only four had received less than 60 percent of the votes in their districts in the 1960 elections, and six of whom didn't even have opposition. These congressmen consistently ran ahead of their party's Presidential candidates. Faced with such secure opposition, the President has his work cut out for him.

Such politically secure members of Congress have usually seen a number of Presidents come and go, and their tenure and experience make them sensitive about their prerogatives. To lead effectively, the President must be both a master politician and an accomplished diplomat. At the start of the 84th Congress, President Johnson announced a thirteen-point legislative "program." He got little party support for his announcement, and even his friend Sam Rayburn complained that he had not been consulted. Such unilateral action by the President may serve to alienate potential supporters.

In the final analysis, the President, for all his difficulties in building support, remains the most effective initiator and mover of programs through the legislative process. More than anyone else in the system, he has the power and the means for establishing the priorities and for directing and manipulating the powerful forces of the nation. In the past only the "strong" Presidents took the initiative and set the agenda for legislative action; today this role is virtually thrust upon all those who occupy the office. Congress, on the other hand, through changes in the system, and to a great degree by default, has been reduced gradually from a vigilant, creative partner in the governmental process to a ratifying or consulting agency.

Checks and Balances

The Constitution which evolved from the deliberations of the Philadelphia Convention reflects the religion of John Calvin, the political philosophy of Thomas Hobbes, and the scientific principles of Isaac Newton. The outgrowth of these influences is a system of checks and balances designed to protect against possible abuses resulting from the human frailties of public officials by balancing the action of those in one branch of government with counter-action in another. An essential part of this arrangement of governmental checks and balances is the congressional-executive relationship.

The Constitution's assignment of functions and powers built into the system an inevitable tension and struggle for dominance between the legislative and executive branches. Through the decades, Presidents and Congress have been locked in an endless duel, with first one branch then the other dominating the scene. Frictions between the two branches were not long in developing. Only four months after his inauguration, Washington and his Secretary of War took a treaty just negotiated with the Southern Indians to the Senate to explain the details and get approval. Refusing to be rushed into approving the treaty without careful examination, the Senate referred the treaty to a committee. In what one witness described as a "violent fret," Washington said the Senate's action defeated "every purpose of my coming here." Two days later he returned to watch while the Senate rewrote the treaty before his eyes. Departing in a rage, he swore he would never return to the Senate again.[5] Following Washington's precedent, no President appeared on behalf of a treaty again until Woodrow Wilson pleaded his case in 1919.

Frequent skirmishes have continued to mark relations between 1600 Pennsylvania Avenue and Capitol Hill, as first the Congress and then the President have appeared to gain the upper hand. "In one hand he holds the purse, and in the other he brandishes the sword of the country. What more does he want?" asked Henry Clay. "He touches everything, moves everything, controls everything. I ask, Sir, is this legal responsibility?" pleaded Daniel Webster, senator from Massachusetts.[6] However, following Andrew Jackson, whom Clay and Webster were chastizing, came a period of congressional dominance. In fact, with the exception of Polk, Lincoln, and possibly Cleveland, the period from Jackson to the turn of the century was one of Presidents largely overshadowed by the Congress. When Woodrow Wilson wrote his book *Congressional Government* in the 1880's, he wrote:

> The President may tire the Senate by dogged persistence, but he can never deal with it upon a ground of real equality. His power does not extend beyond the most general suggestion. The Senate always has the last word.[7]

And around the turn of the century, Senator George Hoar noted, "If Senators visited the White House, it was to give, not to receive, advice."[8]

The early years of the twentieth century brought some changes however, as the growth and increasing complexity of the country demanded more vigorous Presidential leadership. This first came with Teddy Roosevelt, who shocked the Congress with action hitherto unheard of—he presented his own program, The Square Deal. This pattern was followed by Woodrow Wilson, who went so far as to have "administration bills" introduced in the Congress. As President, Wilson also publicly denounced a number of filibustering senators as "a little group of willful men." Outraged by such action, the senators declared this was "unparalleled and unprecedented."

Following Wilson, the pendulum swung in the other direction, as the country embarked on an era of passive Presidents. Franklin Roosevelt re-established the vigorous Presidency, but it was still a touch-and-go contest between the executive and legislative branches.

It was only about forty years ago that H. L. Mencken wrote, "The rewards of the Presidency are mostly trashy. . . . The President continues, of course, to be an eminent man, but only in the sense that Jack Dempsey, Babe Ruth, and Henry Ford have been eminent men."[9] Both time and the Constitution, however, have been on the side of the President, who in the American system has been much more than just an "eminent man." Lincoln's Secretary of State, William H. Seward, once stated, "We elect a king for four years, and give him absolute power within certain limits, which after all, he can interpret for himself." Over the years there has been a cumulative and seemingly irreversible trend toward executive dominance. Today, as acts of the executive grow more arrogant, more arbitrary, the consequences more far-reaching, and as events have eroded many specific congressional functions, serious questions are raised relative to the effectiveness of the system of checks and balances.

The powers of the President have historically been expanded in crisis situations. For the last three decades, we have experienced a permanent crisis situation. This period of American history has witnessed and unprecedented growth of executive powers vis-à-vis those of Congress. In an article entitled "The Twilight of Congress," a writer in *The Columbia State* (S.C.) wrote in 1963:

> By Executive order, by Presidential directive, by bland assumption of powers not heretofore exercised by circumspect Presidents, John F. Kennedy is enlarging the sphere and the authority of the Presidency beyond anything contemplated by the Founding Fathers.[10]

In the fluctuating balance of power between the executive and legislative branches, two principal tools of the Congress have been the power of the purse and the power of oversight or investigation. Today these, as well as other checks held by the Congress, face severe challenges as effective means for controlling the Presidency.

Though Congress still technically must legalize expenditures of public funds by enacting appropriations bills, its grasp on the purse strings has grown more and more slippery. Various factors have combined to make Congress' power of the purse less and less effective as a check on the executive branch. With the passage of the Budgeting and Accounting act in 1921, Congress turned over the initiative in budget-making to the executive. The President and his agencies now prepare the budget and set the priorities for federal expenditures, and Congress sits as a review board. In other legislation Congress has further surrendered some of its control by granting the President and his agencies the authority to obligate funds. Thus, while Congress still must pass the appropriations measures, its discretion in many instances has been substantially reduced.

As expenditures grow larger and larger and programs become

more and more complex, Congress with its lack of staff and expertise becomes less and less a match for the executive branch. While the Appropriations Committees are among the hardest working in Congress, they have the capacity to do little more than take a superficial look at executive requests for money. The understaffed committees are faced by departmental officials, expert in justifying their requests and backed by budget staffs at least as big as those of the congressional committees. In addition, agency officials and the President are assisted by the Office of Management and Budget (OMB) with a staff of over five hundred. Burdened by other duties, Appropriations Committee members become less and less a match for their more numerous executive department adversaries. Neither staffed nor often prepared to make penetrating analyses of executive spending proposals, Congress has been inclined to passively watch its power of the purse wither on the vine. Even the General Accounting Office (GAO), the congressional watchdog over the spending activities of federal agencies, has not been used effectively by the Congress. Now the President further challenges Congress' power of the purse by claiming the right of impoundment. Thus, Congress' role in the budgeting-appropriation process, which James Madison looked upon as the essential counterweight to executive power, has unquestionably been reduced.

If Congress' power of the purse has withered in the twentieth century, its checks on the executive in the field of foreign and military policy have almost completely atrophied. Writing in 1966, James Reston of the *New York Times* observed:

> Something important has happened in America since Woodrow Wilson went to his grave believing that the President of the United States was paralyzed in the foreign field by the overwhelming power of the Congress and public opinion.[11]

Indeed the situation has changed. Today almost unlimited and unchecked power, unlike anything the framers of the Constitution planned, has settled in the office of the Presidency. The U.S. President presently exercises personal power in the field of foreign affairs unequalled by any other political leader in the world. By carefully choosing the right time and circumstances to ask for it publicly, the President can get just about what authority he wants. Case in point: Lyndon Johnson and the Gulf of Tonkin Resolution.

Time and changed circumstances have combined to erode

many of the specific congressional checks. Such developments as the atomic bomb and the ICBM have swung the balance of power toward the President. In the day of the fast-paced military technology of the twentieth century, danger may appear so quickly as to preclude the deliberate procedures of the Congress. In an era of almost continuous world crisis, the President has become the symbol of national unity. He is the spokesman for the entire nation. In the aftermath of World War II with the emphasis on bipartisanism, many legislative leaders viewed it as their duty to support the President on foreign policy.

In the frequently tense situations growing out of the Cold War, the President had numerous advantages. In situations which demanded it, he could act with secrecy and dispatch not possible in Congress. He commanded far superior sources of information. In the Cold War setting, major decisions in foreign policy are more and more embodied in executive agreements rather than formal treaties requiring Senate approval. Diplomacy is most apt to be, not a matter of formal agreements, but of shifting tactics that must be carried out quickly and oftentimes quietly. Thus, not so much because of calculation on anyone's part, but rather because of changing conditions, power in foreign policy-making inexorably shifted more and more toward the President.

In another closely related area, the situation may have been altered even more dramatically. In 1805, Thomas Jefferson proclaimed:

> Considering that Congress alone is Constitutionally invested
> with the power of changing our position from peace to war,
> I have thought it my duty to await their authority before
> using force in any degree which could be avoided.[12]

Other Presidents have felt less constrained to observe the technicalities of the Constitution, and many have exercised their authority as Commander-in-Chief to commit military forces without congressional sanction. In fact, in the period from 1789 to the present, Congress has declared war five times, the last time in 1941. In that same period American troops have seen action abroad on more than 150 occasions, sometimes with congressional approval, other times without. During sixteen of the last twenty-three years, U.S. forces have been involved in undeclared wars, and five times within the last ten years Presidents have launched military interventions without consulting Congress in advance. Congressional opposition was instrumental in preventing military intervention in Indochina in 1954, but subsequent Presidents involved us more and more deeply in this area without congressional sanction, at least until the Gulf of Tonkin Resolution. Nixon's incursion into Cambodia came as a complete surprise to the Congress and was entirely without its assent in any form or fashion.

While recent Presidents expanded their role as Commander-in-Chief, Congress until quite recently did very little to counter the action. Many members of Congress were reluctant, as had been the Founding Fathers, to attempt a precise delineation of the President's powers as Commander-in-Chief. Vietnam and Cambodia were major factors in overcoming this reluctance on the part of many members of Congress. In pushing for legislation providing a congressional check on the President's power to commit troops, Senator Jacob Javits (R. N.Y.) described the existing situation as the "most dangerous imbalance in our constitutional system of checks and balances." After considerable soul-searching and debate, Congress passed in 1974 a measure limiting to sixty days a Presidential commitment of troops without congressional approval. The measure also places upon the President the responsibility of justifying war-like action not sanctioned by the Congress. This action by Congress marked the first pronounced attempt since the Bricker Amendment failed in 1948 to bring about some redress of powers between the executive and legislative branches in the foreign-defense policy arena. A big problem in this area is that any redressing of the President's substantial powers should not come at the expense of his ability to take the action necessary to deter potential aggressors in a convincing fashion.

At times the Congress has seized power at the expense of a weakened executive, but as a general rule, the President is much more capable of warding off potential incursions than Congress is, and in recent years Presidents have displayed a stronger inclination to do so. In the veto, the President has a potent weapon he can use against what he views as unnecessary encroachment by the Congress. Seldom does the Congress succeed in overriding a veto, making it an effective means of asserting executive disapproval. While early Presidents used the veto sparingly, over the years it has been used on numerous occasions. Rutherford B. Hayes vetoed six congressional riders on appropriations bills that in his judgment were attempts to curtail "executive discretion." A bill requiring the approval of the Armed Services Committees of the House and Senate for the Civil Defense Administration and Department of Defense to make any large deals for real estate was vetoed by President Truman. He said Congress was administering as well as making the laws. As President, Lyndon Johnson vetoed a minor flood relief bill because it stipulated that certain projects could be carried out only with the approval of the appropriate congressional committees. In a similar protest against Congressional encroachment, LBJ vetoed a military construction bill because it required the Secretary of Defense to get congressional approval before closing any military installations in the United States or Puerto Rico. In a complete reversal of positions, Johnson asked the Congress to repeal, as an "intolerable encroachment" on Presidential power, a law he had co-sponsored as a senator. The measure required the President to get congressional committee approval before starting specific watershed projects.

On the other hand, Congress has displayed much more inclination to accept, in fact, has frequently encouraged, the expansion of executive powers. In the Nader study group's report on Congress, it charged that Congress "placidly hands its remaining powers over, one by one, to the President and his advisers."[13] Mike Mansfield, while Senate Majority Leader, noted that all Presidents since FDR had taken more power into their hands; he went on to say that he didn't blame the President, but Congress. In recent years Congress has frequently passed what comes close to being blank-check delegations of authority to the President. Commenting on one such piece of legislation passed by the Congress, Senator Robert W. Packwood (R. Ore.) said, "We have delegated this power so broadly to the President that he has virtually carte blanche to set the wage and price policies of this nation. . . ." He added:

> Today, the problem is not that the Executive is trying to steal our powers. The graver problem is that we are prepared to give them away. Congressional power, like chastity, is seldom lost by force. It is usually yielded voluntarily.[14]

In recent years it appears that as executive powers have grown to enormous proportions under the staggering and complex demands of the twentieth century, the Congress has all too often either been subservient to executive power or has engaged in futile forays against it. In the words of Representative Bertram Podell (D. N.Y.), "The legislative branch of government stands by helplessly, waving the United States Constitution at these people as they merrily plunge headlong on their course."[15]

The failure of Congress to assert itself more vigorously invites executive encroachment and even Presidential disdain. When the Senate was considering legislation to curb his power to commit troops abroad, President Johnson remarked rather glibly to reporters, "The Senate Foreign Relations Committee kinda had a big day yesterday. They reported two resolutions in one day."[16] Such an attitude may lead the President to view the Congress as a pesky gadfly to be endured, rather than a co-equal branch to be consulted and relied upon.

The ultimate danger of such an executive attitude is that it may prompt the President to usurp the legislative function out of the feeling that the Congress is incapable of taking necessary action. An example of such executive preemption of power is the present practice of classifying government papers and documents. The present classification system rests solely on executive orders even though there is no statute which gives the President the authority to establish such a system. Such action by the President raises some serious constitutional questions. Should persons be prosecuted for criminal violations under the classification system, the assumption could be made that the President has assumed the power to define criminal acts—a power not granted him by the Constitution nor delegated to him by Congress. Does he have the inherent or implied power to take such action, or is this a function belonging to the Congress? Such an exercise of power by the executive could lead to a serious breakdown in the system of checks and balances.

Another serious threat to the balance of power between the executive and legislative branches has resulted from developments in modern communications technology. Radio and television have wrought significant changes in the Presidency. In earlier times, Congress was the focus of attention, and in the days of the Clays, Websters, and Calhouns, congressional debate commanded nationwide excitement. While congressional debate and discussion can still have considerable impact (witness the Vietnam hearings before the Senate Foreign Relations Committee), it is all too often confined to trivia rather than really vital issues. Too frequently, many members are hesitant to take forthright stands and openly discuss controversial issues. In this heyday of electronic journalism, the Congress is completely overshadowed by the Presidency. The television cameramen and photo-journalists, focusing on the President in his daily chores, have greatly glamorized the Presidency. No other public figure is so constantly exposed to public scrutiny and can so routinely have access to an audience of millions. Presidents have come more and more to realize the benefits of their access to the mass media. Teddy Roosevelt was well aware of the value of publicity but lacked the medium. His cousin, FDR, used radio most effectively, but it was television that gave the President a tremendous advantage over Congress. John F. Kennedy was the first President to have his press conferences televised live, and today the White House has become the subject of an unprecedented volume and range of coverage. Nixon's visit to China was a television extravaganza, and its coverage on NBC's *Today* show provided the kind of exposure other men can only dream about. That it was limited almost exclusively to the President's sightseeing made little difference; it was still news.

In the effective use of the media to influence public opinion, the Congress has played second fiddle to the President. Though the President does have a number of advantages in this realm, much of the imbalance has been Congress' own fault. While the President is *the* spokesman for the executive branch, Congress speaks with many voices. The Senate Majority Leader does not speak for all of Congress, not even all of his party. And the Majority Leader is hardly in the same league with the President. While the President can routinely go on television to present his case directly, views of members of Congress are usually presented second-hand as a brief segment of a news broadcast. Furthermore, much of the really important work of Congress is done behind closed doors in executive sessions of key committees. Neither the House nor Senate allows live broadcast coverage of its floor debates and that fact doesn't help redress the imbalance. If the Congress is going to compete on a more even footing, it must explore ways of taking its case to the masses of voters more effectively. By keeping the broadcast media out, Congress has substantially reduced its own collective influence with the electorate. The Joint Committee on Congressional Operations said that Congress' lack of access to the media "poses a serious threat to the balance of powers between the branches of the national government." If it is to remain an effective component in the governing process, Congress must take some effective action to correct this imbalance.

Legislative Oversight

One of the most vital functions of the legislative branch under the concept of checks and balances is the oversight of the executive branch and its operations. In recent decades effective congressional oversight has become increasingly more difficult as the bureaucracy has grown to enormous proportions and become more and more complex. The fact that we have but one President is a deceptively simple inducement to think of the executive branch as being monolithic, or at least highly unified. Nothing could be further from the true situation; the federal executive is really a congeries of offices with often overlapping functions. This vast federal bureaucracy has the ability to frustrate even the President, as John F. Kennedy learned when he proposed to turn the agricultural aid programs over to the states. He quickly ran into resistance from bureaucrats in the Agency for International Development who saw themselves losing control over some of their funds and programs. Former aide to President Johnson, Harry McPherson, observes that even the Presidential advisor attempting to be totally objective often will fall prey to his own ideological, political or personal biases.[17] This makes both Presidential and congressional supervision extremely difficult.

The tendency in recent years for Presidents to rely increasingly on technical experts has tended both to heighten tensions and widen the rift between President and Congress and to make congressional oversight more difficult. In the abortive Bay of Pigs episode, John Kennedy ignored Senator Fulbright, who opposed the mission, and relied heavily on "experts" in the Pentagon and the CIA. The failure of the mission led to suggestions in Congress for closer legislative oversight of the CIA. Indeed, on some issues the "feel" of the politician with years of practical experience may be more dependable than the fact-filled dossiers of the technical experts. Though the politician has come in for much criticism recently, had Richard Nixon included in his inner circle a real "pro," he might have avoided the embarrassment of a Watergate. None of his top advisors was really a political pro in the true sense; and it is hard to imagine a real pro taking the political risks of a Watergate, considering the meager benefits to be gained from such an operation. When Lyndon Johnson came from a meeting of the Kennedy "brain trust" and was relating to his friend Sam Rayburn, somewhat in awe, all the intellectual power he had witnessed in one room, Rayburn's response was, "Well, Lyndon, I'd feel much safer if just one of those fellows had run for sheriff once."

Not only has the President turned more to experts, but the increasingly complex and technical nature of many legislative issues has forced Congress also to turn for help to the specialists in the administrative agencies. This heavy dependence on executive branch "experts" has, of course, reduced Congress' independence and made the job of effective oversight more difficult.

While the bureaucracy has, indeed, become so vast and so complex as to make effective oversight a real challenge, much of the lack of effectiveness in this area once again stems from Congress' own lack of assertiveness. A close look will reveal that the Congress does not even come close to really using effectively those powers already at its disposal. The General Accounting Office, for example, could be used much more extensively to check on executive-branch spending. Presently, when the GAO makes studies and reports on federal spending, these are often used half-heartedly, if at all, by the Congress. Congressional hearings and investigations, especially in this era of television, could be made into much more potent instruments of Congressional oversight and control. What is necessary for a redress of the ineffectiveness of legislative oversight is a more vigorous Congress using the powers at its disposal.

Summary and Conclusions

Under our system of shared powers, Presidential-Congressional relations always have an element of uncertainty, and at best the relationship between the two branches is one of, in the words of one observer, "creative tension."[18] The Office of the President has come a long way from what one of the constitutional drafters,

Roger Sherman of Connecticut, described as "nothing more than an institution for carrying the will of the legislature into effect."[19] Through the years there has been a cumulative movement toward executive dominance, and the White House and the Presidency are emerging as a new kind of monarchy. Today the strong President takes the initiative in all major affairs of government; it is expected of him. It is he who is credited with prosperity, blamed for recession and inflation, expected simultaneously to make the country prosper, attain full employment, and keep prices down. Even though it is beyond his powers, no modern-day President is likely to greet economic dissatisfaction with "There is nothing I can do," or, "It is none of my business." Separation of powers to the contrary, it is the President who formulates a national legislative program, takes responsibility for it, and fights vigorously for its enactment in Congress. One freshman member of Congress noted that he had heard a lot about lobbyists before he came to Washington and expected to be besieged when he arrived. However, he was rather amazed when the first ten lobbyists who came in to see him were from executive departments, offering assistance, literature and advice on their legislative programs. The power of the President to seize the initiative and establish national priorities is not to be underestimated.

The Great Depression and the New Deal demanded new authority for the President, and once set in motion, the trend was hard to reverse. In the crisis-ridden years following World War II, executive power continued to grow. The seemingly necessary concentration of foreign policy-making in the hands of the Presidency tended to dissolve, or at least weaken, the institutional checks on executive power. Since foreign and domestic policies cannot be neatly compartmentalized, enhanced power in foreign affairs meant more power for the President domestically. Many of the problems of the twentieth century seemed to demand radical and swift changes requiring substantial concentrated authority.

However, executive actions during the last decade have dramatically illustrated the growing imbalance of power between Congress and the President. United States' involvement in Vietnam, the secret bombing of Cambodia, the impoundment of appropriated funds, the misuse of federal agencies, and the invocation of executive privilege have all moved us closer and closer to a constitutional confrontation between the President and Congress. The question is, can and will the Congress move effectively to redress this growing imbalance?

Now substantial numbers of people are becoming concerned that under the pressures of the crisis-filled decades of the twentieth century, Congress has allowed the executive to arrogate unto itself a disproportionately large share of governmental authority. But before the Congress can hope to effectively redirect the executive, it must first address itself to the extremely difficult task of putting its own house in better order. As columnist Tom Wicker noted in a 1965 article:

> The essential fact of the executive-congressional balance today is not that the executive is too big, but that Congress has let itself become too small. The Presidency has evolved in changing times and necessities as a remarkable instrument of governing power; but Congress has not similarly grown and adapted itself to new conditions.[20]

Congress has been, as consumer-advocate Ralph Nader charges, a "continuous underachiever."

While time, events, and technology have tended to favor the President, making the resident of the White House a modern-day monarch, the price of such an enlarged and glorified Presidency has been an overshadowed, sometimes maligned Congress. Since a primary role of the Congress is opposing and checking Presidents, our most prominent legislators—Lodge, Borah, Taft, LaFollette, Fulbright—have made their reputations in opposition to Presidents; Congress has frequently been made to appear negative and irresponsible. Even in American folklore the tendency has been to make the President the hero and Congress the villain. No wonder the Congress has developed an inferiority complex.

Congress itself, however, must shoulder much of the blame for this state of affairs. While not lacking in aggressive impulses, Congress has, especially in the decades of the twentieth century, been primarily on the defensive. Considered objectively, its track record has not been dazzlingly impressive. Faced with the choice, few would be overly enthusiastic about legislative dominance as opposed to executive dominance. However, while the Presidency has been the catalyst for much that has been good, it also must shoulder the responsibility for initiating much that is not so good, The Congress should not be hesitant to point this out.

A key question in any effort to bring about any redress in the executive-legislative balance of powers is whether or not Congress is realistically prepared to accept greater responsibilities. At the start of the 90th Congress, a Democratic congressman said:

> We've had our bellyful of new legislation. The pendulum has swung too far in the direction of the White House, and now it's time for it to swing back.[21]

A Republican colleague chimed in with the warning. "It's going to be rough going . . . around here. Congress will write the laws, not the executive branch."[22] The change is much easier to talk about than to accomplish. As was pointed out in an article in *Commonweal* magazine, ". . . the erosion of checks and balances is so advanced and the centralization of power in the presidency so overwhelming, that any return to traditional procedures is predicated on the cooperation of the President himself."[23] Power is not usually yielded voluntarily; thus, the President must be persuaded or else compelled to agree to some changes.

One prime reason the power of the executive has been almost irresistible the last few decades is that the Congress has offered no coherent alternatives of its own. Congressional nitpicking at executive prerogatives is not a viable substitute for an effective representative function. Currently Congress is inadequately staffed, organizationally unwieldly, and operating with outmoded, time-wasting methods; it badly needs fundamental reforms. Until it takes steps to put its own house in better order, it cannot hope to make much progress toward establishing itself as a co-equal of the President.

While a complete balance of power between the executive and legislative branches is unrealistic and probably even undesirable, some degree of effectiveness on the part of each is absolutely essential to the continued vigor of our constitutional system. The formal powers of the two are so intertwined that neither will accomplish very much for very long without a high degree of cooperation. Redressing the balance of power between the executive and legislative branches is not so much a question of actually reassigning constitutional powers as it is a matter of Congress asserting itself more and exercising more effectively those powers it already possesses. What is needed is not a destruction of Presidential authority necessarily, but rather a constitutionalization of the Presidential exercise of power. The Nixon Presidency, in particular, involved a number of attempts to alter the Presidency as outlined in the Constitution. It is this type of unauthorized and arbitrary exercise of Presidential power that the Congress must curtail.

Both Vietnam and Watergate have produced some encouraging signs of reaction to the misuse of Presidential powers. In 1973 the Congress cut off further funds for the unauthorized war in Indochina, and enacted legislation limiting both the President's power to make war without congressional approval and his power to impound appropriated funds. The Senate forced the appointment of the special prosecutor in the Watergate case, and it was the Congress, with assistance from the courts and the special prosecutor, that eventually brought the downfall of Richard Nixon. As a result of a more determined attitude in Congress, Gerald Ford was compelled to be less defiant than his immediate predecessors. In an unprecedented action, Ford appeared before the House Judiciary Committee personally to explain his pardon of Richard Nixon. In Ford's first four months in office, four of his first fifteen vetoes were overridden. No President since Franklin Pierce had been so rebuked by the Congress. All of these are encouraging signs of a resurgent Congress. The question is whether Congress can maintain its determination and make the lasting reforms necessary to bring the system into proper balance.

In the past, major reforms have come in Congress only in the wake of war-caused turmoil—creation of the Appropriations Committee followed the Civil War; the Budgeting and Accounting Act followed World War I; and the Legislative Reorganization Act followed World War II. Watergate provides the Congress with an excellent opportunity to assert itself and to once again regain its position as a viable and co-equal branch in the federal system. The keys are internal reform and hard work; no statute or constitutional amendment can substitute for the mutual understanding and hard work that must go into the building of a cooperative working arrangement between the Congress and the President.

Notes

1. Abel Upshur, *Federal Government*, 1840.
2. Wade-Davis Manifesto printed in *New York Tribune*, August 5, 1864.
3. James Bryce, *The American Commonwealth* (New York & London: Macmillan and Co., 1893).
4. As quoted by V. O. Key, *Parties, Politics, and Pressure Groups* (New York: Crowell, 1964).
5. Recounted in "The Creative Tension Between President and Senate," *Time* (March 18, 1966), p. 30.
6. *Ibid.*
7. Wilson, *Congressional Government* (Boston: Houghton-Mifflin & Co., 1885), p. 238.
8. *Time, op. cit.*
9. As quoted by Richard Goodwin in "The Shape of American Politics," A *Commentary* Report, 1967, p. 3.
10. "The Twilight of Congress," *The Columbia State* (Columbia, S.C.) July 10, 1963.
11. James Reston in the *Courier-Journal* (Louisville, Ky.), 1966.
12. Thomas Jefferson, Message to Congress, 1805.
13. As quoted in "Senator Mansfield says the Nader Study of Congress has 'Good Deal of Validity,' " *Courier-Journal*, 1973.
14. Robert Packwood, "Congress's Responsibility," *The Center Magazine*, 7 No. 5 (Sept./Oct., 1974), p. 44.
15. Bertram Podell, *Congressional Record*, June 30, 1969.
16. Lyndon Johnson, Press Conference, November 17, 1967.
17. Harry McPherson, *A Political Education: A Journal of Life with Senators, Generals, Cabinet Members, and Presidents* (Boston & Toronto: Atlantic-Little Brown).
18. *Time* (March 18, 1966), p. 30.
19. *Ibid.*
20. Tom Wicker, "The Congress ... What It Its Role In The 20th Century?" *Courier-Journal*, 1965.
21. Democratic Congressman as quoted by Marcus Cunliffe in "The American Presidency a Defective Institution." *Commentary* Report, 1968, p. 8.
22. *Ibid.*
23. "Policing the Presidency," *Commonweal*, 87 (December 8, 1967), p. 324.

Chapter X

Rx: Reform

IN 1974, AT the height of the hearings on the impeachment of Richard M. Nixon, Crystal Lake, Illinois lawyer Richard Zukowski noted:

> I was in the family room watching the televised debates [House Judiciary Committee hearings]. I can look across the field, and there was the Little League. The diamond was jammed with people. I could hear the announcer. I bet there were more people watching Little League in Crystal Lake last night than were watching the committee debates on impeachment.[1]

This observation reveals one of the major challenges facing our governmental institutions for the next decade. Disillusionment with our governmental and political processes is widespread enough to cause concern, and the rising pessimism and cynicism of the American electorate must be reversed.

Though Watergate was a seriously damaging blow to the Presidency, Congress has, as a general rule, inspired even less confidence than the executive. At the time President Nixon rated 26 percent confidence, Congress commanded only 21 percent. As the Congress asserted itself and assumed a more vigorous role in government, it rose in public esteem. In April, 1974, 30 percent approved of how Congress was doing its job while 47 percent disapproved and by August the approval rate had risen to 48 percent while 35 percent disapproved.

Congress should move now to consolidate and expand its hold on public confidence. Legislatures have been the objects of public criticism for years. One critic charged that the Vermont legislature was "hatched from dinosaur eggs." Many feel now is the time for Congress to undertake substantial reform, even at the expense of injuring the feelings of some committee chairmen.

Now, on the heels of Watergate, is the time for the Congress to move aggressively to begin to counter a strongly negative image with much of the public. To a great extent Congress must itself shoulder most of the blame for its poor public ratings and its declining role in government. In a 1973 speech at Oxford, England, George McGovern said:

> I am convinced that the United States is closer to one-man rule than at any time in our history— . . . Today, only the presidency is activist and strong, while other traditional centers of power are timid and depleted.[2]

Congress in this century has been largely a negative force in government—a checking, vetoing, investigating, inspecting institution.

In far too many instances it has been the Congress standing in the way of progress. In the 1940's and '50's the conservative coalition was a stumbling block in Congress, and as a consequence the Congress failed to act on much-needed social welfare measures which could have made our domestic history much brighter. Because it has frequently avoided rather than seized the initiative on sometimes risky and unpleasant issues, Congress has come to be perceived by many as lazy and ineffectual. Russell Baker, writing for the *New York Times*, observes:

> In 1964, Lyndon Johnson's last big year with Congress, it passed a vast quantity of legislation that came to grips with the national problems of the 1940's and prepared the country to meet its needs and responsibilities for the 1950's.

He then asks:

> Why do we need Congress?—Without Congress we would have no way to put off until 1989 what we could do tomorrow.[3]

Columnist Stewart Alsop wrote:

> The only really important law originated, shaped, and passed by Congress since the Second World War is the Taft-Hartley Act, and there may never be another.[4]

It has been easier for Congress to sit back and let the President or the Supreme Court make the really tough decisions and wait to see how the electorate will react. The Congress has been plagued by a failure to be assertive and to provide effective leadership both internally and externally. Because of this, it projects an image of, if not encouraging, at least condoning all sorts of corruption and irresponsibility. While approving pittances for such projects as rat control and air and water pollution, the Congress has authorized the expenditure of $210,000 for studying the Africanized honey bee. When it comes to policing its own house, the Congress is even less assertive. For years Congress ignored the ceilings on campaign expenditures for those seeking seats in Congress. Robert Kennedy spent $3,000,000 to win election in New York, and the Senate didn't bat an eye when seating him. Congress takes disciplinary action against its own members only when the cases such as those involving Powell, Dodd, and Mills become so embarrassing and attract so much attention they can no longer be swept quietly under the rug. Even in a case like Watergate, the Congress was woefully slow in acting, finally getting down to serious business more than two years after the break-in.

It now appears that a continuation of business as usual in the Congress could very well prove disastrous to our system. The time has arrived for Congress to act to clean up a system in which political corruption has been widely exposed. Quick and effective action by the Congress to remedy this situation can go a long way toward improving its image and repairing public confidence in it. This is a much-needed change, as was noted by the Twenty-Sixth American Assembly which urged:

> The vigor of the Congress as a legislative body and the effectiveness of our constitutional arrangements requires that the Congress warrant and command the confidence and respect of the electorate. A Congress able and equipped to discharge its central functions rationally, expeditiously, and with integrity is essential to the survival of representative government in this country.[5]

Needed Reforms

To earn the public's confidence, Congress must take a long, hard look at itself and must make a number of difficult changes.

One of the first things the Congress needs to do is to modernize its structure and procedures. Procedures in the Congress of the space age are as outmoded as the inscribed shaving mugs which stand unused on shelves in the Senate barbershop. While American society has become highly complex, urbanized, industrialized and technological, Congress retains the procedures used to meet the problems of a simple Jeffersonian agrarian society. The scientific and technological advances of the computer and space ages are hardly reflected at all in the structure and procedures of Congress. Industry and the state legislatures have moved much more rapidly to the widespread use of computers than has Congress. Already Congress is years behind the executive branch in the adoption and use of electronic information and support systems. In 1969 the Congress had three computers, compared to 4,600 in the executive branch. The gap has not been narrowed appreciably. Apparently some members see computers as their replacements rather than a means of enabling Congress to make better informed decisions.

Congress lags in other areas as well. Internal communications are haphazard. Even today the telephone remains the most sophisticated instrument of congressional communication. Copies of bills introduced still are stored in metal boxes stacked on shelves reached by ladder. Both houses still rely on stenographers rather than tape recorders to record proceedings. These procedures provide a number of patronage positions for members to fill, but they do little to modernize the machinery of the legislature. Such changes come very slowly in Congress. The Legislative Reorganization Act of 1970 made possible electronic voting but the House did not adopt electronic voting until 1973. Members have been suggesting the need for such reforms for years, but changes come at a snail's pace. Senator Kenneth Wherry (R. Neb.) charged two decades ago that the machinery of Congress was so "appallingly inadequate for modern times that free representative government is endangered." More recently, while still a Senator, Walter Mondale (D. Minn.) observed:

> We need structural reform within the Congress. We need
> more staff. We need computers. We need a greater capability
> to deal with the mass of information constantly developed by
> the executive branch.[6]

At the same time the Congress needs to make fuller and more effective use of modern technology; it also needs to undertake procedural reforms that will enable a majority of its members to act with greater dispatch. Former Senator Joseph Clark (D. Pa.) once said the Senate is "the only representative body in the civilized world which cannot act when its majority is ready for action." The present structure and procedures lend themselves too much to use by a minority to thwart the will of the majority. Such traditional practices as the filibuster and use of seniority for designating committee chairmen must be modified so as to make the Congress more reflective of and subject to the will of the majority. Too frequently in the past, minority, rather than majority, rule has been the norm in Congress. This situation has led to a feeling on the part of many that the Congress is so bogged down and hobbled by archaic procedures and practices that the executive and judicial branches have had to assume primary responsibility for most governmental action. This hasn't helped to bolster the congressional image.

Leadership

To overcome a rather negative image, the Congress must assert itself vigorously and assume more initiative and leadership than it has been inclined to do in recent decades. In recent years Congress has functioned primarily as a processing agency for programs designed by the executive branch. All too frequently it has not even been an effective check in this respect, surrendering more and more of its prerogatives to the executive. Or, when it has got its back up and balked at Presidential initiatives, it has been frequently in opposition to needed social, political and economic reforms.

This negative approach toward major national tasks has prompted columnist Russell Baker to write of the Congress:

> Its central purpose is to make sure that no legislation is passed until its enactment will be irrelevant to national need.[7]

And one of its own members, Representative Richard Bolling (D. Mo.), writes that Congress too frequently has responded ten, twenty, or thirty years after social problems have arisen. Bolling charges that the primary failures in political leadership at the national level occur in the Congress.[8] There can be little doubt that Congress would command more public respect and would be a more effective force in the governmental structure if it attacked the problems facing the nation in a more positive fashion. Had Congress, rather than the Supreme Court, outlawed malapportionment and segregated schools, the legislative branch would be held higher in public esteem currently.

It is important that Congress assume a more responsible leadership role for other reasons as well. The American people at present long for strong, effective leadership in attacking the difficult problems facing our society, but Watergate and other recent actions in the executive branch have made the public understandably apprehensive about unbridled governmental power. The time is ripe for Congress to make the system of checks and balances built into our Constitution by the framers effective again. The system designed by the framers to hem in the exercise of unbridled power works effectively only if the various branches assert their prerogatives. Over the years, Congress has defaulted in so many instances that the Presidency came to wield awesome, and in some areas, virtually unchecked governmental power. This trend culminated in the Nixon Presidency, which was an attempt to alter the Presidency of the Constitution. Congress now has the opportunity, through vigorous leadership, to restore the constitutional balance between the legislative and executive branches. The challenge is theirs, but unfortunately, past performances do not breed much optimism about the potential of Congress for leadership and creativity.

Congressional Ethics

If any substantial progress is to be made in restoring public faith and confidence in the institutions of government, immediate steps must be taken to purify the system. Machiavelli said it was more important for the prince to seem honest than for him to be honest. Many in public life are able to practice this maxim; Dwight Eisenhower was able to project an aura of honesty while accepting over a million dollars worth of gifts. But much of the public is thoroughly fed up with a system which condones the buying of everything from special influence and ambassadorships to favorable legislation and public offices. There is a pronounced need for a strong infusion of moral and ethical standards in politics and government. How can the average citizen have respect for the law and governmental institutions when he sees top officials themselves disregarding the laws?

It would be to its advantage for the Congress to take the lead in a moral and ethical resurgence. Congress has long had the image, rather deservedly, of being the home of the double standard when it comes to ethical behavior and conflicts of interest. While insisting on strict standards for cabinet and other executive appointees, the House and Senate have been extremely reluctant to police the behavior of their own members.

While much of the behavior engaged in by members may not actually be illegal, it raises serious questions about the moral and ethical values of those responsible for making our laws. At a time when we must develop more respect for law and the institutions of government, the activities and attitudes of many of our elected public officials don't contribute much to these objectives. Many of Congress' members apparently subscribe to George Washington Plunkitt's concept of "honest" and "dishonest" graft. In 1906, Senator Joseph Bailey of Texas defended his acceptance of $225,000 from an oil-producing client, saying, "I despise those public men who think they must remain poor in order to be considered honest." Some years later another oil senator, Robert Kerr from Oklahoma, expressed his feelings with these words:

> Now, wouldn't it be a hell of a thing if the Senator from Oklahoma couldn't vote on the things that Oklahomans are most interested in? If everyone abstained on the grounds of personal interest, I doubt if you could get a quorum in the United States Senate on any subject.[9]

Present chairman of the powerful Senate Finance Committee, Russell Long (D. La.), openly admits that much of his income is from oil and gas. He says, "I don't regard it as any conflict of interest. If I didn't represent the oil and gas industry, I wouldn't represent the state of Louisiana."[10] Long's Senate committee has jurisdiction over the oil depletion allowance and imports of foreign oil.

A high percentage of the members of Congress are lawyers by profession, and many retain their partnerships in practicing firms after being elected to Congress. In fact, a survey by the Association of the Bar of the City of New York in 1970 revealed that at least half the lawyers in the House still got $5,000 or more from firms in which they were partners, though most did very little legal work. A not unusual practice is to set up "double-door firms" with the congressman's name on a separate door, but the service actually is performed by the partnership.

Another questionable area is the participation of members in the making of policies from which they personally stand to benefit. Senator James O. Eastland (D. Miss.) is the third ranking member on the Senate Agriculture Committee, which determines government price support policies. In 1970 the Eastland Plantation, Inc. drew cotton subsidy payments of $163,000. When the legislation was changed to impose a ceiling of $55,000 per farm, Eastland split his corporation into six units. In 1971 his plantation's subsidy payments were only $160,000.

Yet another area of frequent abuse is in the hiring of staff in congressional offices. Adam Clayton Powell got into difficulties, among other reasons, for having his wife on his office payroll. Powell was not alone, however; for years it has been common practice to have members of one's family on the payroll. When an anti-nepotism amendment was adopted in 1967, it did not apply to those already on the payroll. Another not uncommon practice is to put on the payroll as staff members individuals whose services to the office are dubious. For example, Representative James Collins of Texas carried a young Texan on his staff payroll at $1,008 per month while the young man finished his final quarter of studies at Stanford University. Asked about the young man's serving on his staff, Collins responded:

> There was nothing illegal about it. I checked. He was supposed to be working for me out there. . . . I'm not sure just what he did. I understand that's the way offices are supposed to run.[11]

On finishing school the young man went on to other work.

Another questionable practice has been for members to have "office funds" provided by private sources to help defray their costs as congressmen. Richard Nixon's famous "Checkers Speech" was an outgrowth of the discovery of such a fund created for him while a member of Congress from California. Senator Charles

Percy (R. Ill.) announced he was raising an "office fund" and any-one who contributed $500 or more would be designated as an "unofficial adviser." Fortunately the scheme did not catch on and was dropped shortly. Such funds raise serious questions about a member's independence and objectivity, especially on issues of direct interest to those who have contributed.

Congress must become more aware of the implications these questionable practices have for public trust and confidence in government, and must move to produce some effective reforms in this area. The development and enforcement of ethical codes for members has gone forward at a snail's pace in Congress; it only took 179 years to produce codes of conduct for members, and the present codes are at best innocuous. What is sorely needed now is a full disclosure by members of personal finances. The present statutes are totally inadequate on this point. The Senate requires its members to report by May 15 of each year all honoraria of $300 or more and all contributions and gifts in excess of $50. Members are required to report only those gifts and contributions made directly to them, not to their campaign committees. The House Code of Official Conduct requires members to disclose interests of $5,000 or more in companies doing business with or regulated by the federal government or income of $1,000 or more from these firms. The code also requires reporting of income for services of $5,000 or more, capital gains exceeding $5,000, honoraria of $300 or more, and creditors owed $10,000 or more. The public has partial access to such disclosures, but some of the data are available only on majority vote of the Committee on Standards of Official Conduct. Spurred by Watergate, twice as many members of Congress made financial disclosures in 1973 as in any other year. Two hundred sixty-seven members listed their income from stock holdings, business interests and law practices. The disclosures were also more complete than usual as 187 went beyond the code requirements.

The Congress cannot, of course, legislate an honest man, and no code of ethics can be drafted that will keep members completely free of conflicts of interest. However, guidelines can be adopted that will reduce members' reliance on sources that could compromise their objectivity and independence. Ultimately the solution lies in elevating the standards of the institution itself, and

Congress is going to reform itself only to the extent that the American people insist that it reform.

Campaign Financing

A closely related sensitive area and one where the Congress simply must assert its leadership and take effective action is the area of campaign financing. In the last two decades, campaign costs have soared to tremendous heights. In 1952, about $90 million was spent in campaigns at all levels; by 1972 the figure had ballooned to $400 million. Today it is estimated to cost at least $100,000 for a candidate to unseat an incumbent member of Congress. These sky-rocketing campaign costs have several far-reaching implications for our democratic system.

Some are beginning to ask if the high cost of political campaigns already has effectively subverted popularly elected democratic government. Theoretically democracy does not lend itself to management by an elite. But as Jesse M. Unruh, former speaker of the California lower house, asks, "Have we reached the point where only the scions of the wealthy can participate in public affairs?" In a system where it takes at least $100,000, in many cases much more, to even hope to be elected, can the system long be considered truly democratic? Do not campaign costs of this magnitude automatically limit access to those candidates of vast wealth or, possibly more alarming, to those willing to mortgage their independence for the necessary campaign contributions?

Furthermore, campaign finance laws as they currently exist work to the advantage of incumbents and of special interests seeking ready access to the legislative process. We need look no further than the data from recent elections to see the implications of the existing regulations. In 1972, 96 percent of the incumbent members who sought re-election were successful. The statutory ceilings imposed on expenditures are a handicap to the usually lesser-known challengers who must engage in intensive and expensive campaigning and advertising to counter the built-in advantages of the incumbent. Well-known incumbents running in relatively safe districts may operate their campaigns on a financial shoestring.

Since no system of public financing has yet been developed for congressional campaigns, the current regulations force the candidates to rely on voluntary private contributions. This makes many candidates heavily dependent upon large contributions from private interests for the financial resources necessary to carry on their campaigns. The strings attached to such contributions, though they may be highly invisible, have grave implications for the independence and objectivity of our elected lawmakers. The Watergate aftermath has brought a flood of revelations of questionable campaign donations. In the 1974 elections the AMA earmarked $25,000 for the campaigns of ten members of the House Ways and Means Committee. Of these ten, six supported a health insurance plan favored by the AMA. Representative Richard Fulton (D. Tenn.), who introduced the AMA-favored bill, received a $2,500 contribution. Omar Burleson (D. Texas), a co-sponsor, got $4,000 and Joel Broyhill (R. Va.), another co-sponsor, received $5,000.

Among the most frequent headline-makers over the last two or three years have been the milk co-ops. Nixon's 1972 campaign was the big beneficiary of the dairymen's generosity, but one of seven congressmen also received donations from the dairy co-ops. David R. Bowen, a freshman representative from Mississippi assigned to the dairy subcommittee of the House Agriculture Committee, received $32,000 over a sixteen-month period. Apparently the dairymen tried to put their money where they felt it would do the most good. In a Missouri primary race, Jerry Litton, a dairy farmer, appeared to be losing. Litton got $150 in dairy money, while his opponent, an urban school teacher, was given $10,000. In all, eighty-two members of Congress received $213,000 from the co-ops, $102,450 going to members of the dairy subcommittees.

Members' chances of receiving substantial support from special interests are considerably greater if they support legislation of particular interest to the group. In the 1974 elections, maritime unions contributed over $300,000 to the campaigns of members who supported a bill to require a larger portion of imported oil to be hauled in American tankers. Russell Long, chairman of the Senate subcommittee handling the bill, got a contribution of $20,-000 and "Tip" O'Neill, House majority leader, received $16,000. In all, 126 House members who voted for the bill got contributions while only three members who didn't support the measure received any funds.

Why are these special interest groups such heavy contributors to the campaigns of candidates for Congress? In the words of former senator from Illinois, Paul Douglas:

> The vast majority of the big donors want something in return for their money. Their gifts are in a sense investments. After election, if their candidates are victorious, they will come around to collect. They will want contracts, insurance policies, jobs for friends and relations, loans, subsidies, privileges, legislation, and so on. Woe betide the officeholders and the party which ignores their claims, for if they do, then the next time the money is likely to be shut off.[12]

Richard Sims, III, a potential candidate for Congress in California, noted, "I spent hours talking to people who wanted to give me money for a campaign. They asked me a lot of questions. But they have yet to ask me a single question about a single issue and where I stand on it."

Special interest groups are willing to invest in a candidates campaign and they are not at all reticent about reminding the recipient congressman what they want once he is elected. Rarely is a congressman's vote actually bought today. But the objectivity and integrity of his vote are severely compromised by his commitment to a particular group or interest because of its heavy investment in his campaign. The end result is still a lack of independence for the policy-maker.

There is no escaping the fact that the large contributors have little trouble gaining the legislator's attention. As long as we retain the present system of financing political campaigns, every candidate for Congress who is not independently wealthy or fortunate enough to represent a "safe" district will be forced to look to those of wealth for his political survival. Inevitably this will place the member in the difficult position of voting on policies affecting his financial supporters. When public officials are placed in the dual role of policy-maker and fund-raiser, the situation provides great potential for abuse. The late columnist Drew Pearson said, "If I were to put my finger on the most corrupting factor in the lives of Senators, I would, without hesitation, point to campaign contributions."

The present campaign finance statutes are so full of loopholes and so laxly enforced that about all they do is encourage evasion of the law and contribute to public cynicism toward politics and government. The Senate Watergate Committee Report documents all sorts of campaign law violations. In Hubert Humphrey's 1970 Senate campaign, Barry Nova, who managed advertising for Humphrey, was told by Jack L. Chestnut to forward some of his bills directly to the Associated Milk Producers, Inc. H. Ross Perot's Electronic Data Systems, Inc., of Dallas, channeled $100,000 through various "dummy" committees to the 1972 Presidential campaign of Wilbur Mills. The committee revealed that the Presidential campaigns of Humphrey and Mills both got thousands of dollars in illegal corporate contributions, and that the Nixon campaign received $780,000 in illegal donations from at least thirteen corporations. George McGovern, the committee revealed, was settling his 1972 Presidential campaign bills for fifty cents on the dollar while at the same time transferring substantial funds to his 1974 Senate campaign fund.

What is the answer? How do we reduce the unequal impact of the corporate and wealthy interests in the legislature? How can the average voter make his voice heard above the huge campaign contributions of the wealthy? Theoretically any taxpayer contributing to a congressman's salary is entitled to just as much of his time and energy as a handful of large contributors. More and more people are coming to believe that there is only one way to achieve such equality of representation—public financing of congressional campaigns.

Speaking to this point, former Senate Minority Leader Hugh Scott (R. Pa.) said:

> One thing is quite certain—private fund raising for political campaigns will have to be abandoned if our system of government is to survive.

He indicated that he felt Watergate would only compound the situation in the long run by drying up the small contributions and thus enhancing the influence of the "fat cats" who would be discouraged only temporarily. He concluded:

> Having witnessed, . . . the gross violations of an even milder law which I did support, I am convinced that nothing short of full public financing will do—. . . .[13]

Public financing of congressional elections has much to recommend it. With this method of financing campaigns, all candidates would compete on a much more equal footing financially. Spending ceilings, which now are largely ignored or serve only to penalize the honest, would become unnecessary, as would the virtually unenforceable disclosure requirements. The undue influence that big money exerts in the electoral process would be reduced and candidates for Congress could campaign for office and cast their votes unencumbered by the cross-pressures of heavy campaign contributions. The honest candidate would no longer be at a disadvantage in competing with a candidate previously willing to mortgage his independence to large campaign contributors. Public financing would go a long way toward freeing members of Congress from the pressures of the wealthy campaign contributors, and would be a small price to pay for more objective and independent lawmakers who could better reflect the interests of *all* their constituents.

Following the Watergate debacle, forty state legislatures passed sixty-seven measures dealing with campaign financing and ethical standards for members. Thus far, Congress has displayed its usual fervor for effective reform. It allowed Representative Wayne Hays (D. Ohio) to water down the 1974 Campaign Finance Bill to where it will have little real effect. As an example of what Congress considers to be reform, this bill reduced the statute of limitations on campaign finance violations from five to three years. If the 1974 efforts are an indication of what Congress feels meets the needs in the area of campaign finance reform, then Congress is not going to command much respect and confidence from a public that expects much more. This is an area where the Congress must act effectively if it is to restore public faith and confidence in politics and government.

Access and Visibility

One characteristic which contributes to a variety of problems in Congress is the secrecy and obscurity which surrounds much of the decision-making. Of course, making the procedures of the Congress more open to public scrutiny has both advantages and disadvantages. The House Education and Labor Committee has admitted the press and the public to its sessions for some time. Some observers are convinced that this has contributed to members grandstanding, which has wasted time, created confusion, and done little in the way of producing sounder legislation. In fact, some feel that members are free to vote on issues much more objectively in executive session.

On the other side of the coin, Congress' penchant for operating behind closed doors makes it more difficult for citizens to get information and raises questions of legislator responsiveness and responsibility. The organization and procedures of the Congress obscure the real centers of power making it possible for the decision-makers to operate with a degree of anonymity. Even the most observant and interested citizen finds it next to impossible to learn what really transpires in the legislative process. The country may be getting extremely poor representation by its legislators, but may be too poorly informed to realize it.

Such obscuring of the decision-making process and those who wield the power also leads to irresponsibility on their part. William Pincus of the Ford Foundation says most corruption occurs when only a very few are privy to the situation wherein it occurs. Opening up the decision-making process to closer public scrutiny can help increase the responsiveness and responsibility of the elected representative.

Here once again the Congress has been guilty of practicing a double standard. While roundly criticizing the executive branch for secrecy and refusing to divulge information, Congress has, until the last couple of sessions, conducted more than half of its own business behind closed doors. The House Government Operations Committee, which drafted the 1967 Freedom of Information Act, voted against open committee sessions. In 1972 the House Comcittee on Standards of Official Conduct held eleven meetings—all were closed sessions. In the 92nd Congress 92 percent of the meetings of the House Appropriations Committee were closed.

On this issue, there are some encouraging signs. In the 93rd Congress, the House Appropriations Committee decided that subcommittee sessions would be open unless a majority voted at the start of a meeting to close the doors. Following suit, both the House Interior and Judiciary Committees opened all their sessions unless a majority of their members vote for an executive session. In the 94th Congress, Senate Democrats endorsed a proposal to open all committee meetings unless a majority on a committee vote to close sessions. The Democratic caucus also endorsed opening conference committee sessions as well. Such increased openness on the part of Congress could help restore public confidence in the legislative branch. One factor Congress has tended to overlook is that an ill-informed public also fails to appreciate what *is* accomplished.

Television Coverage

As a part of its effort to bring more openness to its procedures and decision-making, the Congress must seriously consider permitting television coverage of its activities. Notoriously slow in modernizing its own organization and procedures, Congress embraces new developments reluctantly. It was one hundred years from the time of the development of still photography before Congress permitted itself to be photographed. Now, in the heyday of electronic journalism when most people rely on the electronic media for their news, neither house of Congress allows live broadcast coverage of its floor action. Though the vast majority of American citizens rely wholly upon the news media for their perceptions of the Congress, that portion of the media they rely on most heavily has only very limited access to congressional activity. While the print media have general access, television is not permitted to do what it does best—record action firsthand.

Live television coverage of floor action in Congress has been debated since it first flourished as a communications medium. Still, three decades later, while the President can routinely get on television to talk to his constituents on any topic, Congress' views still are presented secondhand for the most part. As a result of this congressional reluctance to admit television cameras, the balance of power between the legislative and executive branches has been knocked askew. By keeping television out, Congress has given the executive a tremendous advantage and has diminished its own collective influence with the electorate. The President dramatically vetoes actions on television before millions of viewers while Congress debates behind closed doors. In no way can the Congress, speaking with its many voices, expect to have the same impact via television as the President. Neither Ted Kennedy, nor Hubert Humphrey, nor Ed Muskie speaks for all the Congress or all Democrats in Congress, and none of them is a competitor in the same weight class as the President when it comes to the use of television. For as Senator Muskie says, "Congress, speaking in a chorus of contradictory voices, cannot expect to have similar impact, but it should try to obtain similar exposure of its activities." While the Congress cannot hope to compete on an equal footing, allowing televised coverage of its activities could help to off-set the present domination of the media by the President, and it would provide citizens a greater opportunity to identify with the Congress. If the Congress persists in its present stance on the matter, it could, as the Joint Committee on Congressional Operations, said, pose "a serious threat to the balance of powers between the branches of the national government."

Why, other than tradition, has Congress been so reluctant to allow television access to the floor? First of all, this relates to the matter discussed earlier concerning the obscurity and anonymity of the current decision-making process. There are those in Congress, and those outside the Congress, who seek to influence its decisions and who prefer to operate in a closed setting. It is somewhat unsettling to many members to consider that it would be possible for thousands of their constituents to sit at home in their living rooms and see how their elected representatives were performing—or not performing—in the nation's capitol. Not many people carefully peruse the *Congressional Record,* and if they do, they don't really learn that much about what goes on in Congress. Press coverage of the Congress is perfunctory. But, if the TV cameras were there on the floor, then the member might have to be more careful about his speeches, his attendance, and his votes.

There are other considerations as well. Some observers fear that allowing cameras in the chambers would make the temptation to make Congress more telegenic so strong that legislative quality would suffer. Knowing his colleagues in the House, Sam Rayburn opposed television cameras on the floor, fearing that they would cause the grandstanding of members for the folks back home to become unmanageable. Mister Sam also contended that the normal processes for good law making were not dramatic enough to warrant airing across the land. Others have felt as does Representative John Anderson (R. Ill.) that "The legislative process in our democracy is, by its very nature, plodding and ponderous, and not necessarily susceptible to easy explanation by the electronic media."

Most of these contentions do have some validity. Activities in Congress probably would not warrant day-to-day coverage; in fact, this could become quite boring. However, the cameras could focus on major events, key debates, and decisive notes. While such coverage certainly would not reveal all the inner workings of the Congress, it could not help but make millions of Americans more familiar with legislative processes, and more than likely compel some improvements at the same time. Such coverage could be a strong impetus for the Congress to tighten up its procedures, waste less time, stick more closely to its business, and keep its members on the job. Television coverage of the national conventions of our political parties is a good case in point. Television coverage may not have affected who is nominated, but it has brought some streamlining and cleaning up of convention procedures.

High school civics should not be the end of the citizen's exposure to government. In a democracy, the law-making process must be free and open to examination by the public, and the right to know what the legislature is doing must include the right to hear and see, as well as read, about legislative actions. A healthy combination of television and better press coverage could go a long way toward helping the public better understand the Congress and its operations and to be in a better position to make informed judgments concerning the Congress and its performance.

Actually those expressing reservations about televising congressional sessions are probably overly concerned about the potential drawbacks. Twenty years of televising the hearings of various Senate committees has produced some excellent news coverage, considerable public interest and enlightenment, and very few grandstand acts. More recently the televising of the Ervin Watergate Committee hearings and the House Judiciary Committee hearings on impeachment have provided encouragement for televising proceedings. There is little evidence that the admission of television to such proceedings has promoted grandstanding to the extent that it obstructs effective decision-making. In fact, the televising of the Army-McCarthy hearings probably contributed to Joe McCarthy's downfall, and the Judiciary Committee's hearings on impeachment showed that members could appear on TV and seriously attend to their business at the same time. Both the Judiciary Committee and the Ervin Committee proceedings showed that "posturing" and histrionics don't go over very well with TV audiences. Apparently the televising of the Judiciary Committee proceedings helped improve confidence in the Congress as its rating rose to 48 percent approval following the hearings, its highest rating in years.

A study of the effect on Tallahassee high school students of the televising of sessions of the Florida legislature conducted for the Corporation for Public Broadcasting by Bradley Greenburg and Charles Atkin showed that legislators went up in the estimation of those who viewed while there was no change in the attitudes of those in control groups that did not watch the televised sessions. The study indicated there were no negative effects from viewing televised sessions and concluded this was a good way to increase the "trustworthiness" of the legislature. Televising the sessions of Congress would lead many viewers to discover that the body includes some very bright, hard-working and diligent public servants whose views and actions merit more exposure. In its report, Openly Arrived At, the 20th Century Fund asks Congress not to delay any longer in admitting television cameras to its sessions. Senator Lee Metcalf (D. Mont.) has proposed a twelve-month test-run in the Senate. Such a move is long overdue, and could only serve to increase the confidence of a public that for too long has somewhat skeptically watched Congress reform everything in sight but itself.

Improved Efficiency

Because it wastes so much time and its pace is so slow, often dilatory, Congress is perceived by many as being lazy and ineffectual. Unfortunately such an image is not at all undeserved. Though the Congress convenes in early January, very few bills reach the voting stage before April. Between September and the end of the year the 93rd Congress had at least five recesses averaging ten days or more each. As of mid-February, 1975, the start of the 94th "Reform" Congress, the House had been in session less than twenty-four hours and only two bills had been considered. The result is a log-jam of bills near the end of the session necessitating long, hectic sessions which impair efficiency, tempers, and the quality of legislation.

Chairman of the House Education and Labor Committee Carl Perkins (D. Ky.) says:

> Everyone wants to improve the image of Congress. The real problem is that most legislators don't work on Monday and Friday. That's what really needs to be reformed.[14]

Congress is known as the Tuesday-Thursday Club because of the penchant of so many of its members to take "long weekends" back in the state or district. Representative Tom Morgan (D. Pa.), former chairman of the House Committee on International Relations and a physician by profession, managed to find time to treat patients in his district two days a week. Such practices mean that Congress really has only about 150 days of real legislative effort during each session. Much of this time is further squandered on meaningless debate, roll calls, quorum calls and other wasted motion.

The Congress can on occasion act almost precipitously. At 6 p.m. on October 7, 1974, Ted Kennedy introduced a measure, "National Policy and Priorities for Science and Technology Act of 1974." The following morning the Senate subcommittee, chaired by Kennedy, held a half-day hearing and quickly approved the bill. By evening of the same day, the full membership of the Senate Labor and Public Welfare Committee had endorsed the action of the subcommittee. In a series of backstage political deals, Kennedy and his staff had adroitly removed all potential opposition to the measure in advance. They enlisted the support of Senator Peter Dominick (R. Colo.) by grafting on to their own measure a bill he had proposed earlier which he wanted passed before the November elections. Three days after its introduction, S 32 breezed through the full Senate, winning unanimous approval by voice vote. Thus, a measure making substantial changes in the nation's science advisory mechanism was sped through the Senate with virtually no discussion.

This is an example of how the Congress can act too quickly and without due deliberation. The point is the Congress should act with deliberate speed but not without deliberation. Some observers feel the Congress could do its job effectively and still complete its work in six months' time. All the members need to do is employ a full five-day week, invoke effective rules of germaneness and eliminate as much unproductive effort as possible. The use of electronic voting alone can save between one and two months of legislative days per session in the House. If it is to function effectively in a twentieth-century setting, the Congress must adopt rules and procedures which will enable it to function more efficiently.

Effective Reform Difficult

Though legislative reform has been a topic of considerable interest for scholarly observers and writers on Congress for some time, it is not apparently a topic of primary importance for those in a position to do the most about it—the legislators themselves. The number of members in Congress who have either the time or the inclination to think very often or very seriously about the shortcomings of their own body has been relatively small. Also, at least until recently, much of the public was largely unaware of the need for reforms and was not much concerned with the whole matter. Movements for reform have gained momentum very slowly because in those quarters which could bring change, there was considerable satisfaction with the status quo. As former Senator Bill Brock (R. Tenn.) pointed out, "While many of us can agree that various reforms have great merit on principle, it is also true that one change or another will affect each member in a discomfiting manner." Thus, the reformers are bucking a massive power structure firmly rooted in congressional custom and substantial vested interests. Standing and subcommittee chairmen make up about 45 percent of the congressional membership. Add the ranking members who would inherit positions of power should fortunes shift, and a majority have a vested interest in the status quo. Why change a good thing? To alter the power structure would jeopardize numerous positions of power.

Effective reform is rendered even more difficult because all too often when it is attempted, it is somehow subverted and its impact reduced. Representative Elford Cederberg (R. Mich.) observes, "I've been here twenty years, and I've seen a lot of reform bills, and I haven't seen any reform come out of here yet."[15] The Legislative Reorganization Act of 1970 required that roll-call votes taken in committee be made public. The effect of this effort was not to provide the public with more information, but rather that committee chairmen simply quit taking roll-call votes. The Democratic caucus now requires that committee chairmen be elected, a move supposed to make it easier to rid the Congress of arbitrary and unresponsive chairmen. But what really happens when chairmen are elected? Look at the case of Representative Wayne Hays (D. Ohio), one of the most caustic, abrasive and arbitrary chairmen in the House. Certainly not one of the House's most popular members, Hays chaired the House Administration Committee which assigns offices and other favors and he also chaired the Democratic Congressional Campaign Committee which distributes funds to Democrats running for re-election. Though not nominated for chairman by the Democratic Steering and Policy Committee at the start of the 94th Congress, Hays had little trouble being re-elected by his caucus colleagues. He even managed to gain support from some reform-oriented elements by promising Phillip Burton (D. Calif.), chairman of the House Democratic Caucus, to provide that group with funds and office space, something it hadn't had before. It took a widely publicized sex scandal to depose Hays, something his party colleagues had not been willing to do despite his abrasive manner. Bringing real and lasting reform to the Congress is often extremely difficult because simply changing existing procedures may not constitute actual reform at all.

Prospects for Congressional Reform

The Congress does change, but only very slowly and usually never according to any predetermined pattern. Woodrow Wilson's *Congressional Government,* published in 1885, is good testimony to the slowness with which Congress changes. Ninety years old, the book is almost as descriptive of Congress today as if written in 1975. While there has been a growing sentiment for reform among the younger, more liberal members, they have found reform to be a most perplexing issue—easy to advocate but difficult to define and even harder to implement. On the whole, the reform elements have been frustrated in their efforts and have charged the legislative leaders with being less interested in reform than they frequently try to appear. A good example was Wayne Hays' delays on effective campaign reform legislation. The Democratic leadership did nothing to remedy this. Hays' success in delaying campaign reform showed the reluctance of many members to push for really effective reforms, even after the impetus of Watergate, and caused many to question Congress' ability to reform itself. On a rather pessimistic note, Professor James McGregor Burns said:

> . . . I think its institutional drag is so profound, so insidious, so intensive and unremitting that it is not a good institution on which to place our hopes for the future.[16]

Though evidence of any sweeping, revolutionary changes is largely lacking at this time, there are signs that the Congress is moving slowly, inexorably toward reform. The House has been very gradually moving toward becoming a more open, more democratic institution through opening more committee meetings and diluting the powers of some of its committees and their chairmen. The biggest breakthrough came with the opening of the 94th Congress, when the House with an unusually large infusion of younger, more liberal members into the Democratic caucus, made some dramatic changes which shook the seniority tradition and the powerful chairmen to their very roots.

The impetus toward reform had been building in the House for some time. In 1972 a study group under Jonathan B. Bingham (D. N.Y.) had recommended a stronger party caucus. But it took the addition of seventy-five newly-elected Democrats, younger and more liberal than usual, to produce the necessary votes for reform. Joining forces with the incumbent reformers, these newcomers brought a new spirit and confidence to the House. Also, having successfully challenged Richard Nixon, the House was better prepared to face up to its own tyrants.

The first cracks began to appear in the House power structure with the decline and fall of Wilbur Mills, powerful Ways and Means chairman. But the dam really burst when Democratic Majority Leader Tip O'Neill offered the usual motion for the re-election of all committee chairmen. Representative Bingham proposed a substitute motion for separate, secret votes on all committee chairmen. Bingham's substitute motion carried. The reformers then threw House tradition into turmoil by voting to unseat three veteran chairmen, Edward Hebert of Armed Services, W. R. Poage of Agriculture, and Wright Patman of Banking and Currency.

Many observers and members greeted the actions of the Democratic caucus as marking revolutionary changes in the Congress. "The walls are tumbling," said Representative Gladys Spellman (D. Md.). Democratic Representative from Wisconsin, Les Aspin said, "It's an earthquake up here and the Texans are coming off the walls." Reactions of those who see these changes as marking wholesale reform in the Congress are probably premature. The proof will have to come later, and even at this point one has to question how much reform actually occurred. A Steering Committee recommendation for the dumping of at least one other House chairman, Wayne Hays of Government Operations, was rejected by the caucus. While Melvin Price (D. Ill.), who replaced Edward Hebert, may be somewhat less high-handed and arbitrary in running the Armed Services Committee, the degree of reform involved with his choice is questionable. He is almost as old and as conservative in his voting record as his predecessor, Hebert. Also, while key subcommittees have been opened up more to younger members, it remains to be seen whether younger members will actually be selected to fill key slots and will make their influence felt. Many of the older and more experienced members are less enthusiastic than their younger colleagues about the long-range impact of reforms accomplished thus far. They are inclined to feel that with the passage of time, the reforms will become less real. If this happens, it may be more difficult to mount such a reform drive in the next Congress. By the time of the next Congress, the young reformers will have had a taste of the system, will have accumulated some power and experience, and their reformist impulses may be blunted. Now benefiting from the system, they may hesitate to change it. It should also be kept in mind that most of the reforms in the 94th Congress affected only the House. The Senate has yet to be swept by the winds of change.

Summary

The "imperial Presidency" of Richard M. Nixon with his impoundment of funds, secret bombing of Cambodia, improper uses of the agencies of government and the whole Watergate affair vividly underscore the urgent need for a revitalized legislative branch. Our government system of divided powers quite obviously cannot function effectively if the representative branch does not maintain its place and its power as an effective partner. Congress must reassert itself as a viable and effective branch of government; unless it performs better than in the last couple of decades, it will be abandoned by the people.

Presently there is a pronounced need for a revitalized Congress with more independence—independent sources of advice and information on which to base sound judgments and an independent capacity to be more innovative and exert more leadership. Congress must begin to do more than just review Presidential proposals. In recent decades both the judicial and executive branches have been ahead of the Congress in proposing solutions to many of the major problems facing our nation. Congress has usually refused to face up to difficult issues until compelled to do so. Though a variety of reforms are needed in Congress, none of them will really mean a whole lot until the Congress decides to shoulder its share of the responsibility to govern and to occasionally assume a leadership role in grappling with difficult issues. Assuredly there is some risk involved and occasionally some members will be defeated for taking a controversial stand. That, however, is an obligation of elective office.

Currently there exists a wide gulf between what Congress *is* and what it *needs* to be. How can the Congress be made into a modern instrument of effective decision-making? How can the needed reforms be made in Congress to restore its ability to compete more effectively with an ever more powerful Presidency? Can and will the Congress meet the challenge? It appears that if really effective reform is to occur in the Congress, the pressure for it must come from outside and must be so strong as to not be ignored. Are the American voters ready to compel the Congress to do its job? The fate of our democratic system may well hinge on this question.

Notes

1. As quoted by David Hacker in "A Heartland GOP District Sways Toward Impeachment," *National Observer* (August 3, 1974).
2. George McGovern, Speech delivered at Oxford, England, January 21, 1973.

3. Russell Baker, "Modern Saga," *Courier-Journal* (November 18, 1968).
4. As quoted in Larry King, "Inside Capitol Hill: How the House Really Works," *Harper's Magazine* (October, 1968), p. 70.
5. Twenty-Sixth American Assembly, "The Congress and America's Future," New York Arden House.
6. Walter Mondale, "Restoring the Balance" *The Center Magazine* (September/October, 1974), p. 31.
7. R. Baker, "Modern Saga," *Courier-Journal* (November 18, 1968).
8. Richard Bolling, "The House," *Playboy Magazine* (November, 1969), p. 118.
9. As quoted by Warren Weaver in *Both Your Houses: The Truth About Congress,* pp. 231–32.
10. *Ibid.* p. 236.
11. Robert Sherrill, "The Shadow Congress," *Courier-Journal and Times Magazine* (January 24, 1971), pp. 10 ff.
12. Paul Douglas as quoted by Warren Weaver in *Both Your Houses: The Truth About Congress,* p. 211.
13. "Reforming Congress," *Courier-Journal,* April 21, 1974.
14. As quoted by Bill Peterson, "Representative Perkins to oppose House Committee division proposal," *Courier-Journal* (March 20, 1974).
15. As quoted by Riegle, *O Congress,* p. 221.
16. James McGregor Burns, "Don't Go Too Far," *The Center Magazine* 7 No. 5 (September/October, 1974), p. 56.

Bibliography

Bailey, Stephen K. *Congress In The Seventies.* New York: St. Martins Press, 1970.

Bendiner, Robert. *Obstacle Course On Capitol Hill.* New York: McGraw-Hill, 1965.

Berman, Daniel. *A Bill Becomes A Law.* New York: Macmillan Co., 1966.

Bibby, John and Roger Davidson. *On Capitol Hill.* Hinsdale, Ill.: The Dryden Press, 1972.

Bolling, Richard. *House Out Of Order.* New York: E. P. Dutton, 1965.

_____. *Power In The House.* New York: E. P. Dutton, 1968.

Clapp, Charles. *The Congressman.* Garden City: Doubleday & Co., 1963.

Clark, Joseph. *Congress: The Sapless Branch.* New York: Harper & Row, 1964.

Drury, Allen. *Advise and Consent.* Garden City: Doubleday, 1959.

Froman, Lewis. *Congressmen and Their Constituencies.* Chicago: Rand McNally & Co., 1963.

Groennings, Sven and Jonathan Hawley. *To Be A Congressman: The Promise and The Power.* Washington, D.C.: Acropolis Books Ltd., 1973.

Kennedy, John. *Profiles In Courage.* New York: Pocket Books, Inc., 1957.

Kirby, James, Jr. *Congress and The Public's Trust.* New York: Atheneum, 1970. Report of the Association of the Bar of the City of New York Special Committee on Congressional Ethics.

MacNeil, Neil. *Forge of Democracy.* New York: David McKay Co., 1963.

Martin, Joe. *My First Fifty Years in Politics.* New York: McGraw-Hill, 1960.

Matthews, Donald. *U.S. Senators and Their World.* Chapel Hill: University of North Carolina Press, 1960.

Miller, Clem. *Member of The House.* New York: Scribner's Sons, 1962.

Morrow, William. *Congressional Committees.* New York: Scribner's Sons, 1969.

Pearson, Drew and Jack Anderson. *The Case Against Congress.* New York: Simon & Schuster, 1968.

Riegle, Donald. *O Congress.* Garden City: Doubleday, 1972.

Robinson, James A. *The House Rules Committee.* Indianapolis: Bobbs-Merrill, Inc., 1963.

Smith, Frank. *Congressman From Mississippi.* New York: Pantheon, 1964.

Steinberg, Alfred. *Sam Rayburn.* New York: Hawthorn Books, Inc., 1975.

Tacheron, Don and Morris Udall. *The Job Of The Congressman.* Indianapolis: Bobbs-Merrill, Inc., 1966.

Weaver, Warren. *Both Your Houses.* New York: Praeger, 1972.

White, William S. *Citadel: The Story of The U.S. Senate.* New York: Harper & Bros., 1956.

Wilson, Woodrow. *Congressional Government.* New York: Meridian Books, 1956.

Wright, Jim. *You and Your Congressman.* New York: Coward-McCann, 1965.

Index

Abzug, Bella, 15, 139–40
ADA, 184
Adams, John, 9–10, 191, 193, 200
AFL-CIO, 173, 179
Aiken, George, 96
Albert, Carl, 19, 65, 66, 72, 80, 99, 130
Alsop, Stewart, 224
AMA, 174–75, 177, 233
American Constitutional Union, 174
American Petroleum Institute, 181
American Political Science Association, ix
Americans for Constitutional Action, 174, 184
Anderson, John, 239
Apportionment. *See* Malapportionment
Appropriations
  House Committee on, 16, 59, 89, 98–100, 108, 221, 237
  Senate Committee on, 59, 89, 221
Archer, Bill, 101
Arends, Leslie, 97
Aspin, Les, 246
Aspinall, Wayne, 54, 185

B-1 Bomber. *See* Rockwell Corporation
Babcock, Charles, xii
Bailey, Joseph, 229
Bailey, Stephen, xi
Baker, Bobby, 50
Baker, Russell, xii, 109, 224, 227
Baker v. *Carr,* 13, 14
Bankhead, William, 21
Barden, Graham, 108
Bartlett, Dewey, 182
Bayh, Birch, 99
Beard, Dita, 166
Bellmon, Henry, 182
Bentsen, Lloyd, 46, 118, 182
Berger, Raoul, 192
Bibliography, 249–51
Bicameralism, 57–60
Bingham, Jonathan, 245
Blackburn, Ben, 115
Blandford, John, 50
Blatnik, John, 157
Boggs, Hale, 66, 99
Bolling, Richard, xii, 19, 49, 71 82, 110, 115, 117, 127, 141–42, 227–28
Bowen, David, 186, 223
Brandeis, Louis, 195
Breckinridge, John, 143

Bricker Amendment, 212
Brinkley, David, 25, 144
Brock, Bill, 155, 243
Broder, David, 118
Brooke, Edward, 62, 96
Brooks, Preston, 61
Brown, Clarence, 108
Broyhill, Joel T., 99, 233
Burke, Edmund, 4
Burkhalter, Everett, xii, 143
Burleson, Omar, 100, 101, 233
Burlison, Bill, 100
Burns, James M., 152, 245
Burton, Phillip, 244
Bush, George 100
Byrd, Harry, Jr., 158, 194, 196
Byrd, Robert, 63–64

Cable, Bill, 110
Calendars
    House, 125–27
        Consent, 126–27
        Discharge, 127
        House, 126
        Private, 126–27
        Union, 126
    Senate
        Executive, 128
        General, 128
Calendar Wednesday, 127–28
Campaign financing, 232–36
Campaigns, election, 35–45, 53
    Costs, 43–44
Cannon, Clarence, 59, 108
Cannon, Joe, 68, 103, 148
Carswell, Harold, 195
Case, Francis, 179
Caucus, party, 68, 105–6, 148,
    149, 157, 202
Cederberg, Elford, 243
Celler, Emanuel, xi, 7, 54, 185, 186
Chamber of Commerce, 174, 176,
    180, 184
Chase, Samuel, 193
Checks and balances. *See*
    Separation of powers

Chisholm, Shirley, 95
Church, Frank, 184
CIA, xiv, 51, 216
Citizens Research Foundation, 175
Clapp, Charles, xi
Clark, Joe, xii, 104, 227
Clawson, Del, 97
Clay, Henry, 68, 122, 148, 207,
    214
Clements, Earle, 171
Cloture, 132–34
Cole, G. D. H., 2
Colegrove v. *Green,* 12
Collins, James, 230
Colmer, William, 115, 116,
    130, 142
Committee of the Whole, 69,
    88, 126
Committees
    102–10, 113–19, 148, 151
    assignments, 95–102
    chairmen, 16, 79–80, 84, 101
    conference, 58–59, 90
    hearings, 92–94, 135
    investigations, 94, 113, 135
    joint, 88, 90
    on committees, 97–101
    oversight, 17–18, 94–95
    reform, 113–19
    reports, 112–13
    select, 89–90
    staffs, 45, 110–11
    standing, 88–89
Common Cause, 175, 178
Congressional Budget Office, 46
Congressional Campaign
    Committees, 150–51
Congressional Record, 43, 122,
    125, 184, 239
Congressional Research Service, 46
Conservative Coalition, 158–59,
    224
Constituent casework, 17, 18, 19
Conyers, John, 158, 159
Cooley, Harold, 180
Cooper, John Sherman, 6, 162

COPE, 173–74
Corman, James C., 109
Courts, Congress and the, 189–97
Cox, Eugene, 159
Cronin, Thomas, 51
Cunliffe Marcus, xii
Cutler, Lloyd, 170

Daley, Richard, 66
Daniel, Frank, 166
Davidson, Roger, xi
Dawson, William T., 46
Debate, in Congress, 121–34,
    214–15
de Grazia, Alfred, xi, 3
Dellums, Ronald, 53, 101
Democratic Study Group, 77–78
Deschler, Lew, 48, 49
de Tocqueville, Alexis, 122, 189
Dirksen, Everett, 75, 76, 184, 192
Dodd, Thomas, 83, 145, 225
Dole, Robert, 82
Dominick, Peter, 242
Douglas, Paul, 180, 234
Douglas, William O., 193–94

Eastland, James O., 230
Education, House
    Committee on, 16
Ehrlichman, John, 153
Eisenhower, Dwight, 179, 199, 228
Elections, 35, 41
Emerson, Ralph W., 31, 122
Erikson, Robert, 42
Erlenborn, John, 106
Ervin, Sam, 118
Esteem, for Congress, xiii, 25
Ethics, 228
Executive, xiii. See also
    President

Farley, James, 154
FBI, xiv, 192–93
Federal Energy
    Administration, 182
Federalist Papers, the, xi, 29–30

Ferris, Charles, 48
Filibuster, 125, 131–34, 227
Fisher, Joseph, 99
Flood, Daniel, 91, 92
Floor, action on, 121–46
Floor leaders, 67, 73, 75–76,
    148, 151
Ford, Gerald, 193–94, 221
Ford, Wendell, 118
Foreign policy, 210–13, 218
Foreign Relations, Senate
    Committee on, 89, 93
Foster, Augustus, 122
Frank, 43
Fraser, Donald, 99
Frazier, James, 154, 155
Fulbright, William, 7, 51, 54,
    81–82, 96, 166, 216
Fulton, Richard, 233

GAO (General Accounting
    Office), 46, 49, 210, 217
Garfield, James, 60
General Motors, 182
Gerrymandering, 15
Gilbert, Jack, 100
Goldwater, Barry, 156
Gonzalez, Henry, 41
Goodwin, Richard, xii
Gore, Albert, 7, 40, 174
Grant, George M., 171
Gravel, Mike, 172
Green, Edith, 61, 99
Griffin, Robert, 96
Grocery Manufacturers of
    America, 174–75
Groennings, Sven, xi

Hacker, David, xii
Haldeman, Robert, 153
Halleck, Charles, 66
Hamilton, Alexander, 10–11, 151,
    189–90
Hansen, Julia Butler, 82, 110,
    117–18, 141
Harvey, John, 171

Hawley, Jonathan, xi
Hayden, Carl, 59
Hayes, Rutherford B., 212–13
Haynsworth, Clement, 195
Hays, Wayne, 53, 107, 236, 244–45, 246
Herbert, Edward, 101, 106–7, 245, 246
Holifield, Chet, 33, 61, 106
Holland, Spessard, 132–33
Horton, Frank, 106
Hosmer, Craig, 126
House, the, 60–62, 121–22, 125–26
Hubbard, Carroll, 36
Huddleston, Walter "Dee", 118
Humphrey, Hubert H., 19–20, 132–33, 235

Ikard, Frank, 181
Impeachment, 193–94, 223
Incumbency, 41–43, 232
Independent Petroleum Association of America, 182
Interest groups, 111–12, 136, 161, 165–87, 232–36
Introduction, xiii–xiv

Jackson, Andrew, 205, 207–8
Javits, Jacob, 212
Jefferson, Thomas, 29, 193, 201, 202, 211
Jefferson's Manual, 81
Jenkins, Thomas, 49
Johnson, Andrew, 150
Johnson, Lyndon, 6, 41, 66, 73–75, 76, 84, 96, 98, 109, 110, 132–33, 149, 153, 182, 194, 204, 206, 210, 213, 214, 217
Johnson, Walter, 40
Jones, Ed, 186
Judd, Walter, 20
Judicial review, 190

Karth, Joseph, 100
Kefauver, Estes, 94
Kemp, Frank, 173

Kennedy, John, xi, xii, 6, 12–13, 51, 137, 204, 206, 209, 215, 216
Kennedy, Robert, 225
Kennedy, Ted, 63, 242
Kent, Frank R., 32
Kerr, Robert, 182, 229
Keys, Martha, 99
Kilgore, Buck, 122
King, Larry, xii
Kirkpatrick v. Preisler, 14
Kirwan, Mike, 154
Knowland, William, 76
Koch, Edward, 18
Kofmehl, Kenneth, 47
Kuchel, Thomas, 50

Leadership, 63–77, 84, 155, 227–28
Legislative Counsel, Office of, 45
Legislative Reference Service, 45
Legislative Reorganization Act of 1946, 149, 183 of 1970, 105, 138, 226, 243–44
Legislators, roles of
  agent, 17
  broker, 17–18
  campaigner, 20
  compromiser, 21
  educator, 21–22
  lawmaker, 17
  overseer, 17–18
Liberty Lobby, 180
Lincoln, Abraham, 200
Lippmann, Walter, xi, xii, 8, 24
Lipset, Seymour, 3
Litton, Jerry, 233
Lobbying, 165, 169, 170
Long, Russell, 66, 182, 229, 233
Lowenstein, Allard, 95
Lucas, Scott, 171

McCarthy, Joseph, 83, 94, 96, 145, 240
McClellan, John, 94
McCloskey, Paul, 101, 144

McCormack, John, 65, 69, 72, 104, 141, 142, 149, 179
McGann, Joseph, 48
McGovern, George, 224, 235
McMillan, John, 106
McPherson, Harry, 216
McSpadden, Clem, 101
Madden, Ray, 104
Madison, James, 21, 210
Magnuson, Warren, 180
Mahon, George, 16, 104
Malapportionment, 12–16, 190
Mansfield, Mike, 62, 66, 75, 133, 205, 213
Marbury v. *Madison,* 190, 196
Marshall, John, 190, 196
Martin, Dave, 111
Martin, Joe, xii, 6, 19, 38, 40, 66, 76, 155, 159
Mazzoli, Romano, 118
Media, 37, 39, 53, 124, 202, 205, 214–16, 238–39
Mencken, H. L., 12, 208
Merry, George, xi, 15
Metcalf, Lee, 241
Milbrath, Lester, xii, 183
Milk Coops, 186, 233
Mill, John Stuart, xi, 10, 17–18
Miller, Clem, 22, 88, 95
Miller, Dale, 183
Miller, Fishbait, 140
Mills, Wilbur, 66, 82, 84, 97, 99, 109, 115, 181, 225, 235, 245
Minshall, William, 97
Mitchell, Clarence, Jr., 171
Mondale, Walter, 226
Montesquieu, 189
Morgan, Tom, 242
Morley, John, x
Morse, Wayne, 162
Muskie, Edumund, 50, 96, 118, 238, 239

Nader, Ralph, 170, 175, 179, 213, 219
NAM, 184

Natcher, William, 92, 142
National Rifle Association, 166, 176, 184
Nelson, Gaylord, 50
Nixon, Richard, 153, 181, 194–95, 212, 215, 217, 221, 223, 230, 233, 235, 246
Norris, George, 127

O'Brien, Lawrence, 204
O'Connor, John, 129, 155
O'Konski, Al, 15
OMB, 210
O'Neill, Tip, 107, 233, 245
Ottinger, Richard, 43

Packwood, Robert, 54, 213
Parliamentarian, 48, 49, 69
Parochialism of Congress, 11
Parties, political, 30, 31, 32
Patman, Wright, 106, 168, 246
Patronage, 203, 226
Pearson, Drew, 234
Pepper, Claude, 40
Percy, Charles, 230–31
Perkins, Carl, 16, 110, 242
Peterson, Bill, xii
Pharmaceutical Manufacturers Association, 172, 177–78, 179
Pitkin, Hanna, xi
Plunkitt, George Washington, 229
Poage, W. R., 106, 245
Podell, Bertram, 214
Policy committees, 148–49
Political parties, 36–37, 63, 136, 147–62
Polls, 37
Powell, Adam Clayton, 72, 83, 108, 145, 196, 225, 230
Power of the purse, 209–10
President, 25, 151–52, 154–55, 194, 199–222
Price, Melvin, 246
Professional staff, 45–52
Proxmire, William, 96, 118
Pryor, David, 99

Quorum calls, 126

Randolph, John, 122, 193
Rarick, John, 158
Rayburn, Sam, 65, 68, 70–72, 74,
    77, 84, 109–10, 113, 124,
    129–30, 140, 149, 182, 206,
    217, 239
Reapportionment. *See*
    Malapportionment
Recruitment, 29
Reed, Thomas B., 5, 22, 68, 122,
    123, 165
Reform, 33, 149, 220–21,
    223–47
Representation, 1–28
    functional, 10
    proportional, 10
Representative, role of, 3–9
    agent, 4, 5, 6, 7
    politico, 9
    trustee, 4, 7–9
Representative government,
    history of, 1–26
Republican government, 1–3
Reston, James, xii, 72, 210
Reynolds v. *Sims,* 13
Riegle, Don, xii, 32, 52, 54, 101,
    104, 109, 123, 140, 141,
    142, 147
Riemer, Neal, xi
Rivers, Mendel, 50, 54
Robison, Howard, 97
Rockwell Corporation, 178
Rodino, Peter, 101
Rogers, Byron, 173
Rogers, William, 93
Roosevelt, Franklin, 153, 154,
    200, 201, 205, 208, 215
Roosevelt, Theodore, 68, 200,
    205, 208, 215
Rostenkowski, Dan, 66
Rousseau, Jean Jacques, 2, 25–26
Rousselot, John, 144
Rule 22, 132–33

Rules, 80–83
Rules Committee, House, 49,
    89, 116–17, 128–31, 180
Russell, Richard, 73

Sabath, Adolph, 108
Salaries, congressional, 34
Saxbe, William, 143
Schlesinger, Arthur, Jr., xiii
Scott, Hugh, 43, 75, 154, 235
Senate, the, 59, 131–34
"Senatorial Courtesy," 194
Seniority, 16, 79, 102–7, 113–15,
    117, 142–43, 151, 152, 227,
    245
Separation of powers, 189–90,
    195, 199, 209, 214, 216, 217,
    218, 228
Seward, William H., 208–9
Sherman, Roger, 218
Sherrill, Robert, xii
Short, Dewey, 53
Sims, Richard, 234
Single-member districts, 11–12
Smathers, George, 40
Smith, Frank, xi, 8, 22, 96, 159
Smith, Howard, 116–17, 129, 130
Sorauf, Frank, 9
Sparkman, John, 118
Speaker, 65, 67–72, 129, 130,
    131, 151
Staggers, Harley O., 180
Steiger, Bill, 15
Steiger, Sam, 141
Stubblefield, Frank, 36, 186
Subcommittees, 91–92
Sumner, Charles, 61
Supreme Court, 191–92
Suspension of the rules, 128
Sweig, Martin, 50
Tabor, John, 66
Taft, Robert, 76
Teague, Olin, 149
Thompson, Fletcher, 52
Thurmond, Strom, 160, 162

Tower, John, 182
Truman, Harry, 94, 160, 201, 213
Twain, Mark, ix
Twenty-one Day Rule, 130
Tyler, John, 5

Udall, Morris, 67, 102, 185
Udall, Stewart, 60
Unanimous consent, 128
Unruh, Jesse M., 232
Upshur, Abel, 199–200

Vanocur, Sander, 54
Veto, 201, 212, 221
Viet Nam, 93, 96, 122–23, 212, 214, 218, 221
Vinson, Carl, 108
Voting, 123–24, 134–38, 155–56

Waggonner, Joe, 62, 92, 99
Waldie, Jerome, 106
Wallace, George, 158
War Powers Act, 212
Warren, Earl, 193
Washington, George, 200, 207
Watergate, 26, 33, 42, 51, 54, 175, 186, 221, 223, 225, 228, 231, 233, 236, 246
Watson, Albert, 156–57, 160, 162
Watts, John, 80, 100
Ways and Means, House Committee on, 89, 97, 98, 99, 100, 101, 117
Weaver, Warren, xi
Weber, Max, 3
Webster, Daniel, 207, 214
Weltner, Charles, 143, 154
Westburry v. *Sanders*, 13–14
Wherry, Kenneth, 76, 226
Whips, 67, 76–77, 148, 151
Whitten, Jamie, 91, 92, 160
Wicker, Tom, xii, 219
Williams, Harrison, 174
Williams, John Bell, 156–57, 159, 160
Wilson, James, 3
Wilson, Woodrow, xii, xiii, 5, 132, 148, 192, 195, 200, 202, 207, 208, 244
Wyatt, Wendell, 33

Yarborough, Ralph, 40, 174, 204

Carl P. Chelf is ideally equipped to write an inside view of how Congress works and never lose sight of the theory of how it is supposed to function.

This book reflects his experience as a Congressional Fellow of the American Political Science Association and as a legislative analyst for the Kentucky Legislative Research Commission. His close-up examination of Congress probes not only the actions of Senators and Representatives but also their thinking and philosophies.

His experience has been put to practical use in teaching courses in government and political science to undergraduates at Bowling Green Community College of Western Kentucky University. He has been dean of the college since 1973 and coordinates the development and administration of all less-than-baccalaureate programs.

He is the author of *Political Parties in the United States* and co-author of *A Manual for Members of the Kentucky General Assembly*.

STAFFORD LIBRARY COLUMBIA
328.73 Che c.1
Che   Ca   P
C ss i he meri n s en

3 3891 00047 0321

Kirtley Library
Columbia College
8th and Rogers
Columbia, MO. 6

DATE DUE

FEB 9 1981		
DEC 3 1981		
SEP 25		
OCT 2		
PR 1 1		
MAY U 1 '84		
DEC 12		

GAYLORD   PRINTED IN U.S.A.